Human Sociobiology

Human Sociobiology

A HOLISTIC APPROACH

Daniel G. Freedman

THE FREE PRESS
A Division of Macmillan Publishing Co., Inc.
NEW YORK

Collier Macmillan Publishers
LONDON

The Free Press
A Division of Macmillan Publishing Co., Inc.
866 Third Avenue, New York, N.Y. 10022

Collier Macmillan Canada, Ltd.

Library of Congress Catalog Card Number: 78–73025

Printed in the United States of America

printing number

1   2   3   4   5   6   7   8   9   10

Library of Congress Cataloging in Publication Data

Freedman, Daniel G
   Human sociobiology.

   Bibliography: p.
   Includes index.
   1. Sociobiology.   2. Human behavior.   3. Human
biology.   I. Title   [DNLM: 1. Genetics, Behavioral.
2. Social behavior.   3. Behavior, Animal. GN365.9 FS53h]
GN365.9.F73   301.2   78–73025
ISBN 0–02–910660–5

For my wife, Nina,
and for those with whom I share half my genes:
Toby, Tony, Gregory, and 'Granpa' Yankel.

Contents

Acknowledgments

I would like to thank the following colleagues, friends, and students (categories that are not mutually exclusive) for their comments: Bea Neugarten, Darell Bock, Michael Wade, Richard Shweder, two generations of Kayes—Kenneth and Sol, John Pfeiffer, Merri Monks, Alan Fogel, Paul Ekman, Glenn Weisfeld, William Kruskal, Harvey Ginsburg, Mike Csikszentmihalyi, Seymour Larock, Joe Tobin, Charmane Eastman, Fred Kaplan, Dennis Couzin, Richard Savin-Williams, Sharafuddin Malik, James Weinrich, Jeanne Altmann, J. Paul Scott, and Marshall Sahlins. Given so long a list of readers, many of them distinguished scholars, it may be surprising to find any problems at all with the text. Unfortunately, inasmuch as each reader found a separate set of problems and inaccuracies, I have no reason to believe this would not be a permanent process. Furthermore, and in their defense, I did not always respond to a reader's recommendations.

Thanks also to Ron Chambers of the Free Press for his enthusiasm, perspicacity, and for his editorial suggestions; and last, but not least, to Professor E. O. Wilson for his encouragement and for having written *Sociobiology*.

As for research support, the Harry Frank Guggenheim Foundation, whose directors of research are Lionel Tiger and Robin Fox, was most generous just when sources of funding appeared to have evaporated. I am most grateful to the Foundation.

Human Sociobiology

1

Basic Issues

Flower in the crannied wall,
I pluck you out of the crannies,
. . . if I could understand
what you are, root and all, all in all,
I should know what God and man is.

Tennyson

      I have tried in this book to address both a lay and a professional audience, and though this approach may bother both audiences, it has had some advantages. It forced me to pay less mind to that rigorous censor each scientist carries with him and to say what was in the back of my mind, the personal and perhaps unexpected, as well as the tried and true. Its writing has been a personal pilgrimage to sociobiology via the fields of clinical psychology (my first professional interest), genetics, ethology, and primatology.

      As for the question, What is sociobiology? there are a number of possible answers. Mine is simply that sociobiology is the application of recently developed biological principles to behavior. And since biological principles usually are concerned with populations, sociobiology reverses psychology's focus on the individual and views him, instead, as a pawn in broader, evolutionary, population-wide processes. Individual behavior is seen as a unique variation on the species' theme, with the species' theme the primary motif. As for the common objection that man is unique vis-à-vis the lower animals, my answer is that all species are unique vis-à-vis other species, and the human ability to plan and take cognizance of the past is no less a species' characteristic than is hive building in honey bees. We will not be distracted by the frequent claim that man requires new, extrabiological rules to explain his behavior. Ours is a

1

monistic position, and nothing in monism is extrabiological (see Wightman, 1934).

What, then, are the main principles of sociobiology? This book, at least, focuses on seven:

THE PURPOSE OF LIFE. The standard biological position is that life's only purpose is to reproduce itself. Since living things frequently either eat up or edge out other living things, competition and survival of the "fittest" necessarily follow.

GAMETIC POTENTIAL. Sperm and ova are gametes, and since mammalian males produce many more sperm than females produce ova, any given male has far greater potential for producing offspring. He is also more inclined to compete with other males over the "scarce" resource, females.

KINSHIP GENETICS. Closely related organisms have genes in common with one another. Siblings share at least 50% of their genes, parents and children share at least 50% of their genes, half siblings share at least 25% of their genes, and so on. If I give up my life to save three siblings who would otherwise die, I have, in effect, saved 150% of my gene complement, and, in death, I have obeyed the biological commandment to reproduce myself. Such is the logic of biological altruism. This is also called *inclusive fitness,* meaning evolutionary fitness that goes beyond the survival of the individual or its offspring.

THE SOCIAL CONTRACT. All sexually reproducing animals are in some way social; a common feature of animal interaction is competition over "agreed upon" stakes, be it a lush territory or a higher position in the status hierarchy.

MULTIPLE CAUSALITY. Natural selection (evolution) may occur simultaneously at all levels: the individual, the family, and the population. Reductionism, the attribution of evolutionary change solely to selection among individuals (or even among individual genes, as in Dawkins, 1976), is here eschewed.

HOMOZYGOSITY–HETEROZYGOSITY. All populations achieve some balance between homozygosity (complete genetic identity from individual to individual) and heterozygosity (the nonidentity of genes among individuals). Homozygosity gives a population its uniqueness, makes one species distinct from another, and permits appropriate social and sexual interactions to occur. Heterozygosity within a population helps raise the probability that in times of stress or change at least some "preadapted" members of the population will survive.

MONISM. It is assumed in this book that such "dualities" as heredity and environment or biology and culture are merely the products of human manipulations of symbols and that their components are neither opposed nor separable in nature. To give a brief example, "free will" is often counterposed to the "determinism" inherent in a biological perspective. Our position is not unlike that of Spinoza, who said of human free will that not only does man make decisions, but that he is obligated to do so. This aspect of free will —its obligate nature—renders it universal, species-specific, and therefore within the realm of the "biological."

Armed with these principles, I believe the average reader can wend his or her way with me, for the entire book follows from them.

In the remaining sections of this chapter I will discuss some methodological issues and current arguments in the field. They center largely around my intuition that mechanistic explanations will take you only so far before the specter of "circularity" arises.

HOLISM VERSUS REDUCTIONISM

My main theoretical forebear was Kurt Goldstein (1939), a great neurologist, and ironically a man deeply suspicious of Darwinism. Both he and his teacher at Berlin University, the biologist Jacob Von Uexkull, shared the view that life was too marvelously rich and organized to have come about via some chance mutational process, as the genetically oriented neo-Darwinists of their day had it.

This position seems intuitively right, but Darwinism cannot be ignored, and once one joins the ranks of evolutionists, as I have, there is no turning away. The best hope is to reconcile the holism of Goldstein and Von Uexkull and the mechanistic neo-Darwinist explanation of how we got here.

Holism is an approach to the study of behavior that insists that behavior must be considered in its full, natural context. If he studies infants, a holist starts by looking at mothers and their babies in their usual setting, not in the laboratory. Studies of infants hooked up to recording apparatuses are fine, but the results are meaningful only when reconciled with the natural situation. This is the "approach from above," in that it starts with whole, naturally occurring phenomena.

A strict approach from below, though it may uncover many facts, rarely lends itself to the understanding of a phenomenon. It would mean, for example, that someone who had never seen or heard of an automobile could unravel this strange hulk's purpose by scrutinizing its constituent parts. By contrast, the approach from above would have one try intuitively to grasp the object's function and then examine the parts with various hypotheses in mind; intuitive guessing combined with empirical examination would continue until some level of understanding had been obtained.

As a psychologist, I was brought up on this debate, and I sided early with the holists and Gestaltists in their argument with learning theorists. The Gestaltists, after all, dealt with whole phenomena and with intuitive understanding, whereas the learning theorists saw behavior as either "stamped in" or "stamped out" by "association" or "reinforcement." Although I admit that I look with disdain on so mechanical an approach, I also realize one's theoretical predilections are often a matter of taste rather than truth (see Pepper's marvelous book, *World Hypotheses,* on this score).

When ethology emerged as a field in the 1940s and 1950s, with its emphasis on the study of naturally occurring animal behavior in the wild, I was immediately attracted to it. What did the learning theorists know even of their favorites, Norway rats, having seen them only in cages or laboratory mazes! Ethology, in turn, led me to evolutionary theory, and most of my work in the 1960s and early 1970s was concerned with developing a combined evolutionary and holistic approach to human behavior.

With the publication of E. O. Wilson's *Sociobiology* in 1975, following the theoretical papers of W. D. Hamilton (1963, 1964) and Robert Trivers (1971–1973), the field of sociobiology was born. It was immediately attractive and worrisome—attractive because it brought together population genetics, evolution, animal behavior, theoretical biology, and important areas of psychology; worrisome to an old-time holist because it made life seem too mechanically neat and simple. I recall drinking beer with Trivers in 1974 and, as one is wont to do after several steins asking him whether he *really* believed that the survival of genes is what life is all about! As best as I can remember, the answer was "ninety percent of the time." That was enough doubt to satisfy me, and we have been friends ever since.

Let me explain my reservations. In any debate, it is helpful to have contestants whose positions are clear. We therefore owe thanks to Dawkins (1976) for his book *The Selfish Gene.* It is a perfect example of a strict mechanistic approach, and one that is backed by Trivers in his foreword to the book and by W. D. Hamilton (1977) in his review of it. By "selfish gene," Dawkins and other sociobiologists mean that the motive-force of living things is self-duplication. That is, genes and even parts of genes compete so that they, and not a rival, will survive. All the organic complexities that the world has experienced and is experiencing follow from this theorem. In this view, those twisted strands of DNA, the genes, are king, and all organic activity is in one way or another aimed at getting them into subsequent generations. This will usually involve competition between individuals; if perchance one organism helps another, the sociobiologist's assumption is that the two are related and therefore have a shared cache of genes. In this way, by helping another's propagation one can simultaneously help one's own genes to survive. I initially bought this view, hook, line, and sinker, but I have had second thoughts.

As I now see it, the main difficulty with this view is the insistance that changes in *single* genes are the basis for evolutionary change. It is not difficult to trace the source of this bias to R. A. Fisher, the great and influential British biomathematician (see Provine, 1972). Fisher's mathematical prowess is legendary, but he based his calculations on the assumption that evolution consists of advantageous single genes taking over within populations. It is, then, but a short step from Fisher's "superior" gene (Fisher, 1930) to Dawkins's "selfish" gene.

Fortunately, Fisher's is not the only mathematical view of the evolutionary process. Sewall Wright (1940), by contrast, has consistently made the point that the same gene varies in its effect and action depending on the genes in its company, that is, depending on the genetic background! A gene is but a cog in a complex system and it rarely, if ever, acts alone. In other words, Wright is a geneticist-Gestaltist whereas Fisher tended to treat genes as unitary building blocks. Ernst Mayr (1959) has called Fisher's approach "bean bag" genetics because of the assumption that each gene is independent of the others. With his "shifting balance" theory of evolution, Wright has demonstrated mathematically that competition between individuals can be insignificant when compared with competition between families or competition between populations. Furthermore, in his view, evolutionary changes have depended primarily on genetic differences that developed between partially isolated breeding groups. Thus, for Wright evolution has been largely a between-group phenomenon rather than a within-group phenomenon.

Although I am not at all competent to evaluate these two subtheories of evolution at the level of their mathematics, I do find Wright's approach considerably more congenial. His emphasis on the dynamic balance among selective forces at three levels—the individual, the family, and the breeding group—gives his theory the ring of reality. In particular, the postulation of dynamic forces at the level of populations makes his approach holistic and permits insights not as readily available within the Fisherian approach "from below."

J. Paul Scott (1977), a student of Wright's and an important influence on my own research, has put this debate in modern, systems theory terms: "Whereas a mechanistic theory (such as Fisher's or Dawkins's) assumes one-way causation, systems theory assumes two-way or reciprocal causation." That is, there are simultaneous causal networks coming down from the population level and rising up from the individual and familial levels. Although this is a tough model to work with, insofar as everything ends up as multiply caused, it is probably the best approximation of the way biological systems have evolved.

THE INDIVIDUAL AND THE POPULATION

The greatest advance in evolutionary theory since Darwin is the concept of changes via breeding populations rather than via individuals. The idea is that individuals do not beget new forms as a result of their own life experiences, as Lamarck held and as Darwin tended to believe, but that it is the changing genetic pool available to the entire breeding population that leads to evolutionary change (see Hardin, 1959).

I will try first to show some of the interplay between individuals and populations using a simple, one-gene system, the gene that causes sickle-cell anemia. (Inasmuch as only one gene is involved, this example could as well be Fisherian as Wrightian.) This gene when present on only one chromosome lends resistance to malaria; when present on both chromosomes, it results in the often fatal disease of sickle-cell anemia. In America this disease strikes only those whose ancestors came from malarial areas of Africa, and the irony is that were it not for this troublesome gene those ancestors might well have been wiped out. That is, the same gene has been good for the population but tragic for some individuals. Thus, in evaluating this and similar phenomena, we have to juggle two antagonistic value systems simultaneously, one at the level of the population, the other at the level of the individual.

The issue of why schizophrenia occurs in about the same 1% of the population in all parts of the world has long baffled behavioral scientists. Though almost all workers in the field agree that a complex of many genes is at the root of the disease (Rosenthal and Kety, 1968), the question has remained: How can schizophrenia persist at so high a percentage if there is anything to natural selection? Only recently have we found that an old "layman's" explanation is in part true—schizophrenia is associated with creativity. However, it is usually not the patients who are creative, debilitated as they are, but rather their children or siblings (Heston, 1966). Schizophrenia is, so to speak, a price paid by the family and the breeding population for the creative phenotypes associated with it.

Similarly, there is the tragic disease known as infantile autism. One such child is described lovingly and beautifully in *The Child in the Glass Ball* by his own mother, and one can see in this book how autistic children form a protective shield of nonresponsiveness around themselves (Junker, 1964). Parents may make mistakes and help the process along, but basically autism stems from the inborn nature of the child (Rimland, 1964). The disease is relatively rare, afflicting about 1 in 40,000. What are the chances, then, of its occurring in the families of five theoretical physicists in the state of California (Rimland, 1974)? Again, given that the relationship of theoretical brilliance and infantile autism holds up, it is reasonable to hypothesize that autism is a price paid by the population for this sort of exquisite mind.

My last example involves homosexuality. What can be more antievolutionary in a narrow sense than nonreproducing individuals, particularly when there is evidence for genetic predisposition to male homosexuality (Heston and Shields, 1968). However, D. J. Weinrich (1976) exhaustively reviewed all the evidence that relates nonreproductive individuals and intelligence and found a substantial correlation between high I.Q. and homosexuality. Again, if the unit of reference is the population, "nonreproductive" is not a synonym for "unnatural," for the intelligent, productive homosexual is clearly contributing to the perpetuation of his or her society.

CHICKEN AND EGGS

It follows from the preceding examples that when sociobiologists insist that evolutionary change results primarily from competition among individuals (the Fisher world view), they are leaving out something important. For there is no reasonable way to explain the existence of schizophrenia or homosexuality via selfish genes. Yet, at least half the insights in this book are attributable to selfish-gene logic, and we are confronted with two apparently opposed world views, neither of which we can do without.

It is, in fact, the chicken and egg problem revisited. Selfish-gene theorists have brazenly put their money on the gene, or at most the individual, as the "primary" unit and have assumed that genes preceded individuals and that individuals preceded the family. That is, they have seemed willing to say that the egg came before the chicken. Or, to use another chicken and egg example, in the beginning there were monkeys, then came monkey troops.

However, there is no evidence to support this claim and, as far as anyone knows, families, troops, and populations are as primary as are the individuals who compose them. All we know is that social organization varies with species and that differential selection probably occurs at all levels, from individual through family and breeding population. After all, sociality is at least as old as the slime molds, so that even at the level of phylogeny there is no precedence of the individual over the social group. Sexuality, too, resists an explanation based on individual competition, and we simply do not know how it got started.

The chicken and egg problem, whatever its current disguise, has never been solved and sociobiologists who believe they have done so are deluding themselves. Theories from below are, after all, no more than clever games aimed at throwing some light on the mysteries of life. Insofar as they are successful, they are exciting. They become dangerous, however, when, in the words of G. C. Williams (1966), a staunch exponent of the inductive approach from below, they become "the light and the way." For the irony here is that under the guise of maintaining a hardheaded attitude a leap of faith is made, and the empiricist is transmuted into the worshiper of inductive method, whereas the holist-"philosopher" is the simple realist who believes what he sees: that current explanations of life are probably all circular and that the essential mystery of matter and space is as great as ever.

THE CIRCULARITY OF BIOLOGICAL KNOWLEDGE

In truth, much of biological understanding is circular. Every time we think we are on to a basic mechanism of development or evolution, it turns into a circular argument.

Let me explain, starting with the example of DNA (deoxyribonucleic acid). In recent years, DNA, found in the gametic material of all living things, has been shown to carry the blueprint for subsequent organic development. Following this discovery by Watson and Crick, there was great optimism that all living things might be charted and explained in a masterwork of DNA cryptography (Crick et al., 1961). This position, however, has become less tenable with time, and it is now clear that there is no single starting point of life. Instead, DNA is now viewed as a convenient way of sending life on to the next generation, for the very production of this substance remains unexplained. Consider that in order to replicate DNA, the enzyme DNA polymerase is required. DNA polymerase, in turn, is itself encoded in the gametic DNA, so that the very mechanism by which duplication occurs is, necessarily, already present.

Mutation is another case in point. Presumably, genetic variations are caused, ultimately, by mutations in those DNA molecules that compose the "genes." Since variation is the basis for evolutionary change, "random" mutation is said to be the major mechanism of evolutionary change. As best as I can tell, this notion stems from the sheer fantasy that "in the beginning" there was random activity out of which emerged organization. In fact, random mutation has never been observed. Instead, we know that mutation rates vary with genes and between species, so that if mutation rates for man were the same as they are for insects such as *Drosophila*, our genetic load of defects would immediately extinguish our species. Clearly, the mutation rates are adjusted in some unknown way to what the species can stand (Crow, 1959). Furthermore, within any species certain chromosomal locations ("hot" spots) mutate more than do others, and most never mutate at all (Wright, 1977), apparently depending on whether such change is or is not adaptive for the genome as a whole. The picture, then, is one in which a major mechanism of evolution, mutation, is itself controlled by adaptive, evolutionary processes, and instead of an "ultimate" causal mechanism we find ourselves in yet another circle.

A third example involves embryonic development. C. H. Waddington, who started his work in Spemann's laboratories in the 1920s, was fascinated by the latter's discovery of an "organizing center" into which streamed random cells and out of which emerged organized cellular patterns (ectoderm, mesoderm, and endoderm). But as he continued his search for a single organizing substance, Waddington found that even inorganic chemicals, such as methylene blue, could evoke a certain degree of organization. He came to the reluctant conclusion that there is a "readiness" in cells to become organized and that activation and readiness are, so to speak, two sides of the same coin (Waddington, 1947). Again, what started as a search for causal agency ended in what was for many scientists an unsatisfactory, circular concept.

Given that most of Western science follows similar causal models, the limitations of the selfish-gene concept are not damning, and its usefulness is certainly no less than that of mutation theory, with its clearly demonstrated circularity. This is not a doctrine of despair unless one denies that there is more to life than inductive scientific thought. There is, after all, the existential level of day to day living, and it is, in fact, from that level that the more interesting hypotheses in this book are derived; from creative introspection, if you will, in a co-mingling of science and real life. It was Kurt Goldstein's genius that enabled him to incorporate this view into a rule of procedure for biological and behavioral research.

> With our holistic approach, we are faced with a very difficult epistemological problem. For us there is no doubt that the

atomistic method ["approach from below"] is the only legitimate scientific procedure for gaining facts. Knowledge of human nature has to be based on phenomena disclosed in this way. But is it possible to proceed from material gained by the use of this method to a science of the *organism as a whole,* to a science of the nature of man?

If the organism were a sum of parts which one could study separately, there would be no difficulty in combining the parts to form a science of the whole. But *all* attempts to understand the organism as a whole directly from these phenomena have met with very little success. They have not been successful, we may conclude, because the organism is not such a sum of parts.

Holism does not try to construct the architecture of the organism by a mere addition of brick to brick; rather it tries to discover the actual *Gestalt* of the intrinsic structure of this building, a *Gestalt* through which some phenomena may be intelligible as belonging to a unitary, ordered, relatively constant formation of a specific structure, and other phenomena may become intelligible as *not* belonging to it.

We can arrive at this only by using a special procedure of cognition—a form of creative activity by which we build a picture of the organism on the basis of the facts gained through the analytic method, in a form of ideation similar to the procedure of an artist. It is a sort of ideation, however, which springs ever again from the empirical facts, and never fails to be grounded in and substantiated by them. (1963, p. 9)

LEVELS OF EVIDENCE

It follows from Goldstein's statement that there is more to the scientific endeavor than the careful gathering of hard facts, although that task is basic. There is, for one thing, a second level of not-so-hard facts—findings of small-scale studies in which trends rather than firm, repeatable findings emerge. Both these categories, hard and not-so-hard, are well represented in this book, but there is perhaps too much of the second. A substantial number of studies are reported that were the term projects of students. They tend to be short and sweet, interesting if uneven, and never sufficiently persuasive to change one's mind about an issue. It is the sheer accumulation of these softer studies, within the context of the developing argument, that makes them worthwhile.

Then there are the levels that most creative scientists work at, often in secret. I have already alluded to the accumulation of anecdotes, personal experiences, and intuitive truths that shapes each of us and creates the set for further knowledge. Every scientist I respect has free and easy access to these inner levels of information and, furthermore, this personal knowledge plays an important role in the scientific questions each asks and in his or her choice of experiments. This is true of mathematicians and physical scientists (see, for example, Einstein and Infeld, 1938; Poincaré, 1914), as well as behavioral scientists, although the published scientific product rarely acknowledges such roots.

In writing this book, I specifically set out to include the intuitive steps that led to many of the studies reported. I occasionally refer to my parents, my own experiences as a parent, personal thoughts, incidental observations I have made, and the personal experiences of close friends. I assume that most of us construct our view of the world with such materials, and I have therefore made little attempt to disguise this.

I leave it, then, to the reader to do the same as I have done. To cull critically, to take and to discard, and to use this work as he or she will in the service of an objectively based, but personal world view. By my leave or not, you will of course do that anyway.

2

Gametic Potential

Males and females have differing roles in evolution.*
Females generally produce far fewer ova than males do sper-
matozoa, and from this fact flows certain heretofore neglected predictions. A human male overproduces sperm (male gametes) by a
factor of ten thousand and potentially could populate the universe
with his own offspring. Or, to be rather more practical and measure
by the number of emissions rather than by the number of sperm, an
average 17-year-old male (as judged by sexual and masturbatory activity of teenagers in our own culture) has the potential to fecundate
well over 365 women a year.

Human females, by contrast, produce at most 400 eggs (female
gametes) in a lifetime, and women are theoretically limited to some
60 offspring. The *Guinness Book of World Records* reports that one
mother delivered 69 offspring—but most of her 27 deliveries were
multiple births. The same source informs us that the last Sharifan
emperor of Morocco (1672–1727) achieved a modern male record of
888 offspring.

Given the vast difference in reproductive potential, and if the
point of life is to actualize such potential, is it not reasonable to expect that on the average the male pattern of courtship will differ
from the female? Might nature not have arranged it so that men are
ready to fecundate almost any female and that selectivity of mates
has become the female prerogative?

In many species this does appear to be the case. Spieth (1952)
has shown that in various species of the genus *Drosophila*, the fruit
fly, the male will court anyone, whether his own species or another.
True, he prefers his own, but if only females of other *Drosophila*

---

* In this chapter it will be convenient to take the mechanistic selfish-gene approach
and see what it says about the different roles males and females have had in evolution. In chapters 3 and 4, when I start talking about groups, the issue of Chapter 1
("which came first, the group or the individual?") will reappear.

species are present, he will court them. The female, however, will reject all members of other species, as well as many members of her own, and she makes these judgments by as yet unknown criteria.

Bateman (1948) has also worked with fruit flies and has noted some important trends. In a carefully controlled study, he found that whereas almost all females have young, a small proportion of the males in a population do a large proportion of the successful mating. Whereas only 4% of the females produced no progeny, 21% of the males produced none. It is perhaps astounding that we have similar figures among mammals. Koford (1963), working with free-ranging rhesus monkeys imported to Cayo Santiago island (just off Puerto Rico's coast), observed: "Roughly, the highest fifth of the males performed four-fifths of the observed copulations. . . . At least half of the males of breeding age rarely or not at all, apparently because of social inhibition."

It is probably more than coincidence that similar rates of male mating success are found among the polygynous* Yanomamo in the Venezuelan and Brazilian jungles (Chagnon, 1968, 1972). About the same proportions of males have the majority of wives and children: in any village some males will have 4 or more wives and 20 or more children, others rather fewer wives and children; but about one-fourth of mature males will be childless. Chagnon (1968) reports that the variance in numbers of offspring among men of a village can be as much as 10 times that of females. That is to say, among men, the variability from man to man to man is as much as 10 times greater than the variability from woman to woman. This disparity is not peculiar to the Yanomamo for polygyny, by definition, yields a skewed distribution—a few men have many wives, most have but one, and a substantial number have none (see Thomas, 1959, for comparable figures among Bushmen). Thus, in fruit flies, rhesus monkeys, and some polygynous tribes, females tend to cluster about an average number of young whereas males form a greatly skewed curve, some very successful, many not successful at all. And, since most mammals are polygynous (Brown, 1975), this tendency may characterize the entire class Mammalia.

Perhaps the best explanation for such consistencies is that eggs are needed to nourish the developing embryo and they are therefore larger and fewer than sperm; in other words, bearers of ova are the scarce resource for which the bearers of sperm must compete. Males are thus relatively promiscuous, and even in species that are apparently monogamous, as are most bird species, there is a decided tendency for already mated males to seek other females.

---

* Polygyny = many wives; polyandry = many husbands; polygamy = many mates.

In spring, when the gonads are at the peak of their development, there are attempts to "rape" strange females in the mallard and pintail and a few other species. Heinroth describes these raping flights: "In a shallow bay of the pond the female of the mallard, pair A, seeks food by upending; her mate is close by keeping watch. A hundred feet away a second pair B, comes down on the water. Male A quickly swims towards the strange female B, finally flying towards her, but she takes flight at the last moment and a wild aerial chase begins. The pursued duck rises higher and higher, the strange drake A behind her; she tries to escape by swerving and suddenly flying slowly, and both are followed by male B since he does not know where his mate will end up. Thus one sees two drakes following a duck, and this is generally interpreted as if both were chasing the duck; in reality, however, a strange male is chasing the female of a pair which belong together. Gradually male A gives up and returns directly to his mate. (Grzimek, 1972, vol. 7, p. 270)

It would appear that if the mallard drake had his way his would be a polygynous species and, in fact, one does occasionally see a consortship of two females and a male.

In our own species and our own culture, I am asserting nothing startling when I point out that with sexual maturity, most heterosexual males are in constant search of females, and if inhibited about sexual contact, they fantasize almost continuously and fairly indiscriminately about such contact. Like Philip Roth's *Portnoy* (1969), adolescent males in our culture frequently experience life as a nearly continuous erection—spaced by valleys of depression that accompany sexual disappointment.

Although masturbation is the major outlet for middle-class American boys (Kinsey et al., 1948), most mothers cannot believe these data ("My son masturbate nightly? Nonsense!"), for female and male sex drives are substantially different (see Shaffer and Shoben, 1956). It is clear, however, that whereas the frequency of "outlet" for males is greater, female lust and fantasy were greatly underplayed in Kinsey's report (1953). Recent case reports by female researchers have gotten beyond the guilt and reticence many females feel concerning their sexual fantasies (Bry, 1975; Friday, 1974), and it is now apparent that females, too, may visualize a rich assortment of sexual acts either while engaged in masturbation or intercourse or while daydreaming. Additionally, there are data that these feelings of lust are cyclical in women, reaching a monthly peak at the time of ovulation (Benedeck, 1952).

All things considered, however, it would appear that men are indeed more polygamous in their motivation than women, so that it behooves women to become expert in selecting males who will not desert them and their children. Indeed, love and marriage is the usual way paternal involvement in childrearing is achieved, and the evolutionary point of courtship and love is, apparently, to tie the sexes in an emotional bond that is hard to break (see especially Lorenz, 1966).* All cultures, however, have recognized the ephemeral aspects of love, and marriage ceremonies are everywhere a means of adding some external cement to the tie.

In this light, then, it would appear that monogamous marriage fulfills the average female's strategy but that for the male it is often just a first step: all the woman needs to experience full genetic potential is one good protector, provider, and impregnator; but the fact that 75% of the world's culture areas are polygynous (see Murdock, 1957) seems to point to this system as being most in tune with the species' natural requirements (fulfilling both the male and female strategies).

THE NORMAL CURVE

I must at this point address my female readers directly. I know that many of you are bothered with the way this discussion is going. Certainly if I were a woman evolutionist, I would shade these remarks differently, perhaps stressing female solicitation and choice in the mating encounter, as did Callan (1970), but I know no women who are specialists in this field who do not view sex differences in much the same way (see, for example, Hutt, 1972).

On the other hand, my secretary, in typing an early version of this manuscript, refused to continue on the ground that she was contributing to the perpetuation of sexism. She is an intelligent woman of about 24, and in a frank talk, from which we both emerged a little more clearheaded, she felt I was saying all women fit into a single, outmoded mold.

She was right insofar as I have spoken as if there were an Aristotelian ideal man and ideal woman rather than a full and grand variation of males and females. Clearly most American college women of today object to the label "passive and nonassertive," for the current "ego ideal" is the assertive woman. Therefore, let me immediately point out that it is a basic biological assumption that such complex traits as "assertiveness" will vary within the population

---

* Henry Harpending and Francis Purefoy (1978) have pointed out that in gibbons and in humans, unlike other mammals, estrus is "hidden": ovulation occurs in the absence of overt signaling such as colorful swelling or obvious smells. This situation would tend to encourage prolonged consortship since the male cannot simply "love 'em and leave 'em" with much genetic success. In fact, only in gibbons and man do we find copulation occurring at all times in the estrous cycle, even during pregnancy. Like humans, gibbons embrace, coo in each other's ears, "smile" by way of greeting rather than fear, and even purse their lips affectionately (Carpenter, 1940). Male-female attachments are thereby strengthened, and monogamy is the rule in gibbons and common in man.

roughly in the form of a normal curve; that is, the great majority will occupy the middle range and a minority of very passive and very assertive females will fall at either end. Any point on this curve—any form of assertiveness within a population—is, for an evolutionist, normal. Evolutionary change, after all, depends on small, unusual samples from the larger population taking over during times of environmental crisis, so that what was a central tendency in one epoch might be merely vestigial in another—and vice versa. This logic will hold true for all of my subsequent statements about "most men," "most women," "most mallards," and so on.

It is therefore normal to find highly assertive (and highly passive) women but, as we shall see in Chapter 3, women, on average, show less assertiveness and aggression than do men.*

There is, however, a further question. Can the shifting of a cultural ideal for feminine behavior from accepting to assertive actually shift the manifest types found in the population? Of course, it can and it has. But all the evidence indicates that the male curve of assertiveness is capable of even greater shifts toward the aggressive end (e.g., Maccoby and Jacklin, 1974), so that malleability does not in this case mean an interchangeability of traits between the sexes.

The key to most sex differences, I believe, is childbearing, and at least one factor in the present-day shift in ideal type is the dramatic reduction in birthrate. As a geneticist would put it, although the female *genotype* (chromosomal constitution) remains stable, environmental changes are causing a shift in *phenotype* (the manifest traits).

This, in turn, brings up the issue of how cultural settings encourage or discourage female independence and assertiveness? That will be our next concern.

---

* Dawkins (1976) pointed out that any sexually reproducing population will theoretically reach an equilibrium, say, between *coy* versus *fast* females, on the one hand, and *faithful* versus *philandering* males, on the other. In a large population, each variant has a certain advantage, and we do in fact see a great many personality types and courtship strategies in any species we study carefully. That is, no matter what the species' central tendency (e.g., monogamy versus polygamy), careful study always reveals considerable variety in temperament, "personality," courtship strategy, parenting behavior, and so on. No two gulls, or any two humans, are precisely alike. Such variation not only aids in gross recognition but also provides for a mesh of traits and strategies that give the population its dynamism and potential for change.

I must add the usual quibble, for Dawkins talks about genes for coyness and genes for fastness entering the population at different rates, depending upon the genes' relative success. I simply do not think in this way. Such traits are obviously *not* determined by single genes, and the model is wrong at its inception. These traits are, rather, almost certainly polygenic and each of us is a unique blend of opposed tendencies. To my mind, the selection of complex traits is best regarded as a multiply caused process, a response to simultaneous pressures at all levels of selection. Recent evidence, by the way, would make us conceive of a "sociopathic-moralistic" continuum in much the same way (Cloninger et al., 1975).

MATRILINY—PATRILINY

Any discussion of environmental influences in the social roles of men and women must start with a discussion of the two major ways humans reckon biological descent, descent through the mother (matriliny) or through the father (patriliny). There are, in fact, many versions of each: matrilineal but living in the husband's village, patrilineal with variable residence, descent with a matrilineal bias, descent with a patrilineal bias, and so on (see Schuskey, 1974). However, one important fact shines through: a woman's relative freedom of action, her ability to exercise power, and her independence of male authority is bound up with the' fact that everyone in her culture tracks descent through either the mother or the father. In short, descent through the father usually reinforces male prerogatives and power, whereas descent through the mother dilutes that power and increases female freedom and mobility. I must add, however, that no culture has yet been described in which primary political power does not reside with males, so we are talking about relative status and relative independence of females.

The following are examples of matrilineal tribes that exhibit this semiturnaround in female status even though they are all polygynous. The Ashanti of Ghana (Basehart, 1961), the Abouré of the Ivory Coast (Clignet, 1970), the Navajo (Aberle, 1961), the Garo of Assam (Nakane, 1967), and an Islamic group living on the Laccadive Islands off the west coast of India (Dube, 1969). In all these cultures, women, whether in monogamous or polygynous marriages, have a level of freedom and self-respect rarely seen within the far more numerous patrilineal groups of this world.

Among these and most other matrifocal peoples (where the family is centered around the mother), including Navajo and Afro-Americans, the role of the husband in marriage is openly acknowledged as temporary, the easy "come and go" of males is institutionalized, and divorce rates consequently tend to be high (Dube, 1969; Schneider and Gough, 1961). In a study of first marriages, Hilsdale (1962) reported that 40% of Afro-American females were skeptical that the marriage they were about to enter was an absolute action. Comparable skepticism occurred in only 5% of the patrifocal Euro-American females. Similar statistics among the Navajo are not available, but I have found in my work on the Navajo reservation, over some five years, that first marriages that last beyond three years are rare and apparently have been so for at least a century. In other words, in patrilineal, patrifocal systems women regard marriage as a major event and they are ready to pay the price of secondary citizenship to maintain conjugal stability. In matrilineal or matrifocal societies, women are not so bound to the marital arrangement.

An important sociobiological point here is that when relationships and property rights are traced primarily through the female, a promiscuous male strategy is encouraged. This is sometimes countered by high levels of female promiscuity, which, when it occurs, leads to substantial uncertainty about paternity. Kurland (1976) has proposed that if the uncertainty is sufficiently high (if chances of cuckoldry are greater than one in three), males will be safer contributing to the care of their sisters' children, who are indisputably kin. In fact, there are a number of matrilineal cultures in which fathers do provide primarily for their sister's children: the great Ashanti tribe of Africa, Malinowski's famous Trobrianders of Melanesia (Schneider and Gough, 1961), and, to some extent, urban Afro-Americans (see Rainwater, 1966).

Whereas matrilineal societies lend women substantially more independence than do patrilineal societies, the former have nevertheless tended to be polygynous. Thus, there is no necessary connection between a female's status in a society and her being one of many wives. Conversely, no guarantee of women's rights accompanies a monogamous system, as our own Euro-American culture demonstrates.

In the past, men in white American culture had been more ambivalent about marriage than women. The apparent reason was that social and legal sanctions against breaking monogamous vows were sufficiently severe to make him think twice about agreeing to limit, for all time, his sexual access to other women.

Ironically, as severe male-centeredness has shifted toward female-centeredness, marriage vows have been relaxed, even as they are in matrilineal societies. At the same time, the threat of male desertion has risen so that ambivalence about marriage in young white females is probably now approaching the Afro-American figures reported by Hilsdale. This trend is symbolized by the many young American women who are now hyphenating their and their husband's surnames; others are dropping his name altogether. This tendency may be seen as heralding a new era in women's freedom, but it is as well an old, matrilineal story.

If we are indeed going that way, ours apparently will be the first recorded case of a patrilineal culture's switching to matrilineality (Van den Berghe and Barash, 1977).

CULTURAL UNIVERSALS: MALE BRAGGING AND THE DOUBLE STANDARD

Despite such shifting patterns, certain male-female differences can be expected to remain the same. Male bragging about sexual exploits is probably familiar to every anthropologist, no matter his culture area and its patrilineality or matrilineality. I have heard men boast of their sexual activity among the Hausa of Nigeria, the Balinese, Japanese, Navajo, and Hopi, and I assume such tales are to be heard anywhere that young men get together. Men find playing the role of omnipotent lover fun, but women often find this role disgusting because of the double standard.

The double standard seems to be present just about everywhere (Ford and Beach, 1951). Many cultures give considerably more sexual freedom to women than does our own, but even amongst the most liberal cultures, promiscuous men receive fewer sanctions. Consider the pastoral Masai of East Africa. Young men live apart in a special house, and both sexes are permitted considerable sexual promiscuity in and around these quarters. Nevertheless, a Masai girl can be thought *too* promiscuous, whereas a boy has to be unusually active before he is so stigmatized. This is almost exactly the picture among Polynesian youth in Tahiti (Levy, 1973) and among the Hopi in the American Southwest (Simmons, 1942). Despite the fact that in all three cultures there is no stigma attached to a girl who has her first few children out of wedlock, all three groups come down harder on female promiscuity. Why so?

Cultures, after all, did not appear out of the blue, in some spontaneous explosion of symbolic interaction, and we have to assume that cultural universals reflect those aspects of our species that were evolutionarily derived (evolved). Male promiscuity is universally winked at because there is nothing much we can do about it, and Kinsey's (1953) main findings appear to be descriptions of the species: males must have frequent "outlets" for sex, whether heterosexual or homosexual; whereas many females can go for long periods without copulation or masturbation (see also Money and Ehrhardt, 1972). And this difference appears to hinge on the difference in gametic potential that we have been discussing.

JEALOUSY

No one has as yet systematically compared patterns of male-female jealousy within patrilineal and matrilineal societies, but given my previous remarks about institutionalized uncertainty of paternity in many matrilineal cultures, and the consequent subtle encouragement of both male and female promiscuity, it is likely that sexual jealousy in matrilineal groups is less than that in patrilineal groups. There are several nineteenth-century reports by Europeans on the Nayars of India's Kerala state, for example, expressing amazement and awe at the lack of male jealousy over a lover's polyandrous liaisons (Fuller, 1974). The Nayars are famous, however, because they are so exceptional.

The following remarks apply mainly to patrilineal societies, and we will assume that they hold in mitigated form for most matrilineal relationships as well, including *current* Nayar society (Fuller, 1974).

A paradigm for jealousy in patriarchies is provided by the gelada baboon. This example is not presented as a homolog, mind you, just as an illustration. The gelada is a polygynous species in which one-male harems are formed; the surplus males are gathered in bachelor troops, a situation not unlike human polygyny. Within the harem, the oldest, dominant "wife" will not tolerate any extended contact between her male and strange females. Although she will tolerate a quickly consummated sex act, she will attack and bite the female intruder should her male and the stranger start grooming, for therein lies the basis for a relationship (Kummer, 1968, 1971). Although the baboon female lacks the ability to reason this situation out, our own reasoning runs: a relationship means time away from her and her offspring, so that it is in the wife's "selfish" interest to try to prevent such a liaison.

The female gelada also plays an active role in choosing the male's secondary wives and if a new mate displeases the head female, the newcomer will not remain long. This situation sounds sufficiently like human polygynous marriage so that I think we can safely make the following generalization: the problem for the mated female in a patriarchal society, whether the mating is polygynous or monogamous, is to prevent her mate's straying; if she cannot control his sexual activity, it is most important to prevent his becoming attached to another female, specifically a female she cannot dominate.

Thus, in humans, relations with prostitutes are generally tolerated for an attachment to a whore is everywhere deemed unlikely. As in the gelada baboon, in humans female jealousy is based not on the male's sex act with another woman but on his potential attachment to the latter. It is his exclusive or, in polygyny, his favored care for the wife and her offspring that is the primary goal in the female strategy.

Male jealousy is rather different. It is one thing to have (and impregnate) many women, but even the sated sultan makes sure that there are no sexual intruders. Probably all men, and most certainly those in societies that trace descent exclusively through males, fear cuckoldry (the word is derived from the cuckoo, who brazenly deposits her eggs in a songbird's nest and thereby spares herself the trouble of childrearing). Strindberg, for example, was obsessed with the idea that no man can be absolutely sure of paternity, and he brooded about this subject brilliantly and at length in *Miss Julie* and *The Father*. I know a young Harvard man who claimed not to have a "jealous bone in my body" and who treated his girlfriend most casually. But when "his woman" became committed to another, his subsequent remorse and pain put the lie to the original bravado. This is an old plot line, and many a male has discovered his full commitment to a female only when faced with her loss to another. It is the rival who brings out a male's jealousy, and although the response may be oedipal, it also follows the evolutionary logic of genetic descent. Thus, when Roheim (1969) demonstrates oedipal rivalry in matrilineal societies in support of the Freudian concept, the sociobiologists delight in those same apparent universals, for it is important to know that whereas anger over cuckoldry can be reduced with cultural change, it nevertheless continues to lurk as a persistent social force.

The evolutionary point of male jealousy is obvious. It does not make evolutionary sense for the male to invest in a child not possessing his genes, and the murderous jealousy exhibited by a cuckolded male is biologically sensible. Such a response, we can surmise, evolved to minimize female cheating and to assure that the children a man supports are his own. Furthermore, the cuckold's retribution can strike either the female or the male cheater, so that both cheat only with immense trepidation. Even a weakling husband is dangerous when cuckolded, and most legal systems (perhaps *all* patrilineal systems) wink at the ensuing violence.

ADOPTION

As an argument against this theme of genetic descent it may be claimed that as much love can be developed for an unrelated, adopted child as for a genetic child. However, the facts do not appear to bear this out. In a study I am now conducting, even the best-meaning adopting parents can be seen to favor their own blood children. If the results do indeed go this way, the findings that show that adopted children in our society do not do as well as the nonadopted (e.g., Ainsworth, 1967; Bowlby, 1952), presumably because of changes in parenting figures per se, might be looked at again. For although a parent may be scrupulously fair with his adopted children or stepchildren, he or she may not be as all-forgiving or as ready to step beyond the "call of duty" as with blood children, which in turn would differentially affect a child's self-concept. In a remarkable study of Scottish adopted children who were seeking their biological parents, Triseliotis (1973) was impressed by the feelings of "inner emptiness" so many adoptees felt, whether or not they had been adopted at birth and whether or not they had got on well with their adoptive parents. Though his was a selected population, the inescapable conclusion was that "no person should be cut off from his origins."

There are few good cross-cultural data available, but as we shall see in Chapter 6 nonindustrial cultures tend to restrict adoptions to the sphere of close kin. Probably as a result, considerably more adoption and passing around of children occurs among such tribal people as Navajo and Hopi than white Americans generally are accustomed to. Western adoption procedures are also tribal in the sense that there usually has been extensive matching of the adoptive and biological parents on such factors as race, religion, national origin, coloring, schooling, and intelligence. Although there was a brief period in the United States in which transracial adoptions were popular, strong objections raised by black and Indian minorities, largely around the issue of parental matching, have slowed such adoptions to a trickle (Simon and Alstein, 1977).

The best adopters are apparently those who already have biological children of their own (Humphry, 1965; Simon and Alstein, 1977). Once that is out of the way, so to speak, further adoptions can be made on a relatively selfless basis. And even there, the better adopters are realistic about subtle (and not so subtle) differences in their feelings toward their biological and adopted children; they simply do their best to avoid favoritism (Simon and Alstein, 1977; also see Appendix Study 1).

Again, it can be instructive to look at relevant data from other species. In this case, reports by the Japanese primatologists Sugiyama (1967) and Yoshiba (1968) on the Hanuman langurs of India, later confirmed by Hrdy (1977), are of extreme interest. At Dharwar, Yoshiba found that these handsome monkeys existed in two types of groups, in one-male harems with some seven to nine females, their offspring, and an occasional subadult, and in all-male bachelor groups.

All three observers report that from time to time an all-male bachelor group will attack a harem, concentrating their effort on the head monkey. If he is driven off, one of the bachelors usually supplants him, and the other bachelors withdraw. The new head then systematically kills off all the nursing infants by tearing them away from their mothers, one at a time, and lacerating them with his canines. The mothers show no interest in the injured young, and they are left to die. The ex-mothers then come into estrus almost immediately and mate with the new "king," thereby assuring genetic continuity for themselves and the male.

There are potentially relevant human data. It is a fact that in 90% of severe maternal child abuse cases, the biological father is no longer living in the household (Helfer and Kempe, 1968). At what level of consciousness does the motivation for such an act operate? Does an abusive mother tell herself that she would be in a better position successfully to raise young to independence if she were to rid herself of her present child? Does she openly condone the "step-father's" abuse when he is the beater? This is most unlikely. But the parallel facts do hint that in langurs and man, similar nonconscious forces may be at work, and we need some good, careful studies to check on these possibilities.

We have here just scratched the surface of the issue of human adoptions and more will be said of them later. They comprise a crucial theoretical issue for sociobiology, and I will just mention here that a major contention involves anthropological reports, largely of Polynesian peoples, that no attention is paid to blood ties between adoptive parents and adopted child (Sahlins, 1976). For now, let it suffice to say that these reports are greatly exaggerated. The most recent and most complete ethnology of a Polynesian people, that by Robert Levy on the Tahitians (1973), makes it clear that actual blood lines are not forgotten throughout the lives of both the adopting and biological relatives. But the ease of adoption on Polynesian islands nevertheless needs some explanation, and the biological answer is almost too transparent: on isolated islands everybody is related anyway. I shall show in Chapter 6 that any ethnic group is far more inbred than generally realized and that island populations such as precontact Hawaii, which had been in relative isolation for some 500 years, must have had a startling degree of inbreeding. Thus, precontact Hawaiians who were second cousins were probably more closely related, genetically, than are the full sib children of today's average couples in, say, America or Brazil. Rather than detracting from the importance of genetic descent for human populations, lax adoption patterns in island populations (this is true in Melanesia as well: see Malinowski, 1929) become exceptions that support the rule: determining and protecting one's genetic descendants is a number one priority of human populations.

PHALAROPES AND JACANAS

I have pointed out that since males have greater gametic potential, they naturally vie with one another in pursuit of females. But nature refuses to be completely predictable, and there are exceptions. The most famous is the case of the phalarope. In this small shore bird, females vie with one another for the right to be fecundated by a male. The female fends off other females, threatening them and, if need be, attacking them with her beak. Not surprisingly, it is the female phalarope that is larger, more aggressive, and more brightly plumed than the male.

Grzimek (1972) tells us that

> the colorful breeding plumage of the female and her heightened disposition to fight result from a relatively large secretion of male hormones by the ovary. The brooding spots, on the other hand, which are present only in the male are the effect of prolactin, a hormone of the anterior lobe of the pituitary body, which is the same hormone that induces lactation in mammals during the suckling period.

> The majority of females of all species of phalaropes leave the nesting site at the time of incubation, so the offspring are generally reared only by the males until they can fly.... Since there is an excess of males in the breeding season, presumably, the females live polyandrously. (vol. 8, p. 147)

Polyandry has been directly observed in the phalarope's "cousins," the jacanas.

> Alfred Hoffman made a thorough study of the polyandry in the pheasant-tailed jacana at the palace lakes in Peking in 1946. He found that the female is able to present her males with a full clutch of four eggs each, at intervals from nine to twelve days.... Indeed the hen can provide four males with full clutches, each male twice in succession, so that between them they have six or eight clutches with a total of 24 to 36 eggs to incubate. (vol. 8, p. 145)

Needless to say, as in the phalarope, jacana females do not have much time for rearing young—that job is left entirely to the males.

If, then, we wish to make a rule and include phalaropes and jacanas, it must be rather abstract and go something like this: the sex that invests fewer resources in the *care* of the young will invest more resources in competition with others of the same sex. Stated this way, the rule acknowledges that it is indeed possible in nature for females to take the so-called male role if there is an adaptive advantage in doing so. In fact, in one species of coral fish the alpha female will actually become a male when the current single male leader is eaten or injured, thereby continuing the one-male harem arrangement (Robertson, 1972)!

Fish, by the way, offer something of a problem for the above rule in that fertilization is usually external, so that neither male nor female has a clear edge on investment in the young. Thus male sticklebacks not only stake out the territory but also guard the fertilized eggs, whereas in a larger number of species the fertilized eggs are simply left to float to the surface like plankton—as in the marine fishes—or else to sink to the floor—as in most freshwater forms (Grzimek, 1972, vol. 4).

As for an explanation of the relatively high frequency of polyandry in birds (Jenni, 1974) or, for that matter, the high incidence of monogamy (some 90%), any analysis must start with the fact that sex determination in birds reverses the mammalian picture: females are XY and males XX (Darlington, 1958). From here the reasoning becomes somewhat heavy-handed and complex, but having taken us this far, I have no choice but to give it. Let us start with a highly speculative paper by Whitney (1976), who, using the insights of kinship genetics, tried to explain mammalian-bird differences as follows:

1. In mammals, the X chromosome contains about 5% of the total genomic contribution; biologically speaking this is a sizable amount. The Y probably contains considerably less information.

2. Mammalian females with the same father all share his X chromosome; if they also have the same mother, they share her X chromosome half the time. This means females with the same mother and father, on the average, are more "related" to their sisters than to their brothers and may therefore be more inclined to non-competition and altruism with their own sex.

3. Since sex determination is the reverse in birds, the opposite should be true; since males are more related to male than to female siblings, they should be less competitive with other males than are mammalian males. Whitney claims this situation exists at least in a certain number of bird species.

What of the Y chromosome? Although it apparently contains very little genetic information, Bateman (1948) has hypothesized that it becomes the repository for increased aggression in males. Recent work with supernumerary Y's in humans bears this claim out, for there is strong evidence that XYY men who are otherwise normal are convicted for aggressive crimes at a level far above chance (Court Brown, 1969; Hook and Porter, 1977; for a dissenting view, see Witkin, 1976). In birds, on the other hand, the female has the opportunity to specialize the Y, and the frequency of bird polyandry may be in part the result of such "aggressive Y's."

All this must be coupled with sex differences in gametic potential, for in birds (as in mammals) females have a lower gametic production than males. Only then does it become sensible that we find such uniformity in mammalian male aggression and such diversity as to the more aggressive sex in birds. That is to say, in mammals the higher male gametic potential, a Y specialized for aggression, and an X specialized for altruism all lead in the same direction and uniformly produce males that are more competitive and aggressive than are females. In birds, there is a mixed picture: males have a higher gametic potential but an "altruistic" X in place of an "aggressive" Y. And, as a phylum, there is a correspondingly mixed species picture in male-female differentiation: although, on average, male birds are more aggressive than females, the tendency is for both sexes to be about the same size (monomorphism), for relationships to be monogamous (as opposed to polygynous, as in mammals), for the sex ratio to be more nearly equal (Selander, 1972), and for polyandry to occur in a number of species.

Our next concern is, How are the biologically based sex differences handled within the higher mammalian social groupings? In chapters 3 and 4 it will be helpful to look first to subhuman primates and then, given the primate patterns, to see whether they provide us with useful insights into human social arrangements.

3

Social Arrangements among Primates

The idea of selection at the level of the group is somewhat suspect within the biological establishment (see Alexander, 1974; Williams, 1971). However, it is simply not possible to deal with such items as territoriality, dominance-submission hierarchies, or population- control mechanisms without either invoking interdeme ("group") selection or else getting entangled in unlikely single-gene models.

For example, the enormous reproductive potential of a population can lead to its own downfall unless there are constraints on reproduction, and in fact populations rarely reach a density that makes a crash in numbers inevitable. Instead, as Wynne-Edwards (1962) has documented at great length, most populations have worked out controls that circumvent such knockout blows, usually via the mechanism of territoriality or (and this pattern has not been so well documented) via the establishment of dominance-submission hierarchies within and between groups. Groups do seem to have a life of their own that appears at odds with the individualism and competitiveness stressed by the selfish-gene approach.

To take a rough example, the current American consensus that population growth must be limited is quite outside the realm of a selfish-gene mode. The American rich have but 1.8 children per couple, and there is every indication that the poor are joining them in this statistic. If Americans were properly to follow the rule of maximizing their gametic contributions to the next generation we would not be witness to such a clearcut trend. Are we, then, to relegate these facts to the category of special case? If that is so, sociobiology is indeed an impoverished field, dealing with but a fraction of the human condition.

Sex itself is a major stumbling block for the selfish gene. Why bother with sex, which gets half one's genes into the next generation, when simple duplication will produce a 100% look-alike. After all, the goal of every gene is to get as many copies as possible into the next generation. The answer must be that *in the long run*, sexual reproduction is adaptive. But how did this long-run advantage ever become translated into sexuality? If genes are so selfish, how could they ever hold in abeyance immediate gain for subsequent reward? The only currently available answer, of course, is that selection accomplished this feat. Sex, then, is a sort of derivative altruism in this scheme, and the situation is much like the mutation problem mentioned in Chapter 1—quite circular: the major mechanism of natural selection, sexuality, was achieved by natural selection and in a manner not at all predictable from selfish-gene theory.

TERRITORIALITY

The staking out and defense of a territory, usually by the males of a species, and the formation of dominance-submission hierarchies in animal groups are the two most widespread means by which animals achieve a within-species social arrangement. As usual, there are two views of how territoriality and dominance-submission hierarchies evolved—the mechanistic view from below (selfish gene) and the holistic view from above (group selection).

From the selfish-gene view, since the widest spread of his seed is each male's goal, there are bound to be obstacles to his maximizing his genetic contribution to the future. Obviously, males will be bumping into other males in the rush and, leaving aside for now the female's role in mate selection, males will somehow have to work out a more or less orderly system of having sexual access to females. Of course, they might fight one another, but to what end? For while two are fighting, a third may run off with the desired female. The establishment of a defended territory, then, is seen as the individual's solution to such chaos. In this way he can at least assure himself of a bounded place in which he can hunt or forage, mate, and start the young off properly. Within this view, then, those organisms that first developed such territories were at an advantage, and their offspring, who inherited the same territorial tendencies, carried the tradition forward, and so on until this pattern characterized the entire breeding group.

Again, in this view, once the male has staked out a territory, the female would just as soon be the only mate there in order to insure her own genetic potential. So she is most likely to choose a male who is big, strong, and not likely, therefore, to be displaced; in monogamous species, she would want a male who indicates he will care only for her and who appears unlikely to spend energy raising another's young. In polygynous species she apparently has no choice but to settle for the first set of traits.

How does a male prove to a female he is all these things?

1. He establishes a central territory in good ground. For example, if they are urban robins, he stakes out soft ground with lots of worms and a good leafy tree away from heavy traffic.
2. He starts his advertising campaign by display—auditory, visual, or olfactory, or all three.
3. He drives other males out of the area.

In the contrasting view from above, especially as espoused by Wynne-Edwards (1962, 1971), the population is the evolving unit and territory is seen primarily as a mechanism for population control. That is, breeding groups of animals that failed to space themselves into adjacent territories not only experienced the mating chaos described earlier but also in seasons of food shortage might compete to the death were it not for some "agreement" regarding available resources. Without rules of precedence to allot the meager resources, all might die instead of just those in outlying, bare territories.

In Wynne-Edward's view (1971), selection must have occurred in the inevitable competition that exists between breeding groups, and those groups survived in which groupwide population controls were developed. Such a process would doubtless have entailed significant levels of inbreeding, for once everyone in a group is highly related, the development of group homeostasis is (theoretically) facilitated. I shall discuss the hypothetical effects of inbreeding in chapters 7 and 8, so let it suffice here to note that group selection does not involve extrascientific mechanisms. It is, at least, as understandable as is individual selection and simply involves a different level of organiza-tion—the breeding group viewed as a whole. Once again we confront the issue of the whole as more than just the sum of its parts.

As Wynne-Edwards has put it:

> A simple analogy may possibly help to bring out the significance of this point. A football team is made up of players individually selected for such qualities as skill, quickness, and stamina, material to their success as members of the team. The survival of the team to win the championship, however, is determined by entirely distinct criteria, namely, the tactics, and ability it displays in competition with other teams, under a particular code of conventions laid down for the game. There is no diffi-culty in distinguishing two levels of selection here, although the analogy is otherwise very imperfect. (1971, p. 101)

In animal groups,

> when the balance of a self-regulating population is disturbed, for example by heavy accidental mortality, or by a change in food-resource yields, a restorative reaction is set in motion. If the density has dropped below the optimum, the recruitment rate may be increased in a variety of ways, most simply by drawing on the reserve of potential fecundity referred to earlier, and so raising the reproductive output. Immigrants appearing from surrounding areas can be allowed to remain as recruits also. If the density has risen too high, aggression between individuals may build up to the point of expelling the surplus as emigrants; the reproductive rate may drop; and mortality due to social stress (and in some species cannibalism) may rise. These are typical examples of density-dependent homeostatic responses. (1971, p. 98)

For Wynne-Edwards, social hierarchies as well as territoriality play a leading part in regulating animal populations:

> Not only can [social hierarchies] be made to cut off any required proportion of the population from breeding, but also they have exactly the same effect in respect of food when it is in short supply. According to circumstances, the surplus tail of the hierarchy may either be disposed of or retained as a nonparticipating reserve if resourses permit. (1971, p. 100)

Although Dawkins would prefer to explain these social phenomena via the selfish gene, at least Wynne-Edwards's emphasis on the group as an evolving unit (intergroup selection) has the merit of dealing with group phenomena at the group level. My goal in this chapter, then, is to explain what I can by invoking genetic relatedness as the basis for altruistic acts and also to acknowledge the limitations of this approach when they arise.

THE STATUS HIERARCHY

Let us turn now to species that organize themselves into hierarchies based on relative aggressiveness. Actually, there is an interesting gradation from territorial to hierarchical animals. Many apparently territorial species, when forced by either natural or man-made circumstances into crowded conditions in which territories are impracticable, form a dominance-submission hierarchy instead. House cats, for example, are naturally territorial, but if several are kept in a small space either a hierarchy develops or else a despot emerges who dominates the rest. Underlying the establishment of territories, of course, there is an implicit status hierarchy in that territories usually can be ranked from better to worse.

When animals naturally group together, as do lions, wolves, and primates, dominance and submission behaviors are seen. Characteristically, the most aggressive males are at the top and the most intimidated at the bottom. Females are sometimes participant warriors in such a hierarchy, sometimes not, depending on whether female aggressiveness is generally important for that species, as it is for such predators as cats and dogs (felids and canids). Being head male often confers some advantages, and the top lion, for example, has access to all the females in heat and usually scares off any competing males from the pride (Grzimek, 1972, vol. 12). In wolves and wild dogs, on the other hand, a different arrangement holds. Since the pack can usually support only one litter per season and since male canids are unlike solitary cats and must cooperate in a large pack when hunting, a somewhat more democratic approach is taken as to who fecundates whom. Any pair who can withstand the constant kibitzing from and harassment by the rest of the pack may mate and thereby become the parents of that season's litter. In wolves, a male and female who are so enamored as to withstand nips at their flanks while courting have the mating advantage (Mech, 1966, Woolpy, 1967). Chances are very high in a wolf pack that everyone is related anyway, so it is not necessarily an unselfish act when the dominant male allows another male to mate: a substantial percentage of his genes are nevertheless getting into the next generation (Woolpy, 1967).

The adaptive point of this arrangement seems to involve the importance of having only a single litter to feed each season. More than one in a poor hunting season would exhaust the pack and, furthermore, if the litters were staggered the pack's mobility would be greatly reduced. Apparently for this "reason," Cape hunting dogs have been observed killing off a second litter, with the role of major executioner going to the mother of the first litter (Van Lawick, 1974).

Although mating among wolves suggests some human parallels with regard to sexual attachments, it is not until we get to the primates that we see dramatic parallels to human social groups. All species of primates combine varying degrees of amicability and aggression, and there are distinct correlations of these behaviors and the natural ecological setting. Those species that are always in trees, such as the howler monkeys of Central America, rarely fight one another (Carpenter, 1934). All are vegetarian (fruit and leaf eaters); there is usually food enough for everyone; and there are no tree-going predators to ward off. Apparently, because aggression is not at a premium among the arboreal primates, males are not much larger than females (low sexual dimorphism) and male-male aggression is relatively low (Jay, 1968). But in the semiarboreal, semiterrestrial species such as the langurs of Ceylon we see more disagreements within the troop, a rather more rigidly maintained dominance and submission pattern, and more pronounced dimorphism. And, in species on the ground *all day*, as are the baboons of East Africa, every troop member is watchful of his neighbors for all seem engaged in continual reassertion of dominance. Baboons exhibit substantial dimorphism—males are often twice the size of females; they also sport particularly large canines although they rarely eat meat, these teeth serving to intimidate both fellow baboons and potential predators. Even lions treat large baboon males with respect. Clearly, the degree of male aggression in monkeys and ecological adaptation go hand in glove.

It so happens that we know most about the semiarboreal, semiterrestrial genus of monkeys known as macaques, most especially that branch indigenous to Japan. Japanese scientists have been watching and recording the behavior of *Macaca fuscata* since the 1940s, and many monkey genealogies, with accompanying notes on behavior, go back that far (Imanishi and Altmann, 1965). These macaques are tough little beasts, and a visitor to a Japanese monkey park (where the animals are baited in from the adjoining mountains) sees and hears constant squabbling, chasing, screaming, nipping, and biting. I have spent many afternoons at a monkey park just outside Kyoto (Arashiyama), and I have seen the more brazen monkeys steal lunches, purses, and even cameras after intimidating their human victims.

Why so aggressive? Were these animals not fed by the park caretakers, they would spend more time eating in relative peace the leaves and fruit of trees; the tasty food thrown into the center of a throng of monkeys helps create havoc. But this event also brings into relief the macaques' great potential for aggression, as each animal tries to outdo the others in the quest for peanuts or a preferred spot to sit or, occasionally, in just straightforward intimidation. Naturally, it is the larger males who are the most involved in these attacks, with smaller females and juveniles keeping at a healthy distance and grabbing what food they can.

In general, the males of terrestrial primate species sort out the hierarchy with intensity and passion whereas female motivation is extremely variable from species to species and even from troop to troop within the same species. Wherever they get into the action, females occupy the lower half of the dominance order, with some overlap in the middle. Estrus usually makes a difference in that the females become more aggressive, while males, naturally, become more interested and tolerant (Jay, 1968).

But there are species in which females do not get involved at all and just let the males have at it (Kaufman, 1967). Also, within the single species of Japanese macaques, some troops are simply more pacific than others, and in these the females especially eschew fighting (Kawai, 1965).

We may now ask, at a theoretical level, what these findings mean. Because of Hamilton's papers (1963, 1964) primatologists are much more conscious of kinship relationships than ever before, and more and more instances of nepotism have been seen within monkey troops. It has become clear that aggressive attacks are not random: they tend to be directed at nonkin and most especially at males that have recently joined the troop (Kaufman, 1967). These newcomers tend to be either orphans or sons of low-ranking females so that for them there is nothing to lose and everything to gain by switching troops and seeking their fortunes elsewhere. However, their reception is usually hostile as suggested by these mortality figures: within the Cayo Santiago rhesus colony Koford (1963) found the sex ratio (males per 100 females) to be around 100 for ages zero to five, 50 for ages six to eight, and 17 at eight years or older. And this is an island that lacks monkey predators and on which Purina monkey chow is abundantly provided. Imagine what the ratios are in less hospitable circumstances! Koford also noted that about 20% of the males (all high on the status hierarchy) performed almost 80% of the copulations; whereas all estrous females tended to be impregnated. These data make it clear that only males are directly involved in differential selection among rhesus and most probably all the terrestrial and semiterrestrial primates. They are the major competitors, the big winners and the big losers.

We know now that one source of help in the status game is one's relatives. As we learn more and more about the genealogical relationships within monkey troops, we see that consanguineous networks exist in which kin tend to help one another (Kawai, 1965; Koyama, 1970; Sade, 1977). Koyama (1970), in fact, claims that all Japanese monkey troops consist of consanguineous relatives centered around the oldest female relative as a unit of social organization. In the same vein, Kawai (1965) has noted that Japanese macaques who gain the support of relatives in an aggressive encounter achieve a higher rank (if only temporarily) than macaques who challenge an animal on their own. He observed 14 instances in which a mother offered support, 6 in which a brother or sister did, 7 in which an aunt or uncle came to help out, and 1 in which a grandmother participated.

Junichiro Itani, perhaps the dean of Japanese primatologists, noted that just about every male Japanese macaque switches troops at some time in his life. However, there are exceptions. Itani reported on a five-year-old male, the son of a high-ranking mother, who remained in the central part of the troop long after his age mates either had been driven off or had left (see Imanishi and Altmann, 1965).

Similarly, among the rhesus of Cayo Santiago, Koford (1963) noticed that not all maturing males left the central hierarchy of the troop. Some adolescent males remained central and gained precedence over several older and larger males. In each instance the mother of the precocious sub-adult was either the highest ranking female in the band, or nearly so.

Since *all* mature females tend to be impregnated each season by a minority of males, the biological advantage for a female's having achieved a high rank is apparent only through her son's mating activity. Only if he is high ranking and therefore a frequent impregnator is her superior genetic destiny assured.

It also may benefit a female if her daughter achieves a high rank since her grandsons may then become successful impregnators. Accordingly, Sade (1967) found that "as rhesus females become adults they come to rank just below their mothers in the hierarchy of adults. This means that they defeat not only their age mates but also older females who were adults when they were growing up" (p. 113).

This material has been summed up nicely by Alan Fiske:

> Male fitness is highly contingent on obtaining a very high ranking position in the core of a band, and only the highest ranking mothers appear to be able to effect such a status for their sons directly. Lower ranking mothers do not waste their investment on securing a useless middle or low ranking position for their sons in the core of the group, but leave them to pursue the high risk strategy (of switching troops) which is their only chance of reproductive success, despite the high mortality entailed. The males who do most of the copulating protect their presumptive immature offspring, defending the troop from external threats and internal discord. (1973, p. 20)

Another point about rank and copulation: although nondominants may be seen copulating, the dominants tend to take over at the peak of estrus, the normal time of ovulation. There is much species to species and group to group variation in this arrangement, and it may actually work like that among wolves. The more inbred the group, the less the selection pressure for dominants to beat out subdominants in mating, for all troop members are related anyway.

As for female choice of a mate, no one seems to know quite how it works. From the fruit fly through baboons, chimps, and man, it is clear that females choose and even actively solicit from among available males, but the basis of this choice is rarely apparent. As I have said, among primates, dominance is just one (sometimes minor) fact of a male's attractiveness, and many subdominant males do father offspring (Altmann, 1977). It is one thing for a male to win a fight, quite another to have a female baboon accept him. And as far as we know there is no rape among subhuman primates.

One logical requirement of female choice is that she select males who give some promise of future aid such as would be suggested by an emotional bond that develops prior to fecundation. In rhesus monkeys and yellow baboons, at least, this sort of bonding does occur. A consortship develops between a mated pair, who remain together for some weeks at the group's periphery; often the male continues to be seen alongside the female throughout pregnancy and after the young are born. Recent data among yellow baboons indicate that a father may develop a special relationship with his child that lasts indefinitely (Altmann, 1977). Does permanent consortship or its promise increase the likelihood of impregnation, and is that why such behavior evolved? Probably yes. As for the defense of immatures by older males in the troop, this behavior has long been observed in both the baboons (DeVore, 1965) and the macaques (Itani, 1959), but this is the first time such action has been shown to be based upon actual paternity. In addition, there is evidence that adult males of the Japanese macaques form closer bonds with male than with female youngsters, and father-son collusion within the troop is a definite possibility.

In sum, most of our discussion of the macaques and baboons appears to corroborate the notions of selfish genes and gametic potential. As predicted by selfish-gene theory, nepotism abounds in that kin tend to defend kin, mothers help their young attain status, and males tend to favor the offspring of their consort, thus their own children; conversely, males are especially intolerant of males from other troops yet most leave their natal troop to try their luck elsewhere. As for gametic potential, we have considered evidence that high-ranking males often copulate more frequently than low-ranking males and that in general males either make it big as progenitors or do not make it at all; Females, by comparison, show little variation in numbers of offspring.

However, when we start asking questions at the level of the group, selfish genes and gametic potential fade as explanatory tools. We have already dealt with the question, Why do species vary in the level of male aggression? We can get more specific and ask, Why do monkeys form troops in the first place? How did intratroop dominance-submission hierarchies evolve? Why do new troops form from old, and why do the troops then become one another's "enemies"? These are difficult questions. I can say only that I accept monkey troops, sociality, and dominance-submission arrangements as "givens," as somehow having evolved over the millennia at the

level of the group. They are "beyond" the selfish gene and are simply another order of phenomenon. To use Hebb's (1959) analogy, one
does not discover the use to which a steel girder will be put by studying the electron structure of steel for you do not explain one level of
organization by referring to another. Novikoff made perhaps the
clearest statement on this issue when he said, "Knowledge of the
laws of the lower level is necessary for a full understanding of the
higher level; yet the unique properties of the higher level cannot be
predicted, *a priori,* from the laws of the lower level" (1945, p. 209).

With this lesson in mind, then, I shall now address a
phenomenon at the group level, the nature of attention in monkey
troops.

ATTENTION STRUCTURE

Status squabbles so pervade the life of terrestrial monkeys that
they are constantly watchful lest they be punished or miss a chance
to punish. Michael Chance of the University of Birmingham noted
that the attention of subordinates is always on those above them in
the hierarchy, so that if you multiply this effect throughout an entire
troop you get what can be termed the troop's attention structure, and
it is always oriented upward (Chance and Jolly, 1970). Thus, even
subtle behavior at the top is seen by everyone in the troop. The
character of the troop is thereby most readily influenced by the
behavior of the leadership.

As a result of this hierarchical structuring of attention new
habits, say, eating a new food, will descend through the troop in a
matter of hours if started by the alpha animal.* A case in point is the
Japanese monkey troop at Mino: one day the troop leader was seen
eating wheat although it was well established that the troop had
never touched this food before. Despite the fact that animals are normally very cautious about taking to new foods, the entire troop was
eating wheat within a matter of two days (Frisch, 1968, 1970).

On the other hand, a low-ranking juvenile has almost no influence at all—in the short run. The Japanese workers (Frisch, 1968)
have also traced how a new eating habit, the washing of sand from
sweet potatoes, started with a juvenile in an island group of
Japanese monkeys. The potatoes were placed daily on the sand by
the primatologists as a routine matter, when it was noted that Imo
(meaning sweet potato) began washing hers in the lagoon. Soon her
sibs were doing the same. After some months other low-ranking
monkeys were washing their sweet potatoes and the custom slowly

---

*For historical reasons, dominance hierarchies are always given in the Greek
alphabet.

made its way up the troop hierarchy. After four years half the troop had adopted this custom; after six years, some 70%. Nine years after Imo had made her discovery, all but a few were washing their potatoes. We can conclude from this and similar studies (Itani, 1965) that although juveniles because of their playfulness often achieve new and useful behavior, the response from the troop is far from overwhelming; whereas the alpha males, though not terribly inventive, have a very receptive audience.

Another aspect of being the dominant monkey is that the troop, since they are all watching this animal carefully, become attuned to his temperament, character, and mood. In Japanese monkeys, the social structure of the entire troop has been shown to vary with these traits in the leader. In Takasakyama, for example, the lead monkey, Jupiter, was old, tough, and crusty and tolerated only the females (with their young) and his long-standing male friends around him. Consequently, his troop looked something like this:

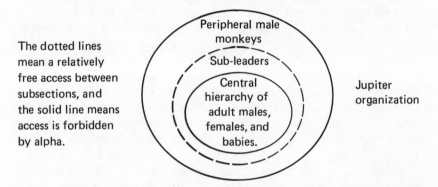

At Shodoshima there was another famous monkey leader called Atlas (the Japanese take their monkeys seriously, and what I am describing is common knowledge in Japan). Atlas was a peaceful sort who permitted easy access to the central hierarchy. As a consequence, his troop looked like this (Frisch, 1968, 1970):

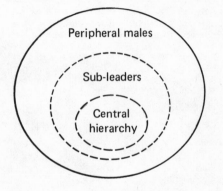

Yet another troop looked like the following; apparently the leader, Gengero, was annoyed by the juvenile males:

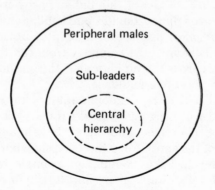

Peripheral males

Sub-leaders

Central
hierarchy

Sometimes leadership involves shifting coalitions of monkeys, usually relatives, and the troop's characteristics will change depending on the coalition in power (DeVore, 1965). The idea of attention structure remains the same, and we will see later that this concept is as useful in the study of human groups as in that of macaques and baboons.

For his part, an alpha male monkey carries himself in a manner that can be described as "lordly." He is erect, rarely looks from side to side but only in the direction in which he is heading, and expects others to get out of his way. His coat is shinier and more fluffy than those of the other troop members, and he looks much heavier than he in fact is. Alpha animals have something extra, something "charismatic" going for them. They apparently feel like winners and expect to be so treated. Actually, even after they are deposed, troop members continue to give them a certain respectful leeway. To repeat, the attainment of *status* seems a goal in and of itself, and

Two rhesus monkeys of a Cayo Santiago troop. They are brothers, but one is dominant and the other, who is approximately equal weight, is an outcast; sometimes with the troop, sometimes alone. The dominant walks slowly and deliberately and his gaze is steady; the subdominant's movements are quick and furtive, and his coat is scruffy. Photos courtesy Donald Sade, Northwestern University.

although there is priority given dominants over choice foods few other privileges come consistently with high rank. There is some evidence, in fact, that an alpha yellow baboon mates less often than do those males immediately below him, perhaps because he cannot absent himself in a prolonged consortship (Hausfater, 1973).

Much of what Darwin thought of as sexual selection, the tendency for traits that are valued by the other sex to survive, we now know to be of primary utility in the achievement of status. Many male secondary sex characteristics in monkeys and man are best understood as devices to intimidate other males, and later I shall present human data to this effect. It is true that female monkeys gravitate to the unintimidated males, but the main purpose of the large canines seen in male baboons and macaques or the colorful mantles of gelada males, which increase apparent size, is to intimidate other males (Kummer, 1971).

Finally, recent physiological studies have shown that the males higher in the hierarchy secrete more testosterone than those lower. However, it is not necessarily the case that these higher levels of male hormone propelled the dominant to where he is. For, when he finally loses a fight and drops a notch or two, his testosterone level goes down, whereas the winner's level goes up. Testosterone change is just part and parcel of the visible behavioral change, and no straightforward cause-effect relationship can be drawn (Rose et al., 1971).

HAREM GROUPS AND ECOLOGY

The gelada monkeys of Ethiopia, although related to the macaques and baboons, demonstrate a special form of male-female social interaction. The males are twice the size of the females, and the basic social unit is a group with one male and several females. I had the opportunity of observing a unique experiment with geladas conducted by Hans Kummer at the Delta Primate Research Center at Covington, Louisiana. Geladas previously unknown to one another were introduced into a large enclosure and immediately began forming one-male groups through the activity of both sexes:

> Immediately after the introduction a male would pair off with a dominant female: the female would present her rear, he would mount her, and she would then groom his cape. From this point on, the pair female would viciously attack any other female who approached her male or whom her male sought to acquire in addition to herself. A second female was eventually accepted, but only after the first, dominant female had gone through the pair-forming process with female number two, with herself in the role

of the male. Number two had to present her rear, be mounted by female number one, and then groom her. Thus the dominant female established herself in the role of the owner of number two, just as the male had established himself as her owner.

As a result, each one-male group comprised a chain of animals each of whom dominated and controlled an immediate subordinate, preventing its interacting with nearly everyone else in the colony. One top female, for example, interfered with every interaction between her male and the number two female to such an extent that the latter learned to avoid the approaching male. Only when the colonies were well stabilized did contacts between the male and the number two female become more frequent. Even then high-ranking females would drive their subordinates back to the group when they attempted to contact members of another one-male group. The dominant gelada female is, as it were, a secondary group leader. She is usually nearest the male, and in encounters with strange males proves to be the most faithful of his consorts. (1971, pp. 109–10)

Kummer also studied hamadryas baboons, who also form one-male harem groups. Among this species, however, the male must prevent his females from straying by constantly herding them via nips on the back of the neck. Unlike the geladas, in which the females develop a "commitment" to the group, hamadryas females require the male's constant surveillance lest they become adopted into another male's harem. Although within both species large numbers of animals come together at night to sleep in a common area, the hamadryas harems, in that they are so precarious, space themselves well apart as units, whereas gelada one-male groups can spread safely throughout the area. In the gelada "attempts to appropriate a female met with the solid resistance not only of her male, but also of most of the females in both groups [so that] the integrity of the one-male groups rests on the joint action of many "(1971, p. 110).

Finally, Kummer discusses a third terrestrial monkey, the patas, who also organizes into one-male harems:

Patas monkeys form no troops. Agile fleers and hiders, they do not depend on large social units; their one-male groups live apart from each other, so that the male is not forced to live near females that are not his own. Such a social system is much easier to maintain than the crowded aggregations of one-male groups of the gelada or hamadryas. First, herding is not required, and patas males in fact do not do it. The exclusion of strangers is not a permanent task but an occasional event that totally separates the groups for a number of days. All that is required is that males be highly intolerant of each other. In contrast, hamadryas or geladas must constantly maintain the discreteness of their one-male groups, though intolerance among males must be moderated so as not to split the troop. (1971, p. 111)

I have presented these details from Kummer's remarkable work in order to show the substantial variation in patterns of male-female relations within these harem living terrestrial monkeys. Three such contrasting patterns should certainly prevent any claims for homologous human patterns, and it is perhaps best that no easy generalizations be drawn. Note, however, that harem keeping species are common; male aggression plays a role in each; and foraging in a harem arrangement probably has an advantage over foraging in large troops when food supplies are low, as in the arid plateau area of Ethiopia where the hamadryas and gelada live. A notion of how this social form may have arisen comes from recent observations of yellow baboons in the Amboselli reserve of southern Kenya. Normally, yellow baboons live in large troops, but in low rainfall years they can be seen to break up into one-male harem bands and bachelor bands (Hausfater, 1973). Analogously, polygynous humans who live under desert conditions, for example, Australian aboriginals, also tend temporarily to separate into one-male harem groups (Meggitt, 1962). There is nothing startling in these parallel facts: each arrangement makes sense and appears reasonably adaptive given the scattered nature of available resources.

To summarize to this point, territorial behavior and the dominance-submission hierarchy are social devices that have evolved presumably to bring order into breeding groups. They also serve to organize allocation of food and other necessities and thereby assure the survival of at least the more redoubtable species' members. Male-male aggression is thereby regulated, and it is typical of both systems that the incidence of bluffing and threat far exceeds that of actual combat. Intimidation is the order of the day, and self-confidence is therefore important in achieving a reasonably high rank or a reasonably attractive territory.

As I have pointed out, in Japanese macaques and in rhesus monkeys such self-confidence is closely related to the mother's rank within the hierarchy. That is, if a youngster grows up with a mother who is constantly harassed, he or she expects to be harassed also. Conversely, a youngster to whose mother other females have consistently given way becomes used to royal treatment, and apparently begins to expect it. Inasmuch as males are bigger and rougher, they occupy the upper half of such a quasi-linear hierarchy, females the lower half, immature juveniles the lowest of all. All younger monkeys are essentially out of the hierarchical scheme, and even their nipping is not taken seriously. Nature has, in fact, seen to it that infants are easily distinguishable, and their light brown coat marks them as "off limits" with regard to serious combat.

A typical picture of ground-living monkeys, then, involves a fairly large group—the great majority of Japanese macaques, for example, are in troops of 20 to 175 members (Nozawa, 1972): potentially highly aggressive males and somewhat less aggressive females, with absolute feeding advantages and some mating priorities for the male dominants and with ulcers and nervous indigestion for the male submissives (Koford, 1963).

I have also discussed other ground-dwelling monkeys whose social arrangement is primarily the one-male harem group. One species maintains the integrity of the harem through constant male surveillance (hamadryas), the second through a thoroughly enmeshing dominance-submission hierarchy, with one male as alpha (gelada); the third species relies on the absolute abhorrence of males for one another, which produces nonoverlapping routes (patas).

The question arises, Do humans follow any of these patterns? Or, as some biologists maintain, are we more like the semiterrestrial chimps—who, after all, are very much like us in serology, chromosome number, and all other indications of evolutionary distance. Chimps form far-ranging groups and have but a loosely constructed dominance-submission structure. Chimps, however, are largely forest dwellers and, like tree-dwelling monkeys of both New and Old Worlds, tend not to fight much. Remember that even the terrestrial macaques are more amicable when up in trees than when in close quarters around a ground level feeding station.

Tree dwelling usually means fruit and leaf eating, and there the best strategy is to spread out, which means less physical contact, less competition over food, and less anger among animals. Chimps do not have to threaten and fight to feel alive, as is apparently the case with most of our ground-dwelling relatives. They are instead content to let each other know where they are with occasional bursts of vocalizing and tree pounding. Even when artificially fed in the wild, as by Goodall's group in Tanzania's Gombe preserve, chimps are respectful of one another. On a visit to the preserve, I saw several instances in which the first chimp to gather "free" bananas became their official possessor; latecomers, no matter their rank, though they might beg, did not fight or try to wrest the food away.

Man, however, is not a tree dweller, nor has he ever been. He is terrestrial, and his social organization resembles those of the terrestrial monkeys more than that of his zoological brother, the chimp. Certainly the chimp's chromosomes, blood groups, and intellect are more manlike, but not his social organization. In the wild, at least, he's just not mean enough properly to herald man.

In closing this chapter, I must admit that anyone can read man's primate ancestory in any way he or she wishes—the evolutionary record is rather like a Rorschach test. It may therefore be no surprise that some female scholars have tended to favor the theory that we do indeed come from a species resembling the more pacific chimpanzees (Tanner and Zihlman, 1976), whilst their more competitive brethren, myself included, have tended to emphasize intragroup and intergroup aggression in our ancestry. Raymond Dart (1956), in fact, has written most dramatically of *Australopithecus gracilis* and claims to have evidence (reconstructed of course) that this man-ape of some three million years ago smote baboons dead with clublike antelope femurs and, furthermore, that he killed others of his own species and ate their brains. Many scholars now tend to buy Dart's story and to point to the corroborating facts that Peking man (our 500,000-year-old predecessor) and recent (if not present-day) New Guineans also enjoyed the apparently delicious brains of enemies. On the other hand, most researchers in this field have been males and they consequently may have tended to overdraw this aggressive pattern. With this caution, then, we will next examine human groups.

4

Men, Women, and the Status Hierarchy

I hope I have by now established that both the selfish-gene approach from below and the group selection approach from above are needed for an adequate explanation of social behavior, no matter the species. When we get to primates, the need for a dual causality model rather than a one-way model is emphasized since primates can act with clear selfishness or in concert, as the situation demands.

For example, among the terrestrial primates, group allegiance is most dramatic. However, among Japanese and rhesus macaques when the troop number goes much higher than about 150 the troop usually splits in two, with a new head monkey leading a substantial portion away. From that time on, the two troops are essentially enemies, the more intimidating (usually the larger) taking precedence over the other wherever they meet (Koford, 1963). Group life, in these instances, seems to imitate individual selfishness and competition, but it can be explained only by starting with the open recognition that a group has a "life of its own."

In this chapter, then, we will examine to what extent our species is or is not behaving in the primate tradition. The most obvious place to begin is the dominance-submission hierarchy.

It should by now be clear that working out a hierarchy of dominance and submission is a way of *avoiding* random and excessive aggression, not a way of encouraging it. It is a social system that permits short aggressive encounters but that depends upon stabilized and mutually acknowledged differences in status to maintain itself.

In this and subsequent chapters, I shall present the results of empirical studies in humans based on the dominance-submission model. Abstracts of these studies and associated data tables appear in the Appendix.

Richard Savin-Williams (1977) turned a job as a summer camp counselor into a doctoral research program by carefully noting the dominant and submissive ranking in four cabins of five or six boys, all 12- to 14-year olds, white and upper middle-class. He found, amazingly, that the boys in each cabin worked out the dominance-submission order within the first hour; thereafter, the tendency was for this arrangement to stabilize over the summer. The sorting, for the most part, was accomplished nonviolently, but a clear-cut hierarchy of who defers to whom was almost immediately apparent in each cabin. The least problematic ranks were the top and bottom boys; both were somehow immediately recognized (within the first half hour!). As judged by their comrades on sociometric tests, alpha boys were the most handsome, the most physically mature, and the most athletic, but not necessarily the biggest or the strongest. They themselves agreed that they were the most handsome boys and the best athletes, exhibiting the confidence we have learned to expect from alpha monkeys. Omegas are more difficult to describe, but they were so readily identified that one might talk of a "negative charisma."

It turned out that the best predictors of overall dominance were three items: verbal ridicule of other boys, verbal commands, and physical assertiveness such as pushing and shoving. If a boy demonstrated these behaviors toward another, one could be practically certain (about 10 to 1 odds) that he would be dominant in most other behaviors, too. He took the lead, had the last word, made decisions for the group, answered important questions, and so on.

The beta position was usually allotted to a boy who got on well with alpha, whereas gamma tended to be number three only because he was big and strong, though disliked—the bully. Each group had a boy described as a "joker," who tended to occupy a middle position, followed by a lad best described as a passive follower, and finally by the omega, the boy the others tended derisively to call the "nerd." "Nerds" tended to be physically immature, short, and the least athletic, but they were the most enthusiastic about camp and in each case wanted to return! Again, as in omega monkeys, belonging to the group was the overriding impulse.

This arrangement of "personality" types was replicated from group to group (see Appendix Study 2). Thrasher's studies of Chicago gangs in the 1920s follows an almost identical "typology" (Thrasher, 1963), and the question naturally arises, What would happen if a cabin were populated with six boys previously described as the same type, say, six "leaders"? Would this arrangement tend to bring out different and complementary facets of their personalities, or would it make for chaos? Such a study is underway, and it does look as if the various roles tend to re-appear in the new hierarchical arrangement.

What of the girls at camp? Savin-Williams secured the cooperation of four women counselors in girls' cabins at the same camp.
They used his notation system and came up with quite another story.
Whereas the girls, too, tended to form hierarchical arrangements, the
process was not as dramatic in either speed of onset or in overt
rivalry. Girls were more indirect in their putdowns and accordingly
used physical methods less than did the boys (physical assertion
represented 15% of the male interaction, 5% of the female). Even
verbal putdowns tended to be indirect among the girls (52% overt
among girls, 86% overt among boys). Boys, like male baboons
(Hausfater, 1973), were far more apt to contest established
dominance relationships than were the girls (or Hausfater's female
baboons).

Athletic ability, although important for the girls, was not as
likely to give a girl the alpha role as was "maternal" assertiveness.
Girls who gave unsolicited advice on proper dress and manners
("Let me cut your hair—it's awful the way it is") were seen as
sources of security and support and so became group leaders. They
tended to be pubertally mature; they were not "most beautiful."
They were described by adjectives simply not used for alpha boys:
confident, loyal, kindhearted, and manipulative.

But let Savin-Williams speak for himself:

> Briefly, females more frequently utilized the verbal and indirect
> indices of dominance-submission behavior; boys were more apt
> to overtly contest each other and to display physical indicators
> of power status. Over time males became more overt and were
> less frequent in initiating dominance-submission behavior; the
> females had the opposite pattern. The female groups fluctuated
> more in their daily frequency rates of dominance-submission
> behavior, which was more subject to situational factors than
> was the male frequency rate. While low ranking boys were most
> apt to shift status positions, the top of the female hierarchy
> tended to show such shifts. As might be expected, physical asser-
> tions and displacements were considerably better predictors of
> male than female group structure; verbal ridicule had the op-
> posite sex pattern. Popularity status accurately predicted female
> but not male dominance-submission position.
>
> These findings are not totally unexpected given the research on
> sex differences in behavior, aptitudes, and skills (see, for exam-
> ple, Hutt, 1972; Maccoby and Jacklin, 1974; Freedman, 1974).
> Most interesting is that while females agreed among themselves
> on how the group ranked on dominance and submission, this
> rank order had little relationship with the behaviorally derived
> dominance-submission hierarchy. The key to this discrepancy
> was found in the notebook of the Cabin One counselor. After her
> cabin completed a sociometric exercise to determine dominance,

she wrote that the girls thought being dominant was a bad thing, synonymous with being "annoying," "talking most," and "standing out." This characterizes not maternal leaders but antagonistic (middle ranked) and compliant (omega) girls. Thus, while girls behave in a dominant manner, they perceive dominance differently than do boys, as a negative evaluation. This may explain why girls frequently underranked themselves on the dominance sociometrics: this was not self-abasement, since to them dominance as a social or personality characteristic was undesirable. When the female counselors were asked at the end of camp to rank order their cabin group on dominance and submission, they invariably selected the antagonistic girl rather than the maternal leader as most dominant. They too were equating dominance with assertiveness/aggressiveness. Perhaps dominance is mentally a masculine term; behaviorally, it is characteristic of both sexes.

If this dichotomy in female leadership—the positive maternal and the negative antagonistic leaders—is characteristic of female leadership in general, it is interesting to note that in the present study the former were perceived by peers and authorities as more likeable; they were also more effective in eliciting peer support and in exerting leadership, and dominance, over them. The charismatic antagonists were more visual, but ineffectual on a long-term basis. When they were in control, cabin life was chaotic, unpleasant, and unproductive.

In the camp Leader's Manual it is proposed that there are four stages in the life of a summer camp group. Not all cabin groups pass through all stages but the sequential ordering appears to be pervasive:

1. Polite: Initially, all interact in a formalized manner. This grace period appears "unnatural" and does not last long because "kids have to be kids."

2. Conflict: Personality styles and behaviors diverge, becoming apparent and conflictual. Depending upon the make-up of the group this varies from slight to intense, occasionally involving physical fights.

3. Resolution: By the last week attempts are made to tolerate individual differences in the name of cabin peace and unity.

4. Together: Few groups reach the point where they move beyond a collection of individuals to a "group." Together they think, feel, and act with conflict kept to a minimum, usually to advance rather than demoralize the group.

While the camp has no empirical data to support this temporal typology, it does provide a useful heuristic model for considering basic male-female differences on a group level. That is, even though in some ways each cabin group is unique and in other ways all groups are similar, it is also true that as male and female groups the two are qualitatively different. The description and analysis below are not based on numerically quantifiable data (which we have in considerable amounts), but on the impressionistic reports of the cabin counselors in their five-week camp diary and in their after-camp interviews with the author.

The polite stage was evident in both sexes but boys were "nice" to each other for only a few short days before full scale conflict developed. Girls, however, were polite to each other for several more days, often to the consternation of their counselor who deplored the lack of genuine relations during the first week.

Male groups experienced conflict more quickly, frequently and overtly than did the female groups. While this is supported by the empirical data, there is another element that more clearly separates the two sexes: the conflict among boys can best be described as "mean"; girls were not so much mean toward each other as they were "vicious" or "cruel." All four female conselors felt this in their group; they hated it and tried to fight it, but all were unsuccessful. At one point or another all four said that the conflict was so pervasive and uncontrollable that they cried or wanted to go home. One said, "Now I know why no one studies junior high-school girls! They are so cruel and horrible that no one can stand them! I remember my own adolescence as that way, and this summer was like reliving it. Never again!"

The conflict among boys was potentially more physically injurious (towel flipping, wrestling, and throwing eggs, oranges, peanut butter, and the like), but it was also short-term. Grudges were rare since after physical fights or verbal arguments attempts were made to reconcile differences, or at least to tolerate them.

All male groups made a concerted and successful attempt at resolving the large interpersonal conflicts during the last weeks of camp. This is reflected in the decrease in the per hour frequency of dominance-submission behavior in cabins Five, Six, and Seven. Even though the frequency increased in Cabin Eight, by the end of camp this "impossible" group of boys was getting along in a verbally and physically teasing manner. One boy commented to another the last night of camp, "You aren't such an ass-hole as I once thought you were. You're even an okay person, though you'll never be my best friend."

Only one of the female groups approached the resolution stage; in the others conflicts appeared to multiply and not decrease over time. In two groups this was rather dramatic, resulting in a pair of crises known as "the silence" and "the detention." Whether the girls were incapable of resolving conflicts or just unwilling needs further study. . . .

The chaotic time reported by all four counselors was attributed variously to the programatic structure of the camp, the lack of free time that the cabin could spend together, the general "geist" of the camp, the nature of the individual girls, things they did wrong, and situational events. While it is likely that all were contributory factors, the extent to which the camp and its programs were to blame is perhaps overly drawn.

The most common complaint of the counselors was that scheduling was too tightly controlled so that girls were too physically and emotionally exhausted to form cohesive groups. Yet, an examination of the daily schedule of the two camps reveals that in actuality the girls had more free time (3.5 hours per day average) than did the boys (2.8 hours). During this time campers could choose whether or not to be with their cabin since no all-camp activity was scheduled. It was rare for girls to spend this time with their cabin group, preferring instead to associate with sisters, cousins, home-town friends, and extra-cabin friends, or with no one. On the other hand, boys in a cabin frequently spent their free time together playing basketball or tennis, hiking or talking. It was unusual to see brothers, relatives, or old friends together after the first week in boys' camp, since the cabin group appeared to be paramount in the life of the boys.

This female resistance and the male proclivity toward forming cohesive same-sex groups are theoretically congruent with Tiger's (1969) speculations on group bonding. He proposes that male-male bonding is a positive valence or attraction serving group defense, food-gathering, and maintenance of social order, purposes that are a direct consequence of pre-hominid ecological adaptation.

In summary, the impressionistic data clearly indicate that noteworthy differences between males and females exist at the group level of analysis. Girls were more polite, and for a longer period of time; their conflictual confrontations were more vicious than mean. Boys were more apt to resolve their conflicts and to form a cohesive group. Despite many plausible reasons one could give for the higher level of chaotic conditions that existed in female rather than male groups, the one adopted here is that it reflects a fundamental (biologically based) sex difference in the ease by which same-sex bonds are formed.

After the first week of camp the sociometric exercises had to be discontinued in three female groups because they were said to be the cause of unrest and resentment. The girls considered such information to be private. The boys' perspective was the opposite; they wanted more of "those fun things." This may reflect a basic socialization difference: what is in the sphere of public information may be considerably greater in males than in females. (1977, pp. 109–115)

I have presented these results in some detail so that the reader can gain the flavor of the differences. Assuming these results are repeatable,* where and how do such sex differences start and develop? We are in an era in which environmental explanations predominate, so the expected rejoinder is that we have *learned* to behave in these sex-specific patterns and that they have little to do with a primate heritage. How to solve such opposed explanations, our environment versus our evolutionary biology? As has often been the case in science, a solution lies not so much in obtaining a crucial bit of evidence as in changing a way of thinking. Unless we start with the recognition that behavior is wholly biosocial, unless we think of it as determined simultaneously by proximal and historical factors (including evolutionary history), there is no solution to the culture versus biology conundrum. The holistic approach is certainly my predilection, but until such thinking becomes general (and in order to help it along), we can accumulate and examine four lines of evidence. (1) We can look at very early development, especially newborn behavior, to see whether intimations of later patterns are present in this obviously unlearned and "precultural" behavior of infants. (2) We can look at developmental patterns in children to see how closely they follow the lower primate patterns. (3) We can look for worldwide consistencies in behavior, assuming a biological underpinning for those traits that are universal. (4) Finally, we can resort to experimental techniques; for example, we can modify standard psychological projective instruments in order to test evolutionary hypotheses.

In this chapter, it will be convenient to deal briefly with sex differences in infancy, with the development of these differences through early childhood and adolescence, and finally, with cross-cultural data. I shall save for Chapter 5 a discussion of the pertinent experimental studies.

BABY BOY AND BABY GIRL

What I shall say here covers a good deal of accumulated study by a large number of baby watching and baby testing scientists (and it is more or less an abstraction of data reported in Freedman, 1974).

In general, differences between the sexes are subtle at birth, and usually large numbers are needed before a trend is apparent. But differences are there. As soon as babies are in the light of day, boys are giving parents a more difficult time. They cry more, respond less to vocal cajoling, and require more holding. Thus, within the first days,

---

*Tiger and Shepher (1975) found very similar differences between adult same-sex groups within an Israeli kibbutz.

boys are giving intimations of the temper tantrums they will have at greater rates throughout later infancy and childhood.

Boys are rather more interested in inanimate, nonsocial objects than are girls. For example, infant boys are as attracted to a bull's eye as to a drawing of a face, whereas girls clearly prefer the face (Lewis et al., 1966). They also show interest in problem-solving sooner, so that if a toy is put behind a barrier, nine-month-old boys will reach for it; girls often will sit, watch, and wait (Kagan, 1971). Later in the first year, when dolls are given children, boys tend more often to take theirs apart (to see how it works?). Even in children blind from birth, boys more quickly pick up on how gadgets work and can, for example, easily replace a wheel on a wagon. Blind girls appear to be particularly helpless about such chores (Burlinghame and Robertson, 1967). Boys thus seem very early to evince interest and ability in mechanical tinkering (see Appendix Studies 3 and 4).

Darrell Bock has discussed the considerable evidence that such abilities (called spatial-visualization skills) are inherited via a major recessive gene located on the X chromosome (Bock, 1973). In overly simplified terms, boys need but one dose of this gene to show the trait, whereas girls need two. This model accounts for the observed facts that only about one quarter of girls are as good as the average male on tests of spatial visualization and that males are generally more successful mechanics and engineers (Bock and Kolakowski, 1973). More is involved here than social pressure for in research we are now conducting, biographies indicate that female engineers were good at spatial tasks from an early age, and apparently because of subsequent rewarding experiences these women developed the strength to withstand the inevitable social stereotyping. In this same regard, Munroe and Munroe (1971) found that among East African children, the tendency to wander away from the home was related to better performance on tests of spatial ability: boys ranged farther from home than girls, yet those few girls who were found farther from home than typical for their sex outperformed the boys on the measures of spatial ability.

Another long-term trend is heralded when girls are found to be more responsive to their mothers' voices in the first weeks of life. Throughout childhood girls are more alert to vocal sounds. Furthermore, they form words before boys do and throughout their lives do better at all verbal and linguistic tasks—spelling, speaking fluently, or learning new languages (Freedman, 1974).

Recently, a large number of studies have appeared that relate these differential skills to sex differences in brain organization, specifically to differences in hemispheric dominance. In brief, the left hemisphere is said to control verbal tasks, the right hemisphere spatio-visual tasks. Doreen Kimura (1967–1969), who is one of the

most active workers in this field, has presented evidence that left
hemispheric dominance for speech occurs earlier in girls than in
boys and that, by contrast, boys eventually show right hemispheric
superiority over girls to go with their better spatio-visual and
arithmetic skills. But let us not overstate the fatedness of these sex
differences, for modifications can occur. Hoffman and Maier (1966),
for example, were able to enhance female performance in problem-
solving by expanding the linguistic presentations of the problem;
conversely, Michael Long developed a reading test that requires constant problem-solving so that it actually favors boys (Appendix
Study 5).

There are other sex differences to note. Girls start off life more
cuddly. In three separate studies of newborns, hardheaded scientists
dared to rate babies on how cuddly an infant feels when held (see
Freedman, 1974). In all three studies, in three different places,
newborn girls were found to mold into the arms better, to kick less,
and in general to offer less resistance to being cuddled.

Women have the same tendency. Susan Blanck, observing
students in the University of Chicago library (see Appendix Study 6),
found that only females tucked their feet under themselves, only
females typically hunched under coats, only females tended to hold
their heads to one side while rounding their shoulders. That is, even
when older, females tend to curl into compact, spherical
shapes—cuddly shapes, if you will (see also Appendix Studies 7 and
8). Males, by contrast, usually were squarely planted in their chairs,

Male and female col-
lege students in typical
reading positions. See
Appendix Study 6.

with shoulders level and head unbent. Both feet were often on the ground, with legs spread apart. (Wickler, 1972, asserts that this leg-apart position typifies primate males, and he presents evidence that its function is to display the penis.)

Female newborns are also more sensitive tactually. They react to a fine, camel's hair brush that hardly affects males, and they cry more readily when wet. That is, they react more immediately to any change of skin temperature or to touch. It is interesting that Kinsey found that women are more typically aroused sexually by touch rather than by vision (the male mode). Have we yet another possible thread that runs from birth through maturity? Here, however, we must note dissenting arguments by authors who attribute Kinsey's finding to "culturally induced" repression (Bry, 1975; Kronhausen and Kronhausen, 1964).

As for the link between girls' interest in dolls and eventual motherhood, we have compared how little girls *and* little boys play with dolls. Boys are interested at first in the doll generally but soon become interested in mechanical aspects, sometimes taking the doll apart. Girls personalize the doll, and it more often becomes a "baby." For some reason (the soothing effect of the mother's heart-beat?), mothers, whether right- or left-handed, usually hold babies on the left side despite the fact that most are unaware of this preference. Richard Perline (Appendix Study 9) found that females at all ages have this non-conscious tendency more than do males. But then evidence that females of our species take more readily to the role of infant caretaker than males should not be surprising (see also Appendix Study 26).

THE SMILE

Perhaps the most interesting and most significant sex difference found at birth involves the "reflexive" smile, that is, smiling in the absence of any apparent sensory stimulation. Several studies have found that *newborn* girls smile more than do newborn boys (Freed-man, 1974; Appendix Study 10). By newborn, we mean between 12 and 72 hours of age; by smile, we mean the unmistakable but fleeting smiles that babies exhibit as they fall off to sleep after a feed. It is the sort of expression that makes everyone laugh, and when a baby on the newborn ward does it a lot, nurses and aids typically gather around, watching for the next eyes-closed, self-contented smile.

There are some doubters, even among professionals, who claim these early smiles are "gas" induced. Accordingly, we carefully noted the facial expressions of infants just preceding smiling and just preceding a gas burp (Freedman, 1974). Just before the smile, there is complete face and limb relaxation and a state that must be termed "serenity." Just before the burp, the face reddens, the mouth twists and contorts, and there is full-body and limb writhing. Then the gas is expelled. This state is not serene, and there is simply no relation between early smiles and gas induced grimaces.

Yet early, "reflex" smiling is clearly related to later social smiling: babies who do much of it turn out to be the more smiling, friendlier children in the family, at least in our extended studies of twins from birth through the early teens (Freedman, 1974). Unfortunately, of all longitudinal studies of children heretofore conducted, none has examined continuity in the amount of smiling.

Are there other indications that female infants are more socially oriented? Jerome Kagan (1971) and Michael Lewis and his co-workers (1966) have found that infant girls, but not boys, can differentiate adult male and female voices; that girls prefer to watch

Arturo and Felix, fraternal twins at two months. Arturo smiles readily to sound and touch, and has done so since birth. Felix is much more sober. In follow-up visits at five years of age, similar differences are seen. Arturo is open and smiling; Felix is reserved, hiding mouth with hand over much of play session (see Freedman, 1963 and 1974).

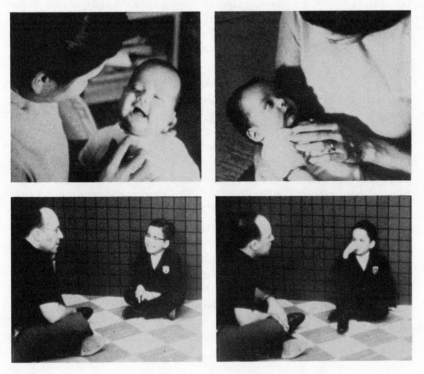

faces whereas boys are equally interested in nonsocial objects; and that at nine months, girls more than boys will babble back when spoken to. Baby girls react differently to adult males and females long before boys make this distinction, and it is not surprising that girls are also more worried by strangers (even as are rhesus monkey females) (Freedman, 1974.) We must conclude that girls are more socially oriented right from the start.

Do females actually smile more than males beyond infancy? We have conducted several studies with young persons and adults and in each case females smiled more readily and more often than males. Try it yourself: watch people in a supermarket or even on the street and count the number of male and female smilers—or, as two of my students did, station yourself at a busy thoroughfare, smile at people coming by, and record the number of returned smiles (Appendix Studies 11 and 12). Whether you are male or female yourself, more women than men will return your smile. Of course, if you are an unusually attractive person, sex may enter the picture; indeed, the only exception to the above finding was the fact that slightly more men than women smiled at attractive, young waitresses.

Perhaps the "cleanest" study we have done along this line was to examine high-school yearbooks from many schools and containing many ethnic groups (Appendix Study 13). We have yet to see a yearbook in which there are not more females smiling than males. Even in the days of prolonged exposure photography, when the subject had to hold a fixed expression for several seconds, one tends to find more adolescent girls than boys with fixed smiles. (We have not yet looked at prepubertal groups.)

These findings, then, coupled with those rather astounding newborn differences, seem to indicate that females are biologically predisposed to smile more readily than are males.

As for what this difference might mean, the best hints come from the primatologists. Their findings are that the "fear-grin" facial expression in monkeys, which calls off an attack by a dominant animal and therefore is labeled an "appeasement gesture," is more often exhibited by females (DeVore, 1965). The explanation has been that since females tend to occupy the lower half of the hierarchy, they have become more adept at warding off attack. But the human newborn data suggest that monkey and ape females, too, may have *innately* lower thresholds to grinning.

In Jane Goodall's famous film of chimpanzee behavior at Gombe stream in Tanzania (1967), there is a scene in which a female and baby from a distant chimp troop hesitantly enter the local troop. The female is seen to extend her hand to a large male, obviously seeking reassurance. This sequence is very clear and one of the most touching, most "human" moments of the entire film. What cannot be

Female chimp entering strange troop extends hand to male and grins. Single frame from Goodall and Van Lawick, 1967. Courtesy National Geographic Society.

seen without a stop-motion projector is that the female is nervously grinning throughout the entire sequence. Observing the hand touching coupled with the fear-grin, one cannot resist the notion that this sequence is homologous with similar human behavior.

If we look at human smiling analytically, it must be admitted that it is more than just an appeasement gesture. Human smiling is perhaps the highest expression of interpersonal unity, as when two friends who have been parted find reunion in mutual smiling and embrace (Goldstein, 1957). But in addition, like the touching of hands, the smile does act as an assurance just about everywhere that "I mean you no harm." True, princes have been stabbed by smiling supplicants, but that is outright deception. We are discussing how smiles are normally used and what they ordinarily mean. This, after all, is what makes the deception possible.

Thus, it appears that women are prepared at birth to emit more readily this expression of so-called appeasement, and they do so the world around. In some cultures, for example, the Navajo, smiles are more difficult to come by than, say, among the Australian Aboriginals. Indeed, the count of smiling faces in Navajo and Aboriginal high-school yearbooks yielded the lowest percentage of smiling among Navajos (18.5%, sexes combined) and the highest among Australian Aboriginals (73%). But in each culture, females smiled more than males (Appendix Study 13).

There is one more thing to report about smiling. As we shall see, children of six years and older readily arrange themselves into hierarchies of "who is *toughest*." We found that when we paired children into tough and not-so-tough twosomes, the not-so-tough child consistently smiled and gazed more at the tough child in both boy and girl pairs. This finding appeared to bear out the supposition that smiling is a gesture of appeasement. However, there is one ex-

The Navajo feel that too much smiling means falseness, and this pose is a typical one. Australian Aboriginal children, by contrast, usually smile readily and easily. See Appendix Study 14.

ception. When a girl who was rated by her mates as tough was paired with a not-so-tough boy, she nevertheless smiled and gazed at him. In other words, although the girl was judged physically stronger and tougher, there was a tendency to act as if the reverse were true in the heterosexual pairing (Freedman, 1975; Appendix Study 14).

Though these observations were made in six- to eight-year-old children, they seem to have a world of implications for male-female relationships in general. We have long known that when women are better at something, they tend to avoid lording it over the male. In order to examine this disconcerting tendency in detail, Carol Cronin conducted a study in which 12-year-old, middle-class, Afro-American girls and boys were independently assessed as to their prowess in dodgeball. In this game a child stands in the center of a circle of players who try to hit him or her with a ball. A hit is counted as a tally for the thrower. Two teams were composed, one of the best girls and the other of the worst boys, and the teams were matched against each other. Although the girls had the greater talent, they collapsed completely, allowing the no-talent boys to retrieve the ball at will and thereby rack up more points. They clearly did not try as hard as when playing a girls' team, and the boys, thus encouraged, tried harder than when playing a boys' team. Cronin then repeated the study with another group at the same Chicago school and then with a group of Hopi children on the Hopi reservation, and in both cases there was about the same outcome (Appendix Study 15).

What is going on here? Are these examples of social learning or have culture and biological predispositions conspired together? From all we have so far seen, the second alternative is right. Not only are girls poised on the threshold of a smile, but they also exhibit at greater rates than males all the behavior that goes with smiling: conciliation, appeasement of aggression, and avoidance of physical combat (especially vis-à-vis males). In other words, the evidence is that females are more specialized in disarming behavior than are males. More on this subject later.

MALE MORTALITY

Male offspring are a gamble. We need to start with more of them in order to achieve a 50–50 ratio at maturity. Thus, at conception, the ratio is 130 males to 100 females; through spontaneous abortions the ratio at birth becomes some 104 to 100; with higher male mortality parity is reached by age 20; thereafter there are more and more women alive compared with men—and that is true wherever such statistics have been compiled and as far back as Neanderthal man (based on skeletal estimates; see Birren, 1959).

The usual biological explanation for these differences is that the male XY constitution exposes lethal genes on the X chromosome, whereas in females the double XX serves to mask them. Unfortunately for this theory, there is also greater male mortality in birds (Trivers, 1972), where sex determination is reversed, males being XX, females XY.

As we have seen, males are more aggressive and they kill each other off at far greater rates; they even kill themselves (commit suicide) three times more often (see any U.S. almanac). Males also suffer more from heart failure, cancer, and schizophrenia. But not all men are so badly off, and a certain number are as long-lived as are average women. Males, in fact, exhibit a greater range than females in almost any attribute—from mortality statistics (more die early, yet males hold the longevity records) through performance on I.Q. tests (Terman and Tyler, 1954). More males score very low and very high (more neurological disorders, more achievement of eminence); females adhere more to the center of the distribution (Dale, 1970). The fact is that because of the mammalian male's XY constitution, any trait influenced by a sex linked gene will probably have greater variance in males.

In Chapter 2 I related this state of affairs to differences in gametic potential and to greater intrasexual selection among mammalian males. The point there and here is that most males are relatively expendable, that they are both born and obliterated at relatively greater rates, so that differential selection occurs primarily through that sex.

Although the sex ratio generally favors mammalian male births, these ratios vary depending on the state of the economy.

There is ample evidence to show that when nutrition is good, fewer male embryos abort and therefore the ratio is higher (Trivers and Willard, 1973). Conversely, when nutrition is poor, relatively more females are born since male fetuses are more likely to abort. Also, a female born at, say, three pounds is less vulnerable than a male at the same level of pre-maturity. Selfish-gene logic would indeed favor more male children when things are going well, since a healthy male may turn out to be a highly successful impregnator and leave behind him a plethora of grandchildren. In evolutionary terms, healthy male children are a good gamble. On the other hand, when a family is in a bad state, daughters will at least assure a parent of an average number of grandchildren. That is to say, given the all or none nature of males, daughters are a safer, more conservative vehicle for mammalian parental genes.

At the least, this logic has the merit of explaining the facts. Teitelbaum and Mantel (1971), in a large U.S. study of sex ratios at birth, found that in all the ethnic groups studied, families of lower socioeconomic status produced 8–9% fewer males than did middle and upper income families. And in population studies, 8–9% is a sizable and highly significant difference. Also, if American presidential families may be construed as socially successful, it is interesting that they have produced some 80 sons compared with 55 daughters (see Appendix Study 45). In the same vein, Figurski (Appendix Study 16) surveyed 29 countries on all continents, using life expectancy as an index of socioeconomic status. He found a substantial correlation (+ .61) between a sex ratio that favored males and overall life expectancy.

This state of affairs tends to work out well sociologically as well as biologically, for it is well known that with marriage, women, more than men, tend to rise in social rank (Sorokin, 1959; Trivers and Willard, 1973). Thus, it "pays" for poorly nourished, lower classes to have more daughters than sons, since daughters will, on the average, improve their socioeconomic status, while sons will not. Indeed, it all fits together remarkably well.

THE DEVELOPMENT OF STATUS HIERARCHIES

Having established that human males and females either are born with or soon exhibit behavioral tendencies that characterize them thereafter, let us pursue a second line of sociobiological evidence. This we can call the comparative approach. How close to primate social patterns do humans come? Particularly, how do we compare with regard to the development of dominance-submission relationships? (Much of the work to be discussed here is drawn from Freedman, 1974; Omark and Edelman, 1977; and Appendix Studies 17, 18, 19, and 20.)

As I have said, it is obvious that boys are more prone than girls to temper outbursts by the end of the first year, although there are indications of this tendency even in the earliest days of life. By three years, where peers are available, boys are ready to run in groups and to play more aggressive games than do the less mobile girls. This pattern can be observed even in settings that overtly try to suppress aggressive behavior. I recall visiting a Hong Kong churchschool in which toy guns were forbidden and in which all parents espoused a religiously motivated antiwar position. Nevertheless, the three-year-old boys (not the girls) daily fashioned guns out of handkerchiefs, excitedly shooting at each other over the entire play period. We videotaped one such play period, and only a single girl can be seen (peripherally) participating in this activity.

It was a similar story in our visits to playgroups at the Sri Aurobindo Ashram in Pondicherry, South India, an experiment in cooperative living, where the aim is to rear "children of the future"—that is, children steeped in cooperation and nonsexist attitudes. Despite the fact that these sentiments were deeply felt by both parents and teachers, we found that the behavior and drawings of the Aschram boys and girls were differentiated in about the same ways as those of boys and girls in any other setting (Donaldson, 1972).

Probably as a result of basic temperamental differences, boys and girls, like monkey and baboon youngsters, tend to play with others of the same sex—from the first moment that such a choice is possible. Look at any sandbox or playground: two-year-old boys will be near boys and toddler girls will be near girls (Appendix Study 21; see also Study 22). By two and one-half years, the boys' groups have become more mobile; by four years, they are all over the playground, even as four-year-old girls tend to play in the sandbox. The boys clump into rather larger groups as well, and by six years they already have the looks of what we eventually call a gang. Even at six, girls gather in groups of rarely more than four playmates and often congregate in the sandbox, side by side, talking and "baking" pies (Parker and Freedman, 1971).

What about other cultures? In 1971 I had the opportunity to travel around the world with a group of college juniors under a junior year abroad type of arrangement. We stayed about six weeks in each country, observing and videotaping four- to seven-year olds at play in school playgrounds, looking for boy-girl similarities and differences. We observed Japanese children in both Tokyo and

Four-year-old boys typically form larger groups than do four-year-old girls. Here five four-year old boys form one group and two four-year old girls form another. From Parker and Freedman, 1971.

Kyoto, Chinese in Hong Kong, Balinese in a small village in Bali, Australian Aboriginals in and around Darwin, and Ceylonese in Kandy; in India we worked at the aforementioned ashram in Pondicherry, as well as in several New Delhi schools (including a school for the blind); we finished our trip in Kenya observing Kikuyu and Masai youngsters. We also managed to get drawings from these children to the translated instructions of "draw anything you wish."

Boys and girls in the sandbox tend to do different things. Here girls are independently baking pies; boys are building a connecting tunnel. From Parker and Freedman, 1971.

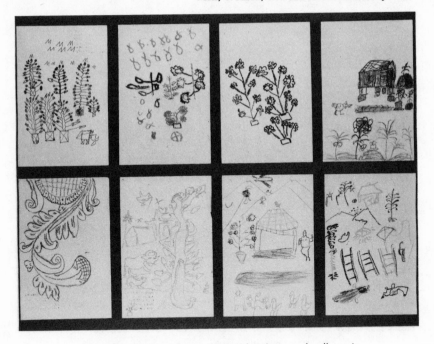

Drawings by five- to seven-year-old Balinese schoolboys in response to the teacher's request to "draw anything you want." Batuan, Bali, 1972.

When we returned to the United States, I made similar observations and obtained drawings at Navajo and Hopi school settings in New Mexico and Arizona (Freedman, 1976; see also Table 1).

There were of course differences in each place, making each unique and memorable. But, in every single setting, including the school for the blind, boys tended to be with boys, girls with girls; boys tended to cover more space in their play and to engage in more rough physical contact. Boys were louder, more frenzied, more disorganized, and less neat; girls tended to play in smaller groups and to engage in less spread out, quieter, more orderly games. Girls tended also to stay closer and to be more obedient to the teacher and to rely more on adults to settle disputes than did boys (even as Draper, 1975, has found among !Kung Bushmen children). Boys had shorter attention spans and, if not playing a competitive game, they were far less content to stay with one activity for long periods of time; by contrast, we clocked girls swinging upside down from parallel bars for 20 minutes and more. These observations were made by both male and female observers, and in every place video or film samples were made that corroborate these generalizations.

Although boys were often rough, we also saw affection exhibited

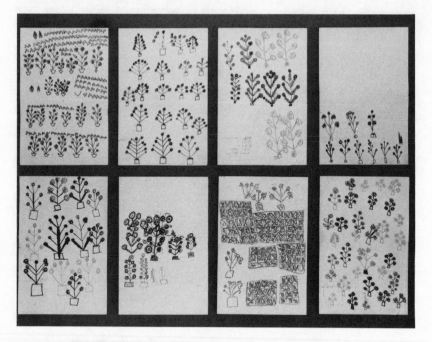

Drawings by five- to seven-year-old Balinese schoolgirls in
response to the teacher's request to "draw anything you
want." Batuan, Bali, 1972.

everywhere by both sexes. In all cultures, children of either sex can
be seen holding hands or keeping their arms around one another. But
cultures seem to push boys to greater extremes in this regard, some
encouraging, others discouraging their affectionate display: in Bali
this was exceedingly common behavior; in Chicago, relatively rare.

Boys everywhere were more interested in how our cameras and
recording equipment worked than were the girls. Also, boys tended
to ham it up when being filmed, whereas girls everywhere tended,
initially, to coyness and embarrassment when the camera was on
them. Eibl-Eibesfeldt (1970) found the same differences in his extensive filming around the world.

With regard to inhibition of aggression, all the children seem to
have developed choose-up games (for example, odd or even fingers
in the United States, paper-stone-scissors in Japan) for the purpose of
defining who shall first occupy a resource such as a slide. In this,
however, there was considerable variation. For example, in Nigeria,
among the rigidly age-graded Hausa, Jerry Barkow (1969) reports
that the older of any two children always goes first.

As for the drawings, boys everywhere were obviously more attracted to and intrigued by vehicles of transportation: trucks,
airplanes, and rockets (and also horses among the Navajo). Even

TABLE 1: SEX DIFFERENCES IN FREE DRAWINGS OVER NINE CULTURES: COMPARATIVE PERCENTAGES IN THE FIVE MOST CONSISTENTLY DIFFERENTIATING CATEGORIES[a]

	Sex	American (Chicago)	Ceylonese (Kandy)	Aboriginal (Arnheim)	African (Kikuyu)	Indian (Delihi)	Balinese (Batuan)	Chinese (Hong Kong)	American Indian (Navajo)	Japanese (Kyoto)
Vehicles	M	15.0%	68.4%	48.6%	86.4%	33.8%	41.6%	17.0%	54.0%[b]	33.3%
	F	0.0[b]	7.1[b]	3.5[b]	61.9[b]	11.6[b]	1.0[b]	6.0[b]	29.0[b]	12.12
Monsters	M	15.0	0.0	5.4	0.0	5.6	10.5	10.6	2.0	57.1
	F	3.1	0.0	0.0	0.0	12.5	0.0	4.0	0.0	12.5
Flowers	M	10.0	63.2	5.4	3.7	73.2	80.2	19.1	2.0	23.8
	F	21.9	78.6	31.0[b]	3.2	79.1	95.1[b]	54.0[b]	9.7	75.0[b]
Male figures	M	40.0	21.1	5.4	3.7	18.3	1.2	25.5	32.0	19.0
	F	3.12[b]	14.3	6.9	1.6	12.8	1.0	4.0[b]	22.6	0.0
Female figures	M	5.0	10.5	8.1	4.9	4.3	1.2	4.2	0.0	4.8
	F	65.6[b]	14.3	44.8[b]	3.2	33.7[b]	0.0	22.0[b]	9.7	93.8[b]
Number of subjects	M	20	19	37	81	71	86	47	50	21
	F	32	14	29	63	86	70	50	31	16

[a] Twelve categories were scored. Except for the Japanese children, aged three to six, all the children were five to seven years old.
[b] $p < .05$.

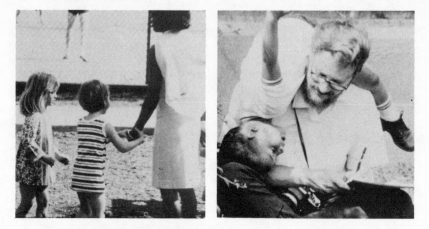

In all the playgrounds visited, more girls tended to stay close
to the teacher whether the teacher was male or female. This
girl overdid it a bit. From Parker and Freedman, 1971.

among the Kikuyu, where girls were rougher than any other girls in
their play and where they, too, drew many moving vehicles, boys
were even rougher and drew even more vehicles.

Flowers also provided some interesting comparisons. Whereas
girls everywhere were more prone to draw flowers, *all* Balinese and
most Ceylonese children had flowers in their drawings: Balinese
boys, however, would intersperse airplanes and other vehicles
among their flowers; Balinese girls never did so (Table 1; see also
Appendix Studies 23 and 24).

Australian Aboriginal boys reacting boisterously to being
filmed.

WHO'S THE TOUGHEST?

Certainly, it was our experience that children were everywhere far more alike than different. In fact, the sexes differ far more than do the cultures. Although Balinese boys may appear softer and gentler than, say, Kikuyu boys of Kenya, the contrast between boys and girls as just recounted was far more consistent than were such cross-cultural contrasts.

Now, a finding of immense importance: if one asks two four-year-old boys, "Which of you is toughest?", in 80% of such twosomes both children will answer, "Me!" As Berry Brazelton, the noted Harvard pediatrician, found when I asked this question of his four-year-old son and a friend, not only is the response given with gusto but the two boys may also feel compelled to demonstrate the truth of their answer. In this case the boys began pelting Berry and me with handy objects, and I had made the point better than I had wished. Yet I have never seen a pair of girls, or even a boy-girl pair, react with anything but embarrassed giggles or lack of interest when asked the same question.

Girls are just not as concerned about demonstrating superior toughness, nor are boys particularly interested in demonstrating that they are tougher than girls. Culture-specific? We have tried the "Who is tougher" question with four-year-old boys and girls in Zurich, Ethiopia, Nigeria, and among the Navajo, always with similar results (see Omark, Omark, and Edelman, 1975). True, American boys are given much leeway for demonstrations of aggression, whereas Nigerian Hausa village boys are careful of such spontaneity and tend to act as if older equals tougher, but the greater male interest in the question is unmistakable.

By six years of age, a tremendous change occurs in the answers to this question. Boys now agree about 80% of the time on who is tougher and, more than that, the group as a whole is in agreement

Tenderness is readily displayed by Balinese males; witness this Balinese father and son. Balinese men often wear flowers behind the ear, and flowers appear frequently in boys' as well as in girls' drawings there.

Boys on playgrounds, everywhere, wrestled one another to the ground, girls much more rarely so. Kikuyu boys in Tigoni, Kenya, and Navajo boys in Crown Point, New Mexico.

right down the line. A hierarchy has been formed, known to all, whose order is acknowledged by everyone. Such clear-cut hierarchies of toughness exist in every interacting group of children over six we have observed and are present in rudimentary form among four- and five-year olds. More often than not, teachers are completely unaware of toughness hierarchies, and in our experience they usually do not believe they exist until their students so inform them. Usually, the hierarchy is linear: boys at the top, girls at the bottom, with overlap in the middle.

It is an absorbing fact that within these groups everyone pays much attention to those high in the hierarchy and little to those at the bottom. Everyone can readily name the boys at the top and tend to agree more on their rank than on the lower ranking boys or girls.

Kikuyu girls parading around playground and Navajo girls in game of jacks. It was rare to see boys engaged in these activities.

That is, there is simply greater accuracy in ranking the upper half of the hierarchy. As I mentioned in discussing subhuman primates, Michael Chance (Chance and Jolly, 1970, 1976) has called this phenomenon "attention structure," inasmuch as a dominance-submission hierarchy may be ascertained by noting who pays attention to whom. Certainly, if the leadership is constantly reasserting its dominance with random attacks, as among the macaques, a potential victim had best keep his attention upward. But in humans something similar happens without physical attacks. Most of our attention, most of our talk and gossip, is directed to and about dominants in our lives. Among graduate students, for example, the favorite topics of gossip are the professors. Among the professors, it is the chairman or other perceived bigwigs in academia. One puts down those above him, complains about them, makes jokes about them, and tries to learn all about their personal foibles. In this way one can partially equalize the difference in status, but the net result is a lot of time spent on the topic of the head men and women.

The popularity of gossip columns involves the same principle. About whom do we read? The mighty, the rich, the beautiful, the acclaimed, and the powerful. And which of us can resist at least a glance at these personal tidbits, particularly when they take the hero or heroine down a notch or two. Like grade-school children, all of us simply pay more attention to and know more about those at the top (Omark and Edelman, 1977; Appendix Study 25).

We have tried to establish hierarchies other than toughness with our school children—who is smartest, the best athlete, the most handsome—and in each case we found that although there may be overall agreement on hierarchical positions the arrangement is kept in dynamic flux by the tendency for each child (especially boys) to think he or she is better than anyone else! We have called this practice *overrating* and in boys it is clearly a carry-over from the four-year-old male's feeling that he is the greatest. Each six-year-old boy (and, as we shall see, each male of any age) tends to rate himself several slots higher than the group has done. It is as if a male achieves a preeminent concept of his invincibility early in life and, thereafter, external circumstances must serve to modify this initial sense of limitlessness.

Consider the boyish charm of former heavyweight boxing champion Muhammad Ali. It consisted of his continual and often rhymed avowal, even as he undoubtedly maintained as a four-year old, that he is Number One, or the best in the West, and the coincident proof that, in fact, he probably was ("Liston is great, but he'll fall in eight"). Thus, Ali represented fulfillment of the four-year-old male's sense of omnipotence, living proof that it can really happen. Cocky and arrogant, he dared anyone to depose him.

As far as I can see, the male sense of omnipotence is part of an evolutionary heritage among hierarchically arranged species. It is the crux of what motivates the hierarchy, the psychological basis for male vying with male. Without overestimation of self, there can be no hierarchy, no challenge to the establishment. It is the basis for sibling rivalry, for father-son competition, for the Oedipus complex, and for the substantial psychological literature supporting the existence of that complex.

Primatology has in fact supplied a biological basis for father-son rivalry to replace Freud's literary one: if the male child, as a member of a hierarchical species, initially must have a sense of invincibility, a part of him will always consider all other males as less than himself. And only a father who has himself achieved some equilibrium around this issue can deal reasonably with his sometimes insulting and defiant youngster. Thus, few fathers achieve the level of empathy with sons that mothers do (Appendix Study 25) because they are natural competitors. First sons, since they are next in line, generally are the toughest for a father to handle; the second son finds the first son the biggest challenge; and so on. Unfortunately, I know of no good statistical data to confirm these observations. Although unique family constellations would complicate the research, a statistical study in this area is feasible, and it would have the merit of combining into one paradigm the issues of father-son rivalry and male-male sibling rivalry.

If males exhibit an overblown sense of self-worth and competitiveness, does this not lead to greater disorganization in all-male groups? Here we come back to the Savin-Williams (1977) study. As we saw earlier, although there were more challenges within the male groups, the boys nevertheless arranged themselves almost immediately into followers and leaders. By contrast, the all-female groups often had the problem of identifying their leaders. Friends in the feminist movement have complained to me about the inability of fellow activists to make quick decisions and about their reluctance toward taking leadership roles. In Savin-Williams's cabins, alpha girls were, after all, more a source of advice than leadership. It is easy to see the adaptive value in war or big-game hunting of the rapid organizing of male participants into followers and leader, and so it is tempting to make the logical jump that Savin-Williams (1977) did: have men evolved to behave in this way? Indeed, Tiger (1969) has written an entire book on this theme, stressing the ongoing importance for males of affiliation within all-male groups.

What of those male hierarchies that started at six years of age? Is there much change over the years, and do more intellectual endeavors replace athletics as the major criteria of ranking? One might suspect that in an academically oriented high school such as the University of Chicago Laboratory School (populated largely by the children of professors) an academically oriented pecking order would take over. Not so! Glenn Weisfeld has studied high-school boys first observed at age six (Omark and Edelman, 1977): the hierarchy developed among them at that time, based largely on athletic ability, still holds at age fourteen (Appendix Study 27). Alphas and betas are still near the top, and the omegas are still down where they were when the hierarchy formed originally. What will happen when these lads themselves become professionals and academics, as the majority will doubtless become? Will the peer experiences of the past eight years evaporate or are expectations set for life? My guess takes us somewhere in between, but the answers lie with further studies.

We have no comparable longitudinal data with girls, but one can anticipate that such a study would not yield the clear-cut results obtained with boys. Try as we might, we have never found a trait or any traits around which girls hierarchize themselves with the same emotional intensity that boys exhibit over toughness, athletic ability, or even good looks. Certainly, either a boy or a girl feels better having won a contest than having lost it, but most girls are apparently not as preoccupied with competition. Even Maccoby and Jacklin (1974), in their heroic attempt to dampen out sex differences, agreed that the overall evidence indicates that boys are more aggressive and more attracted to its display. That is, boys are more involved both directly and vicariously in social competition, whether it be fighting, play, or comedy (see Appendix Study 28). (Maccoby and Jacklin's [1974] compendium on sex differences has been roundly criticized by Block [1976]. She rightfully points to a consistent trend in that book to turn away from demonstrated sex differences, insisting we just don't know when it is more justified to say we probably do know.)

As I have discussed elsewhere (Freedman, 1967), even when a male courts a woman it is with one eye on the status hierarchy. If he perceives himself as low, his confidence as a lover is commensurately low, and failure seems inevitable.

As for modern women, transmuted as they may be in the "male" direction of assertive competition, only a relative few seem to be playing the status game with the gusto and involvement of males. This is not to say that working women do not derive a sense of worth from their work. For one thing, as families become smaller, today's woman needs more and more to achieve a sense of self-worth via extrafamilial channels. More female status groups are developing, and more women are entering traditionally all-male hierarchies; some already occupy alpha positions in such mixed groups (for example, Meir and Ghandi in politics), and many more will do so in the future.

This is probably the first time the world has witnessed such similarity in male and female goals, so that it is perhaps surprising that things are going as well as they are. However, before we welcome a millennium of sexual equality, let us consider some further facts.

WOMEN WITH MEN, WOMEN WITH WOMEN

It is time to discuss those dodgeball games again and to try to explain why a team of girls, although athletically superior to a team of boys, nevertheless collapsed and allowed the boys to win (Appendix Study 15). When playing other girls, of course, these exceptionally fine athletes were competitive, coordinated, and in total control. It is as if there were two sets of personalities—one reserved for female-female competition, the other for male-female noncompetition. No complementary schism characterized the boys, who merely enjoyed winning for a change, although they tried harder when they realized the girls were giving way.

Following these studies, it was pointed out to the experimenter that dodgeball may be defined by both sexes as a boys' game. What would happen in a spelling bee, in which activity girls are notoriously better? Cronin thereupon conducted a spelling bee using the same twelve-year olds, but a comparable collapse was not seen among the boys. Although consistently outspelled, boys, on average, exhibited excessive self-confidence, far more than warranted by their relative talents.

In general, women often find this male hubris baffling (see, for example, Crandall, 1975), and it is by now a well-known fact that women's groups must exclude men if the average woman participant is to speak openly. The very presence of men, however silent they remain, is inhibiting, especially to younger women. It can be described as a sort of reflexive "insignificant little me" response. If anything, this attitude encourages male competitiveness, and, on the contrary, males in the absence of females appear less competitive (Appendix Study 29).

On the other hand, our data show that girls aged six to eight in all-girl classes take "toughness" more seriously; furthermore, they are more prone than coed girls to overrate their own toughness. In fact, they did so at higher rates than did boys in mixed classrooms. These young girls were more outspoken than their coed counterparts, engaged in more vigorous gymnastics, and in general were more spontaneous (Appendix Study 29). These effects are apparently not limited to younger girls: there are data that women of comparable backgrounds will develop rather different personality traits depending on whether they enter an all-women's or a coed college.

My own introduction to this phenomenon was through a boyhood friend who had left Chicago to take a job with IBM in Poughkeepsie, New York. There he encountered a type of woman he had never before known, the Vassar woman, and I still recall the awe with which he spoke of these independent, immodest, potent women. Mervin Freedman, reporting on a large and thorough study of Vassar alumnae who had attended between 1929 and the late 1950s, noted:

> The alumnae who were attending graduate or professional schools displayed a rather impressive picture of accomplishment. For the most part these students found the academic demands made upon them to be no greater than those to which they had been accustomed as undergraduates; in some cases the work was even a bit easier. Moreover, these women had learned that academic competition with men presented no great difficulty. (1962, p. 870)

Similarly, the Carnegie Commission on Higher Education (1973) asserts that an unusually high proportion of successful women come from the smaller women's colleges (see also Tidball and Kostiakowski, 1976). Yet the trend is toward coeducation. Is this not ironic? For according to the evidence, coeducation increases inequality, despite the greater opportunity for specialization in large coed schools. Consider the famous women's college Smith, which briefly became a coed institution. They found, however, during an experimental period, the lesson we, too, have learned—the presence of males changed performance and attitudes toward the self in a way not conducive to the female's sense of independence. Smith has since returned to the all-female format. Sarah Lawrence is another example. Now torn in two by forces for and against coeducation, it cannot return to the all-female format for financial reasons, and its future as a major institution of learning is now in doubt (Roiphe, 1977).

We cannot have it both ways. If we want women oriented primarily toward childrearing and male supremacy, coed schools are perhaps best. If we want outspoken, independent women, all-female schools seem to be in order.

What do all-boy schools do for boys? In an experiment outside Washington, D.C. a formerly coed school was split into same-sex classrooms (Yolles, 1967). The boys' rooms became noisier and noisier, until one teacher described the situation as resembling a boiler factory. The boys, however, were more spontaneous and less inhibited about questioning the teacher; moreover, they reported enjoying school much more. The girls in this experiment, like girls in other all-girl classes, found themselves less shy and more talkative in class; they also said they enjoyed school more.

Have we made a mistake in mixing the sexes and allowing them to inhibit one another? To answer this question, we have to ask ourselves a whole series of questions. For example, do we, as a society of both men and women, want more dominant women? The answer is not simple, and I would like to close this chapter by noting some of its complexities.

For one thing, if behavior at lower phyletic levels is a predictor, then dominant women will probably mean lowered birthrates. Indeed, psychiatric clinics are reporting increases in cases of male impotence, which case workers (intuitively) relate to the rise in women's independence. Here we must invoke the behavioral "law" Konrad Lorenz somewhat playfully called Beatrice's Law after his daughter-in-law, who first thought of it while watching fish. She found that as long as the female cichlid was awed or even frightened by the male, copulation proceeded normally. But if the male for some reason was awed or fearful of the female, copulation would almost certainly not occur. Similar observations have since been made among other species, including the rhesus monkeys of Cayo Santiago (Sade, 1968).*

The human male is no exception. It is apparently imperative for the male to feel superior to the female—or at least unafraid—for continuously successful copulations, and it may well be for this reason that males everywhere tend to demean women, belittle their accomplishments, and, in the vernacular (clearly laden with symbolism) "put them down." I have not heard of a culture in which the males do not engage in this chauvinistic sport, although cultures certainly vary with regard to women's rights. And, as I have already implied, women more often than not go along with this strategy, agreeing to hold in abeyance the anger that would appear to be inevitable. This is, then, the setting for those recurrent and familiar battles between men and women, for the female's sense that "he never listens to me" and for the male's sense that women are not to be taken seriously.

David Gutmann (1973) has observed similar changes in males and females over the life span in five different cultures: the Navajo, Druze (Israel), Lowland and Highland Maya (Mexico), and a Kansas City middle-class population. In all these cultures, he found that in the early years of marriage women tended to abrogate their own egoism and instead to enhance their husband's self-esteem. Only as the parenting years were ending, again in all five cultures, did females tend to be outspoken and more assertive. Males tended to develop complementary changes, becoming more passive and giving

---

*Such cases of impotence can probably be explained at the physiological level by sympathetic-parasympathetic nervous system interaction of the sort generally found in fearful animals (Selye, 1956).

with age; consequently, marriages tended to reach a new stability. On the other hand, those males who continued to insist on enhancing their own egos, Gutmann asserts, were those prone to heart attacks and other diseases usually associated with stress and early demise. Whereas Gutmann speaks of a "parental imperative" and gives these events a psychoanalytic interpretation, the pattern lends itself even better to an evolutionary explanation.

A young male's motor is fueled by a sense of omnipotence and ample supplies of testosterone; as a young adult, his ego soars, and the world is his oyster. Everything appears possible. The female, in the cause of childrearing, yields and caters to this frequently insufferable egotist, for only in this way can she be sure he will stay. As I have suggested, there appears to be something reflexive in young women that causes them to defer to men. Although not necessarily aware of her behavior, the marriageable female tends to massage the male ego so that he will care for her and her children and proceed up the golden ladder of success, however success is defined by the culture. But once the young are raised, when the parents are about 45 years of age, *relative* testosterone levels rise remarkably in females as levels fall in males (Birren, 1959). The time for female leadership has then arrived, and Gutmann indeed found just this turnabout in each of his five cultures.

My interim conclusion? For true equality of the sexes, we need a world of 50-year olds and older. Because of the consequences of gametic competition, younger men and women are at existential odds. No matter the culture, the sexes simply have different ideal solutions for getting their gametes into the next generation, and it is for this reason, despite love and the "parental imperative," that they tend to see life in different ways.

5

Interlude: Further Thoughts on Polygyny and Monogamy

Hygamous, hogamous, men are monogamous.
Hogamous, hygamous, women are polygamous.

This is the couplet of the thwarted male and the unattached female. For only when a man is heartbroken, or at least uncertain, is he psychologically monogamous. Once he has her corralled, so to speak, and her shopping around has stopped, the couplet can often be reversed.

Let me hypothesize on the basis of very limited data. For many males, one devoted girlfriend makes him feel good. When he has two, he feels great, and three smacks of fantasies of omnipotence come true. That seems true not only among us in the West but also throughout Africa and most probably among men everywhere. Thus, in Africa it is a common saying that there is no difference between a man who has one wife and a man who has none (Clignet, 1970, p. 30).

Sleeping with two women at a time is a favorite male fantasy, and in Paris, for example, it is common for prostitutes to hire out in tandem. Males I know who have had this experience rave about it, for apparently it is the fulfillment of deep-seated polygynous feelings that most heterosexual men share. From what we know so far, heterosexual women tend not to have polygamous fantasies. Nor should one be misled by nude male centerfolds in *Playgirl* and other women's magazines. These are parodies, comic imitations of male lust, and it is interesting that they have served to increase the circulation of these publications among male homosexuals. Female pornography, Money and Ehrhardt (1972) point out, consists of the "true romance" and "true confession" type of magazines. This is not to deny that many women are indeed attracted to a bulging male crotch (Friday, 1974), but most women want more than anything else to be loved by a man she in turn loves or, minimally, to have a man help rear her children—and one man normally will suffice (Simon and Gagnon, 1969).

As people living in monogamous cultures know, there are problems within just about every mated pair, and often such difficulties derive from this difference in the psychology of the sexes. As discussed in Chapter 1, this sex difference in basic mating strategy appears to stem from the sex differences in gametic potential. All males and all females find the other sex strange because each is built toward rather distinct ends, and different cultures and different economic systems modify, but do not determine in any significant way, these basic tendencies. To put it baldly, females are more readily monogamous and males more readily polygamous.

What of polyandrous (many husbands) social systems? First, let us get rid of the amazing Amazons, who always arise in such a discussion. They are the inhabitants of a Roman myth and they are not to be found in some obscure ethnographic report, as many perfectly intelligent people believe. The definitive work on polyandry was written by Prince Peter of Greece some thirty years ago, and it is based largely on his studies in northern India and Tibet, the only part of the world in which polyandry flourishes. There is none to be found anywhere near the Amazon River, whose peoples tend toward polygyny, (as do the Yanomamo Chapter 2). On reading Prince Peter, it is immediately apparent that a polyandrous wife is no Amazon. Just the opposite, in fact. She is usually married to several brothers, and it is her role to cook, mend clothes, and keep house for everybody. Such a system solves certain problems of land apportionment, but these cultures are male dominated, and a married woman obviously works considerably harder than do her monogamous or polygynous counterparts. Thus we can write off polyandry as an anomalous adjustment to specialized circumstances.

Polygyny, on the other hand, as the most prevalent marriage arrangement, requires considerably more thought than we in the West have given it. We assume that monogamy is best. But we know, from statistics and experience, that our system does not work well, and perhaps we can find some answers to our difficulties by examining what each system does and does not do for individual fulfillment. Clearly, polygyny means some men will not have any wives and most will have only one, as it is in current polygynous societies. Thus, the potential losers would benefit by monogamy. But young men being what they are, few believe, given hypothetical circumstances, that they will be the losers; so that most males in polygynous societies cannot be expected to vote for monogamy.

The female vote is a better bet. If a reasonable economic future with one man is predictable, she will doubtless choose a monogamous union. Only in societies with severely skewed wealth is polygyny reasonable from the woman's point of view, for then it becomes difficult to find a man who can help raise the young. Few women living in polygyny cannot be cajoled into admitting they would prefer an economically sound monogamous marriage (see Thomas, 1959). In fact, such marriages are more fruitful for women: Clignet (1970) found significantly more children produced by monogamous women than by polygynous women in the same society, and it thus makes good biological sense that women prefer monogamy.

As I have indicated, polygyny, when supported by a *patrilineal* descent system, is much rougher on women than polygyny in a setting where descent is traced through the mother (*matrilineal*). In patrilineal polygyny a woman's well-being depends largely on how pleased her husband is with her. Usually, close ties with her own family are cut off after marriage, and divorce tends to be much more difficult. The world revolves around the man, and competition and suspicion among co-wives is almost always present. Separate huts (or chambers) for each wife is the rule, and men tend to complain about the problems engendered by bickering wives (Clignet, 1970). On the other hand, the patrilineal polygamist may fear that co-wives will unify against him and in China, long a patrilineal polygynous culture, the pictograph for "plotting" or "scheming" is identical with that for "three women."

By contrast, in matrilineal polygynous societies, a wife's ties with the family of her birth are never broken; the bride price to a wife's parents is lower than among patrilineal groups; and divorce is much easier. Furthermore, if the wives are from the same or related clans, as in Navajo polygyny, it is as if they were blood sisters with all the loyalty that relationship implies. Here there is a communal rearing of children, and the half sibs mix easily with one another. Among the matrilineal Abouré of the Ivory Coast, the man is still considered most important and residence is in his village, but, according to Clignet (1970), the feeling in a polygynous compound there tends to be one of community and togetherness rather than suspicion and competition, seen in the patrilineal Bété of the same area. As an example of the different marital roles played by women in these contrasting groups, among the Abouré the wife comes to sleep with the husband on a schedule set by the head wife, whereas among the patrilineal Bété the husband can go to the hut of the wife of his choice. In other words, it appears that co-wives in matrilineal societies enjoy a degree of independence, respect, and freedom that is in striking contrast to the situation of their patrilineal counterparts (see also Dube, 1969, on an Islamic matrilineal group; Fuller, 1976, on the Nayars of India; Nakane, 1967, on two Assam tribes; and Richards, 1950, on the Central Bantu of Africa).

The level of suspiciousness among co-wives in patrilineal polygyny was brought home to me by a Sudanese graduate student. His father is a wealthy man with five wives and 26 children. The wives are keenly suspicious of one another and foster the same feelings in their children. Black magic is rampant, as each wife suspects the others of using either love potions to obtain the husband's exclusive favor or poisons to get rid of an already favored wife. Traveling medicine men do a booming business, as potions, antidotes, and special prayers are in almost continuous use, but they do not stay long in one place since co-wives would then suspect them of colluding with their rivals.

Women are so deprived of active self-expression in the Sudan that a special institution has evolved—secret clubs at meetings of which women dress and act as men; they swear and stomp about in an orgy of self-assertion, accompanied by obvious pleasure and much laughter. Now, in retrospect, my Sudanese student sees this regular event (which he first happened upon by chance as a young boy) as a natural response to the strongly male centered lives all women there must endure.

Another difficulty with polygyny, this student points out, is the father's aloofness. His own father, since he had to be as evenhanded as possible to avoid further problems, tended to be impersonal with all of his children. This student, as can be imagined, learned to hate and continues to hate a system that left him emotionally isolated from his father and half sibs, and he is now committed to a monogamous marriage. He washes the dishes, cares for the children, and insists he would have it no other way. And yet I see a light in his eye whenever we discuss supernumerary wives. Certainly his *wife* would have it no other way.

Which ecological settings seem to be best suited to polygyny, which to monogamy? In discussing the genetics of populations, zoologists distinguish between two major types of evolutionary selection, r selection and K selection (Wilson, 1975): r refers to a high *rate* of increase of a population; K refers to a population that has already achieved an equilibrium, so that its *carrying capacity (K)* is approximately equal from generation to generation. Chagnon (1978), working among the Yanomamo, points out that relatively little effort is needed in the jungle to make a "living," and the trend is toward expansion of population. Chagnon suggests that the very lopsided polygyny practiced among the Yanomamo, with relatively few males fathering the majority of children, is in the service of r selection. The so-called civilized nations, on the other hand, with their large populations and limited resources, are on more of a holding pattern, or K equilibrium; this must be at least one source of our emphasis on limited fecundity and our antipolygynous social mores.

Clearly, the worldwide trend is toward monogamy. Since Murdock published his atlas in 1957, in which 75% of culture areas were described as polygynous, a vast area of population has switched from polygamy to monogamy: the People's Republic of China. And that drives home a point: where there is a political system founded on the rights of little men, where the masses rule, there can be no polygyny. From this viewpoint, socialist, communist, and democratic nations are much closer to one another than any are to traditional Muslim nations with their skewed distributions of wealth.

But taking a second look at the great Muslim nations we see similar trends. President Sadat of Egypt has but one wife, an outspoken advocate of women's rights. The top political echelon of Egypt are all monogamous. All the young intellectual leaders of sub-Saharan Africa are monogamous and tend to be socialists. Only a few old-timers such as Amin of Uganda rule as did the sultans of the past. Everywhere the masses are coming into their own, and the principles of the Magna Carta have, by now, been incorporated into the constitutions of all the nations of the world. Without doubt, the day will soon come when Muslim polygyny will be no more than an "interesting" historical phase, as the democratization (the K equilibrium?) of the Muslim world becomes complete.

We have, then, heard the death knell for polygyny. Is there anything to say in its favor, if only a historical note? Of course polygynous women themselves rarely complain publicly about the system. After all, they usually have known no other way. They accept their husband's concubines, usually help choose his other wives, and may even encourage his extramarital sexual exploits, so long as they respect cultural proscriptions.

Jomo Kenyatta (1938), founder and first president of independent Kenya, wrote a spirited defense of polygyny, citing some of the specific advantages it had for women of his own tribe, the Kikuyu. Not the least of these advantages was the absence of male-female bickering as monogamists know it. For the setting that purports to make men and women equal also eliminates the institutionalized superiority of the man. With dominance constantly in question, bickering is inevitable. Kenyatta concluded that wife beating is probably much more common in monogamous marriages, where submission must be enforced from time to time. It is a coarse but common remark, usually attributed to European peasants, that women should be beaten weekly, whether they need it or not. There are no data, but I would guess there is much less physical abuse of wives in polygynous groups, where sex roles are more clearly delineated. In this regard, we should not be misled by rituals emphasizing male supremacy within some polygynous groups. Although the polygynous Hadza of Uganda, for example, have a dance in which young men whip young women, the interaction is formalized and both sexes clearly enjoy the interplay (see Gardner, 1974). As already discussed, no male can exhibit consistent sexual potency when his dominance over the female is in doubt, and both Hadza men and women appear to joyfully acknowledge that fact in their dancing.

In polygynous marriage it is understood, at many levels, that the male is dominant. The very fact of having to share one man is in itself a direct message that each woman is proportionately less than her husband, and the issue of who is dominant is simply not a problem. A polygynous colony founded by an ex-Marine, ex-Mormon, Alexander Joseph, was much in the news in 1977–1978. Joseph and several of his twelve wives are young, articulate, and apparently frank. Joseph points out that after he had three wives, it became easier and easier to acquire more; now that he has twelve he receives a constant stream of applications. Clearly, being a winner is attractive in itself.

This case brings up an advantage for females that is characteristic of some polygynous marriages. Joseph's wives make much of the sisterhood that they enter upon becoming his wife and of the safety and support they feel in joining such a family commune. Several had, in fact, been members of other communes, but this family commune provided what was absent in the others—a shared sense of belonging because of the communal marriage to one man. It has been said by members of the women's movement that the major effect to date has been the breakdown of social barriers between women. It is then ironic that polygyny, too, can accomplish the same task but within the proven and fruitful setting of heterosexual marriage.

Polygynous sisterhood can be a powerful force. It was the Hausa women of Nigeria, banded together, who first faced down the British occupying forces at the end of the nineteenth century. In a massive protest march, they advanced on the British troops, expecting them not to shoot a group of women. The British fired, women were killed, the English back home were humiliated by and incensed at their own troops, and a major step toward independence had been achieved (Lugard, 1905). It is difficult to imagine monogamous women so easily banding together to do battle, the temporary togetherness of women's rights campaigns aside. Polygynous households with their small women's bands doubtless set the stage for this landmark in Nigerian history.

Having shown some of the strengths of polygyny, is it possible that we were wrong, that polygyny is not on the way out but that it will instead become the next step for many who are now monogamous? There is one such experiment in Chicago involving an offshoot of the Black Muslim movement. A number of well-educated women in the movement found that there simply were not enough educated, responsible men to go around. The solution? A polygynous sisterhood; heterosexual households of several women, their children, and one man. Illegal, yes. But apparently this arrangement is working well. Although I see little possibility of such polygynous experiments turning the tide because of the massive political trends already spoken of, it is clear that there have been problems with monogamy.

At a practical level, polygynous households would even appear economically preferable. In these days of runaway costs, a communal arrangement with one working man and several working women could conceivably work well. (I hope it is by now clear why the opposite, polyandrous arrangement is not likely to work.) The occasional maternity would put but one breadwinner out of work, and if two can live as cheaply as one, four can multiply that advantage and provide one another insurance against unemployment as well. It would be most ironic, would it not, if the sisterhood encouraged and achieved by the women's movement will have set the stage for experiments in polygyny!

6

Signals of Status

HEIGHT AND DOMINANCE

In a recent talk about her research (1977), Rutgers anthropologist Heather Fowler brought down the house with a description of the sex life of fifteen leaders in the women's movement and most particularly with a description of the traits these women sought in a man. The fun came from the discrepancy between the audience's expectations and Fowler's findings. When asked what in their men aroused them sexually, all the women used words that meant "powerful." He was either "very rich," a "genius," or "brilliant"; there were many references to lavish dinners and large tips, Jaguar cars, and stunning suits. In other words, these women of status needed superdominant males to keep them happy. Furthermore, it was clear, if only from the frequency with which the description "genius" was used, that these women were building up their men with a substantial pinch of fantasy.

Women often prefer dominant males but sometimes refuse to acknowledge this preference. One of my female students was tall (5' 10"), fine looking, politically liberal, and guilty over her discomfort with short men. Why, she had asked herself, should a University of Chicago graduate student, well read and presumably liberated, continue to be so enfettered by "middle-class values." Instead of recommending psychotherapy, I worked with her to devise the following study based on a diagnostic test used by clinical psychologists, the Thematic Apperception Test (T.A.T.). The subject is shown a picture and asked to make up a story about it. The story is then analyzed not so much for its content as for its general flavor and for the themes running through it so that we may learn something about the storyteller's "unconscious" motivation (see Murray, 1938).

We drew a man and a woman, obviously out on the town together: in one case he was taller; in the other, she was (see figure, below). In another rendition of these drawings the male sported a moustache because we wished to determine how that feature might interact with height. We also devised a questionnaire to get at more conscious, openly stated, and avowed attitudes toward dating.

The respondents were twenty female graduate students at the University of Chicago, and, as predicted, there was a decisive difference between what their stated attitudes were on the questionnaire and the less conscious themes evident in the stories. The very same women who professed, in strongest terms, that the size of the man makes no difference to them, would give us stories with a

Female graduate students were asked to invent stories to these drawings, and the stories' themes were then analyzed. The stories to *a* and *c*, in which the female is taller, had a negative tone compared to the stories given to *b* and *d*. Also, the short man with the moustache, but not the tall man with the moustache, tended to be described as "sleazy" by this group of women.

a

b

c

d

dismal outcome to the short man/tall woman drawing. By contrast, the outcomes of stories about the second drawing, the one with the taller male, were either bland or reasonably optimistic (Appendix Study 30).

On further interrogation, when confronted with these contradictory data, most of the women admitted that they rarely had a second date with shorter men. In the same vein, a friend of mine who is six feet tall had had a lengthy love affair with a shorter man and found that they argued less and were far more relaxed when not in public. Social pressure and his sense of disgrace, she acknowledged, played a major role in their eventual breakup. Indeed, whether the pressure is primarily external or internal is a thankless argument—the pressure is always there and present in all cultures we know of; husbands are consistently taller than their wives everywhere in the world. It is true that age and its sometimes correlates, power and wealth, may make up for a number of deficiencies, including a man's being shorter than his spouse. But these feelings run deep, and tall men in all societies appear to be at some advantage.

Leland Deck (1968) followed the careers of graduates of the University of Pittsburgh and found a positive correlation between height and starting salary. College graduates who were 6' 2" or taller received an average salary 12.4% higher than those below six feet. In the same vein, a marketing professor at a university asked 140 job recruiters to make a hypothetical hiring choice between two equally qualified applicants for a sales position. The only variable was height—one candidate was 6' 1", the other 5' 5". Seventy-two percent chose the taller, 1% the shorter, and 27% expressed no preference (Kubey, 1976). As far back as 1915 Gowin published pertinent data on a variety of professions, and two of his tables are reproduced here (Tables 2 and 3). One point seems pretty well made, then, that height per se lends men an economic and social advantage and, as we shall soon see, this advantage is not restricted to our own culture.

Given the advantage of being tall, there is a tendency to form one's noncompetitive relations (friendships) with persons of about the same size. I had for a long time noticed a homogeneity among best friends and, conversely, that tall men and small men rarely hit it off. I therefore suggested to a student that she station herself at a local bistro frequented by university people and note heights, weights, and ages of all-male and all-female pairs or groups coming in for a drink. The homogeneity in the average height of a party was striking in that persons averaged less than two inches of difference from their companions; it was rare to find tall and small in the same party (Appendix Study 31).

Being short is itself a problem, at least for men, largely because

TABLE 2: COMPARISON OF MAJOR AND MINOR EXECUTIVES WITH RESPECT TO AVERAGE HEIGHT AND AVERAGE WEIGHT[a]

Class	Average height	Difference	Average weight	Difference
Bishops	70.6	1.8	176.4	17.0
Preachers in small towns	68.6		159.4	
University presidents	70.8	1.2	181.6	17.6
Presidents of small colleges	69.6		164.0	
City school superintendents	70.4	0.7	178.6	21.0
Principals in small towns	69.7		157.6	
Sales managers	70.1	1.1	182.8	25.8
Salesmen	69.1		157.0	
Presidents of railroad companies	70.9	1.5	186.3	31.7
Station agents in towns of 500 population	69.4		154.6	

[a] After Gowin (1915).

TABLE 3: COMPARISONS IN HEIGHT: LEADERS RANKED ACCORDING TO HEIGHT[a]

Rank	Name of group	Height	Rank	Name of group	Height
1	Reformers	5:11.4	21	World's work list	5:10.3
2	Superintendents street cleaning	5:11.3	22	Inventors	5:10.2
3	Wardens	5:11.3	23	Authors	5:10.2
4	Governors	5:11.2	24	Sales managers	5:10.1
5	Chiefs of police	5:11.1	25	Artists	5:10.1
6	Socialist organizers	5:10.9	26	Mayors	5:10.0
7	Railroad presidents	5:10.9	27	Factory superintendents	5: 9.8
8	University presidents	5:10.8	28	Insurance presidents	5: 9.7
9	Economists and sociologists	5:10.8	29	Psychologists	5: 9.7
10	Bank presidents	5:10.7	30	Presidents fraternal orders	5: 9.6
11	Senators	5:10.6	31	Chief justices state courts	5: 9.6
12	Bishops	5:10.6	32	Philosophers	5: 9.6
13	Presidents state bar	5:10.5	33	Merchants	5: 9.4
14	City school superintendents	5:10.4	34	Roundhouse foremen	5: 9.3
15	Presidents labor organizations	5:10.4	35	Anti-saloon league officials	5: 9.2
16	Presidents religious organizations	5:10.4	36	Lecturers	5: 9.2
17	Corporation directors	5:10.4	37	Manufacturers	5: 9.0
18	Chiefs fire departments	5:10.3	38	Labor organization	5: 8.2
19	Anti-saloon league organizers	5:10.3	39	Publishers	5: 7.9
20	YMCA secretaries	5:10.3	40	Musicians	5: 5.6

[a] After Gowin (1915).

it is an automatic sign of subdominance, and being tall is automatically a self-esteem booster for the opposite reason. I suspect there is no culture in which such feelings do not attend differences in height, and in fact, even at the level of intergroup relations, relative height often plays a decisive role.

Consistently, across northern sub-Saharan Africa, taller tribes are feared by their shorter neighbors. Thus, in Nigeria, the tall Fulani, although a minority, have long been rulers and enslavers of all neighboring groups; similarly, the Masai have always been the most feared warriors of East Africa; and in Burundi a minority of supertall Watusi (some 15% of the population) had long enslaved and later governed the more numerous Wahutus. In the Congo, the pygmies have been perfect targets for enslavement, and a sort of working relation was established with neighboring Bantu tribes whereby pygmy women were available as tribute (Turnbull, 1965).

Nor need we confine such an analysis to Africa. Sorokin (1959) has made a rather complete review of the European literature, and the consistency of the correlation between height and social class is remarkable. Sorokin concludes that nutrition alone could not account for such a gross, widespread phenomenon and that hereditary tallness must be at its root. Class difference in height in England, with a full head separating the Oxford working class and the Oxford dons, is frequently commented on. The correlation between a Cambridge-Oxford accent and height must be enormous, and, although Sorokin reports only older statistics, I must assume, given about equivalent nutrition in recent generations, that in England class and genetic tallness are highly correlated. The probable history of this pattern is not difficult to reconstruct—and it likely goes back to the Saxon and Norman conquests and subsequent appointments of the tall to high places. I think it safe to conclude that taller peoples have tended to hold sway over their shorter neighbors, even as within-group differences have similarly favored the tall.

I received some insight into the psychological meaning of height when I was investigating the "fear of strangers," sometimes called the "eight-months anxiety," in babies. Some time in the second six months of life almost all babies start to cry when approached suddenly by a stranger, and the taller the stranger, the more frightening he or she appears to be. One of my students sought to test this notion by dressing a child of seven exactly as she was dressed, including makeup, hairdo, and clothing. The child, who was well rehearsed in aping the adult's actions, drew completely different reactions from the six- to twelve-month-old infants. Whereas they would freeze or cry in response to the adult, they would smile and even babble at the strange child. None of the 20 infants cried when approached by the little girl; seven cried with the adult stranger (Appendix Study 32).

A very similar phenomenon occurs among animals at a comparable stage in life. Soon after they have made initial attachments to their parents and those with whom they are in daily contact, most animals begin to show fear of strangers, including strangers of their own species. The reaction is considerably more pronounced with strangers of equally large or larger species. It is most obvious in birds like ducks and geese or in mammals like sheep and goats, that is, animals who are on their feet soon after birth. When such *precocial* animals are confronted with strangers they flee and we know immediately that they are frightened. In *altricial,* or slow developing animals, a fear response to strangers also develops but it is stretched out over time and therefore not as clear-cut. Dogs provide a good example of this process. We raised several litters of puppies in acre pens with their tame mothers and despite the fact that the tame mothers greeted our weekly visits into the pens with tail wagging, the pups (beagles and cocker spaniels) grew progressively more and more fearful of the human intruders. By twelve weeks of age, they were as wild as foxes and had to be captured using the same trapping methods one would use on a wild mammal (Freedman, King, Elliot, 1961). It appeared, moreover, that *the taller the human stranger, the farther the wild pups ran* before they dared stop for a second look. That is, they tended to maintain a safe distance that varied with the stranger's size.

Heini Hediger, director of the Zurich zoo, has found this "safety distance" to vary with each species (Hediger, 1951). Man, because he

Critical period study (Freedman, King, and Elliot, 1961): beagles raised in a one-acre pen from birth to twelve weeks became so fearful as to be untrainable. Only five days of socialization to humans before ten weeks' of age produced trainable animals. Second animal was socialized during his fifth week and returned to the pen.

stands tall, gets a wide berth, and this is clearly one of the evolutionary advantages of walking erect: though a lightweight, man could draw the same "respect" (induced fright) as could an animal many times his weight—both look equally imposing trudging over the bush. By the same logic, the typical bush hunter crouches low so that even if seen he is not too imposing.

A simple experiment can be performed with domestic cows to see how this reaction works: if you approach a grazing cow, she will move off a certain distance before again grazing; now hunch down a bit, and she will let you get closer and, crawling on all fours, you can come right up to her. Throughout nature the rule is the bigger, the more dangerous. There is a lesson in this for the visiting, out-of-town grandmother, for her grandchildren are not much different. The worst thing she can do when visiting her eight-month-old grandchild is immediately to grasp the child in her arms. More often than not, the infant will cry. The proper approach is to avoid the child's eyes completely for a period; only when the baby has had a chance to investigate the visitor from afar, approach slowly and tentatively, retreating if the baby is not yet ready.

This awe of tall people has some practical implications in the schoolroom. My older son's Montessori class of eleven- and twelve-year olds was particularly unruly and the principal and teacher were hard pressed for a solution. The teacher was inexperienced, but she was smart and competent and very sweet. A self-assured young man, 6'3", and sporting a substantial beard was introduced to the class. His name was Ruud Van Velthoven, and to this day he is famous in our family. The boys in the class immediately complained about his "meanness" although in fact he was gentle and rarely chastised anyone. Despite their complaints, they hung about his desk as if magnetized. They were in awe, a bit frightened, but attracted, and the deportment problem was solved in a day! We are all in awe of people who tower over us, and the first manifestation of this reaction is the fear of strangers in the first year. It is clearly an evolved reaction shared by all animals, save a few species on the predator-free Galapagos Islands, that has the obvious adaptive function either of summoning a protector (as does an immature primate's squeal or cry) or else triggering escape to potential safety.

Finally, lest the case for tallness be overstated, it is clear that if one is too far beyond the population's average, disadvantages begin to accrue. In the aforementioned study by Deck (1968) of University of Pittsburgh graduates, as height rose above 6'2", salaries began again to decline. And one has only to recall Thomas Wolfe's personal experiences around his 6'6" to achieve some insight into the plight of the very tall man.

He would be going along a street at five o'clock when the city
was pouring homeward from its work, and suddenly he would
become conscious that the people were watching him: would see
them stare at him and nudge each other, would see their
surprised looks travelling curiously up his frame, would hear
them whisper to each other in astonished voices. . . . This feeling
of shame and self-abasement and hatred of his flesh is the worst
thing that a tall man knows, the greatest inequity that his spirit
suffers. (1935, p. 139)

EYES

In almost all primates and in many predators, looking each other
full in the eyes is an act of aggression. The great horned owl can be
angered by a human stare and has been known to gouge its keeper's
eyes in response (Linblad, 1962). Anyone who works with macaques
or baboons can attest to the fact that their reaction to a human stare,
especially in close quarters, may be very frightening even though the
animal is in a holding cage. Depending on its rank and confidence a
monkey may react to the human's stare with fierce baring of the
canines or an averted face and lazy yawn, also baring its canines. A
third possible reaction to the stare, particularly if the animal is a
juvenile or a smaller female, is lip smacking and fear-smiling, both
signs of fear and acknowledgments of submission.

For field researchers, staring into a large male primate's eyes is
simply the wrong thing to do. George Schaller (1963), told me that
his most frightening experience while investigating the mountain
gorilla was a chance encounter in the bush with a large female. They
found themselves face to face at about three yards, and Schaller in
retrospect is sure she was as frightened as he, for both left in a hurry.

The sudden flash of a set of eyes appears at various phyletic
levels, and it invariably functions to frighten the viewer. Gelada baboons, who scatter over the terrain in one-male harem groups, have
white outlines to their eyes so that a flick of the brow can be seen
across a long distance as a white flash. Since such flashing usually is
directed by males at other males, its purpose is apparently to warn
that "this is my territory" (Kummer, 1965).

Among birds, fish, and insects imitation eyes, or eyespots, have
evolved as one of the most widely used defenses against predators.
Usually, eyespots are located at otherwise unprotected areas, and
they are most effective when suddenly exposed, just before the
predator attacks. I experienced the way this device works while
swimming under water with a face mask at Ala Moana beach in

Hawaii. The water was dark and murky, and I was probing about the sand with a stick when suddenly two large red eyes flashed in front of me. My initial reaction was panic. To my relief, I realized that I had encountered a bottom-feeding fish and that the "eyes" were spots on the normally retracted dorsal fins, which flash open at the first sign of danger. If I were a member of a less reflective species, I would certainly have darted off. All living creatures seem to react to staring eyes in about the same way: to be stared at means attack may be imminent. Consequently, the red eyespots are universally effective and appear on a wide range of preyed upon species. (See Appendix Study 33, for the frightening effect of a red mask on human infants.)

In man, paranoid fantasies abound with accusing, staring eyes, and probably in every culture, a stare without a smile is taken as a sign of unfriendliness or even evil intent. Alice Dan has demonstrated very nicely how sensitive we are to another's stares. In her initial observations, she merely placed herself at various angles to persons eating alone in a neighborhood lunchroom, stared at them, and noted their reactions. All were affected, and some persons seemed to have eyes in back of their heads, picking her up from "impossible" angles. Then, in a more formal study she enlisted the aid of 2 males; the 3 proceeded to stare at some 40 lunchers. The results support her initial findings and are reported as Study 34 in the Appendix. I would like to quote Dan's description of the experimenters' subjective experiences that were perhaps most revealing of all:

> In an area as little explored as human visual interaction, these phenomenological data seem particularly relevant. When an observer's direct gaze was returned by a subject, there was invariably a feeling of tension reported by all observers. In 2 cases the tension was dissipated by a subject's smile, but more often it was broken only when one of the starers looked away.

> Male observer No. 2 reported that when a male subject stared back, "My heart beat faster, I felt adrenalin going all over the place. I felt he was giving me a sinister stare. I felt the same as if I knew he were going to hit me." This observer also reported that he felt a strong urge to smile or laugh, but restrained himself from changing his expression. The female observer (me!) felt a similar hostility in the returned stares of female subjects, but I was not aware of such a violent physiological reaction. When confronted with the direct gaze of a male subject, however, I did experience those physiological "alarm signals." I felt that the male stare seemed "invading," but not necessarily hostile—more like an unwanted intimacy. (Appendix Study 34, p. 10)

A white high school student in Chicago's Hyde Park area wrote a treatise for the school paper on how he survived while traversing the black slums surrounding the University of Chicago. The problem was to avoid being challenged by territorial gangs. Four years of experience led to the following advice: never stare another adolescent male in the eyes, preferably keeping your eyes on the ground. By exhibiting such an extreme of deference and nonbelligerency, one greatly reduces the chances of being accosted. Needless to say, the fact that this student was white lent him some neutrality for it was clear he was not a member of a rival gang.

What of the black gang member in the nearly all-white university protectorate? What are his reactions? I learned something of this from a former student, an Afro-American brought up in the great Chicago slum known as the West Side, where he himself was a gang leader. He recalls a visit to the University of Chicago area as a youth during which he found himself smiling so much and so broadly that he could not believe this was he. His reaction was, of course, the universal hominid display when on strange turf, assuring all that "I love you, so forgive my intrusion."

Some further insights into these phenomena come from Dan Scheinfield (1973), an anthropologist who has worked with a territorial gang on Chicago's West Side. He found that within the gang there was a "looking" order that appeared to follow the pecking order. Those on top considered it "uncool" to look at those below them and did not deign to do so. The rule was that attention must be paid the hierarchy's leadership and to receive attention one must earn it. By noting who looks at whom, Scheinfield was able to construct a dominance hierarchy that followed, fairly closely, the gang members' ratings of one another's prestige. As among the macaques, when a dominant did look at a subordinate, it usually meant the latter was in trouble. Scheinfield, in fact, was so struck by the parrallels with rhesus monkeys that he has been reluctant to publish his observations lest someone feel hurt by the comparisons. In my view, however, no one group need feel stigmatized since we all are primatelike in our use of eyes to signal aggressive or submissive intent (Appendix Study 35).

But this is only half the story of eye contact. Particularly in man, eyes focused on eyes can also designate attraction and interest, and no one has yet described a culture in which such behavior is absent. The attractive pull of a pair of eyes looking at one is elemental and Carolyn Goren et al. (1975) were able to show that as early as *nine minutes* of age, human infants are more attracted to eyes than to any other visual stimulus. Goren first constructed a series of cards with drawings of faces, parts of faces, and mixed-up faces (figure, p. 96). The study, which was disarmingly simple, consisted of placing the baby on the lap with a cardboard protractor above the baby's head like a 180-degree halo. The cards were shuffled so that their order

Newborn infant partially following a "mixed-up face." The organized face was followed considerably better.

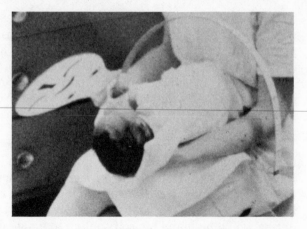

was unknown to the experimenter, and she slowly moved each from the center to one side and then the other. This procedure was repeated three times, and the baby's farthest head turning to either side was taken as a measure of interest in the drawings. (Such research with newborns is possible because for about six hours after birth babies remain awake and unusually alert, probably because of the circulating hormones resulting from the birth process. In drugless births this period offers a marvelous opportunity for mother and infant to establish initial bonds.) Goren tested 20 babies in this way, with an age range of 9 to 17 minutes, with an average age of 12 minutes, and the results paralleled those of her previous study on day-old babies (Appendix Study 36). As in the figure on page 97, the newborns preferred a moving face to any other stimuli, and when Goren separated out parts of the face for the twenty-four-hour olds, the eyes were clearly the most important aspect. This finding is not just an artifact of the experiment: newborn babies picked up for the very first time frequently turn their eyes directly to those of the adult. This is illustrated on page 98 in a series of stills taken from 12 seconds of film. A crying newborn is picked up and cradled in the arms for the first time, whereupon the eyes of the baby come to rest on those of Goren and crying immediately stops (see also Appendix Study 37).

At the end of the first month, eye contact with a baby can be established with greater and greater regularity, until adult and baby are having staring contests (page 98, below), and some ten days after the onset of staring, usually during one of these staring bouts, the baby starts smiling.

The smile is the first firm, recognizable sign of pleasure at the social presence of another. A two- or three-month-old child will not smile at a profile but only at someone turned full face, and therefore, save in the blind, smiling and full facial contact are almost always

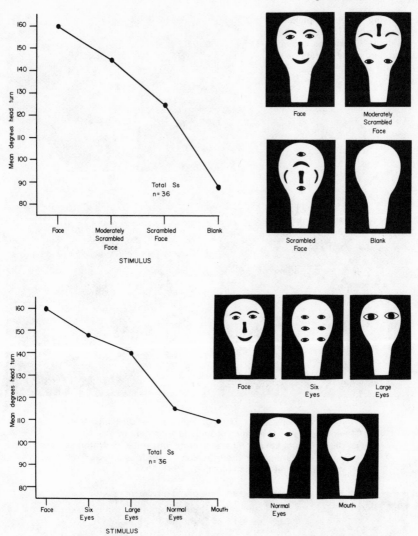

Newborns were shown a variety of cards while held in the lap (see Appendix Study 36). The card was moved to either side three times, and the longest excursion left and right was recorded (perfect following = 180°). It was considerably easier to get infants to follow a regular face than any of the other configurations, and the results at twelve minutes of age paralleled the results at twenty-four hours. It would seem that humans are born with a preference for the human face.

associated (Spitz and Wolfe, 1946). Blind infants also smile socially, usually to a familiar voice (p. 99, top), but in the early months it is not quite as full and steady a smile as in seeing children. In fact, the smiles of persons blind from birth are never as full and warming as

A crying newborn is picked up
and consoled for the first time
in its life. She stops crying as
her eyes come to rest on the
adult's face.

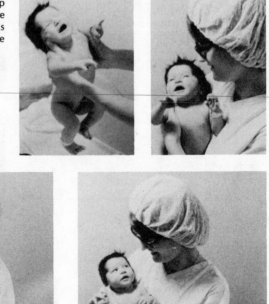

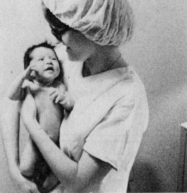

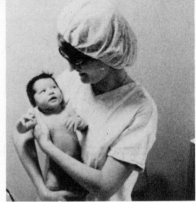

Identical twins, one month of age, each staring into their
mother's face. The timing of such development events is very
similar in identical twins and quite dissimilar in fraternal
twins, indicating that these behaviors are to a great extent
"preprogrammed" (see Freedman, 1963, 1974).

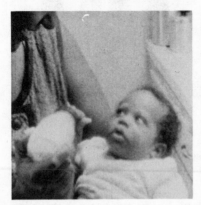

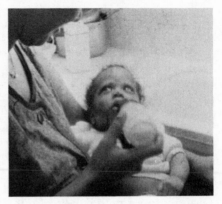

Three-month-old Yvonne, blind since birth, smiles momentarily to her mother's touch and voice. Her sightless eyes fix in the direction of her mother's voice (see Freedman, 1974).

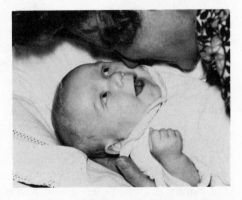

those who become blind later in life. The meeting of eyes is, then, a most important development event. By the same token, when babies begin to fear strangers later in the first year, the worst thing a stranger can do is to look into the baby's eyes, for that assures a full-scale fright response. Thus, both attachment and fear are mediated by the en *face* experience in the seeing.

On this score, a small percentage of babies habitually turn away from the caretaker's face. Although all babies do this occasionally, babies who do so consistently are often diagnosed eventually as "autistic," a psychosis of childhood (Rimland, 1964). No one knows the cause of autism, but it is a heartbreaking condition in which the child cannot relate with normal warmth and affection but becomes

An eight-month old smiles at her mother (a), but recoils from a staring stranger (b). The second child is her identical twin, and her reactions were much the same (see Freedman, 1963, 1974).

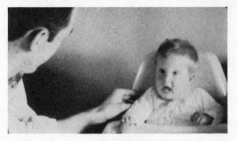

more and more turned into himself. Again, the first symptoms involve the head and eyes.

There is another aspect to eyes that deserves mention. Ekhard Hess of the University of Chicago has long been fascinated by the fact that the pupils contract and expand depending on one's interest in what is under scrutiny (Hess, 1976). He found, for example, that the picture of a nude female usually results in enlarged pupils in young men, that nude male figures do the same for male homosexuals, that animal pictures do the same for naturalists, and so on. One of his most fascinating experiments involved making two copies of the same photo of a pretty young woman (page 101) and enlarging the pupils in one. When asked to judge the woman's character by checking the most appropriate adjectives, male respondents described the woman with the enlarged pupils as warmer, nicer, more feminine, and more attractive than the woman in the undoctored photo. Rarely could a respondent explain why these differential judgments were made, but they clearly were based on differences in pupil size since only that feature was varied.

At a practical level, women have long known that the eyes are an important aspect of attractiveness, and the history of cosmetics involves disproportionate attention to the eyes. Perhaps the most striking testimony for this assertion is the drug belladonna (Latin for beautiful woman) used in classical Greece and Rome by courtesans (Hess, 1976) and to this day used as a beautifier. A few drops in each eye enlarges the pupils, and Hess's message is that we get cues about another's disposition toward us by noting, at a nonconscious level, that person's pupil size. In general, pinpointed pupils mean dislike; enlarged pupils, acceptance and interest.

In order to see whether this disposition to judge intent by pupil size is "precultural," Janet Bare performed an interesting study with five-month-old infants. She visited each infant twice, once with her eyes pharmacologically dilated; once, constricted. In each case she held the baby in her lap, attempting to get it to smile. As Hess had discovered with adults, the effect was clear only in the males, who smiled significantly more at Bare when her eyes were dilated. The boys also showed a greater negative response when her eyes were constricted, exhibiting more fearfulness and crying (for further details see Appendix Study 38).

Although it is intriguing that males responded more to Bare's dilated and unstricted eyes, especially in light of the discussion of courtesans and belladonna, the major point is that infants as young as five months of age apparently react differently to persons with dilated or constricted pupils. This finding appears to be evidence that reaction to pupil size is a low threshold response; which is to say, even if it is not built in, it is very easy to acquire.

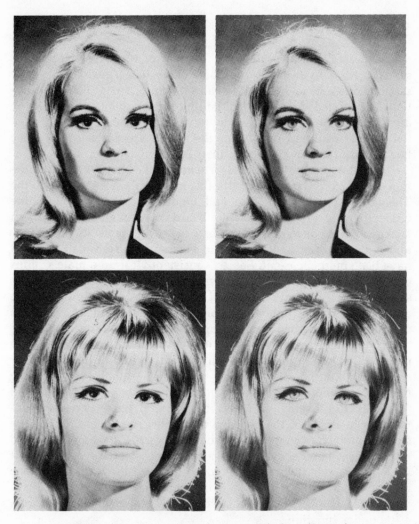

Photographs of two women were retouched so that each
woman had large pupils in one photograph and small pupils
in the other. Male subjects were shown eight different pairs
of the photographs: all the possible combinations of the two
women. As subjects viewed each pair, they were asked in
which of the two pictures did the woman appear to be more
sympathetic, more selfish, happier, angrier, warmer, sadder,
more attractive, more unfriendly, and so on. When the question concerned a positive attribute, male subjects tended to
choose the photograph of the woman with the large pupils.
When the question concerned a negative attribute, they
tended to choose the photograph of the woman with the
small pupils. Neither woman, however, was consistently
chosen as being the more attractive or the more unfriendly.
The selection in most instances appeared to be made unconsciously on the basis of pupil size. Courtesy of Professor
Eckhard H. Hess, The University of Chicago.

HAIR

In general, the evolutionary function of the male's secondary sexual traits is to awe and intimidate other males, even as they may serve also to awe and attract females (Guthrie, 1970). The two functions are related, for the intimidation of males implies clearing the area of rivals for females. Remember that it is generally the differential success of males that forms the main basis for selection since females are relatively equal in their reproductive success.

The first question to address is whether the beard is an intimidation device. In order to deal with this question, we went back to the Thematic Apperception Test and modified pictures used in the clinical testing situation, drawing beards on a number of the clean shaven males (page 103). We then asked students to tell stories about the bearded and unbearded versions. The results could not have been more clear-cut. Beards consistently raised a male's status or else lent him emotional independence not found in the clean shaven men (Appendix Study 39). Thus, in the picture of a young and an old man, the unbearded young man was a "son asking advice of his dad." In the bearded version, however, he became "a lawyer conferring with an older colleague." Or, in the picture of a young man and an older woman, an unbearded "grandson feeling guilty over something he said" became a bearded "young Freud leaving home." In keeping with the hypothesis that beards are intended primarily for display vis-à-vis other males, these perceived differences in status of the bearded and unbearded held only for the stories obtained from males. Beardedness versus shavenness seemed not to affect females' responses in any consistent way, although it would appear that women can indeed be awed by facial hair. Since beards affected the assessment of status in men only, it seems a reasonable hypothesis that facial hair evolved with male-male threat as its major function.

Friends who have shaved off their beards have reported decided differences in how they were generally regarded. In one case, a friend came bearded and beardless to the same busy restaurant at which he had been served by the same waitress over a substantial period of time. His bearded presence meant quicker service and, furthermore, he was recognized as a steady customer as opposed to the anonymity he experienced when shaven (see Appendix Studies 39 and 40).

Shaving, of course, means retaining youth, removing secondary sexual distinctions, and, it follows, advertising subdominance, nonintimidation, and friendliness. Said another way, shaving masks the testosterone in the mature male's bloodstream. Small wonder,

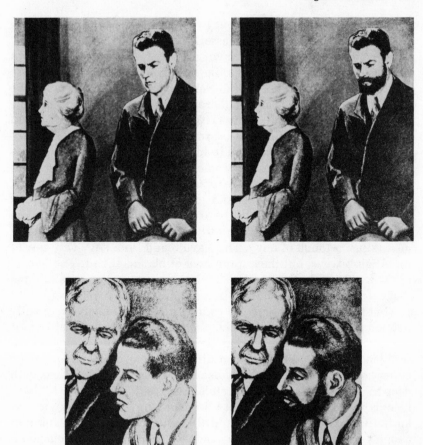

Card 6BM of Thematic Apperception Test, original and doc-
tored version with beard.

Card 7BM of Thematic Apperception Test, original and doc-
tored version with beard.

then, that Alexander the Great insisted that his soldiers shave, allowing only his generals to retain their beards. A well-oiled army, then
and now, is a well-governed army, in which men are at once shorn of
hair, individuality, and within-group competitiveness.

Bureaucracies in general seem to require shaving. Ancient Rome
did so, and Western businesses do so today. Some time ago, I received a letter from a man of 44 who had grown a beard, to the
chagrin of his boss. The boss insisted he shave and this 44-year-old
wrote me for advice. Somewhat in the spirit of Dear Abby, I
answered that he had three choices: quit his job, ignore the boss, or

shave. He actually chose number two and succeeded in acclimating the boss to his new-found self-assertiveness.

Peoples who themselves have sparse facial hair, the American Indians, for example, appear to be as affected by facial hair as are Caucasians. A colleague, Carl O'Nell, worked in Mexico among the Zapotec Indians. After a year there, he began growing a beard. As the beard grew, so did what O'Nell (1969) described as "social distance," and by the time the beard was full and flowing, few spontaneous remarks were directed to him. By his own introspective account, he had become too awesome a figure to joke with.

I have worked and continue to work among the Navajo and Hopi in the American Southwest, and inasmuch as both are relatively beardless peoples, my own beard draws considerable comment. The jocular putdowns are made mostly by older males, and there is always just a touch of envy. The Navajo and Hopi envy very few of the Anglo's ways, but they are in awe of his facial hair. The barber at Crown Point, in the heart of the Navajo reservation, has told me that false moustaches and sideburns sell unusually well there.

In the days of their glory, of course, American Indians frequently painted their faces, most especially when preparing for a raid or for a battle. The intent was without doubt both to lend courage and to frighten the enemy. Sub-Saharan Africans, many of whom tend to be either beardless or else sparsely bearded, often scarify the face, with deeper, fiercer scars for the males. Negroid skin tends to form keloids when scarred, and these permanent marks readily identify an individual's tribal and clan affiliations. The point is, then, that peoples who cannot grow beards achieve the same psychological effect in various ways.

A few words about the moustache are in order. You will recall the experiment in which we added a moustache to the drawings of a tall and a short male, each in the company of the same woman (see figure, p. 86 and Appendix Study 30). The respondents generally indicated that the moustache made the short man appear more *active* and *sexual* but also *sleazy*. It was as if the smaller man was seen as buying status not rightfully his by sporting a moustache; the same moustache on the tall man simply made him more mature and sexually appealing. The moustache, then, does appear to change a male's image in a more provocative, sexually potent direction, and once again height creates a halo effect in that sleaziness was not usually attributed to the taller man.

Finally, there are two other normally visible areas of hair growth we have not yet discussed, head and chest hair. In one of our studies (Appendix Study 41) the Afro hairstyle, on both men and women, was clearly perceived as intimidating. European female hairstyling in which the hair is piled up on the head, as in the pompadour, usually described as "regal," yields some of the same feeling tone. Among American Indians a bonnet of feathers was clearly meant to intimidate and was worn solely in battle. The Western ten-gallon hat seems primarily to have the same function since protection from the sun, its ostensible purpose, can be more economically accomplished with other headgear. Desmond Morris (1967) has written about the function of military headgear, to which he gives a similar interpretation.

Exposed chest hair, too, appears to intimidate other males and to be somewhat attractive to females (Appendix Study 42). In general, then, the display of male hair seems to have such a dual function. Conversely, the nonhairiness of females and youths complements our findings that mature males specialize in threat and intimidation.

VOICE

One of the more striking changes at puberty is the full octave drop in voice pitch that occurs in males over a relatively short period. Frank Winstan (1973) studied this phenomenon in much the same way we had studied the psychosocial effects of beardedness. In place of the visual stimulus cards he developed an Auditory Episode Test, a series of dramatic encounters on tape, each with two versions—one with a naturally high-pitched male voice (a prepubescent actor) and the other with an actor whose matured voice was pitched about one octave lower. Both actors were, in fact, of approximately the same age. Some of Winstan's methods and data are described in Appendix Study 43, and it is clear that the lower pitched voice, with its fuller harmonic, was found more interesting and attractive by the adolescent girls in this study. Additionally, both boys and girls tended to accord the postpubescent voice more status. Thus, we now have statistical corroboration for an event we all know intuitively to be true: the changing voice signals a changed life status and, like facial and bodily hair, serves to intimidate and impress males and to attract postpubescent females.

BREASTS AND BUTTOCKS

Among primates, only human and gibbon females are found continuously attractive by their male counterparts, a necessary correlate of the prolonged consortship and covert estrus typical of these two groups. Thus, female beauty is of continuous interest to males and not just of passing fancy, as it is in those species typified by overt estrus and temporary liaisons (for example, chimps, macaques, and baboons).

The human female's lack of facial hair, her higher voice, lower muscle to fat ratio, relative shortness, cuddliness, and smiliness all suggest nonaggression and subdominance. These traits certainly help disarm male aggression, but there is more to a female's attractiveness to males, and female breasts are an obvious first consideration.

What is their function? To feed babies? Breast size is in no way related to milk production, so that the only possibility is that breasts are prominent in order to do that which we already know they do—attract males.

It is perhaps an uncomplimentary commentary on modern psychology and anthropology that one should have to prove such an assertion. Nevertheless, and as usual, we used TAT type cards to this end (see below). In the first study (Appendix Study 44), we presented a scene in which a male and a female, large-breasted in one version and small-breasted in another, are waiting for a bus. The male subjects, all college undergraduates, tended to see the large-breasted woman as a very provocative, sexual object who might possess "liberal" attitudes and who was "on the move." The female

TAT-like stimulus cards. The second card (b), differing only in the outline of the breasts, received substantially more courtship stories from male respondents than did the first.

undergraduate respondents chose adjectives emphasizing the large-breasted women's naivete, warmth, and understanding—maternal qualities in contrast to the males' perceived sexual ones.

The small-breasted version evoked descriptions of sweetness, youth, and innocence from the males; for the females, this *small-breasted* version was considered more feminine, sexually attractive, and appealing. Obviously, these undergraduate women, in the middle of their own maturation, divided womanhood in quite a different way—maternal and mature versus attractive and immature.

In a second study, people 35 through 50 were asked to tell stories to two versions of a photo of a young woman behind a man in a wheelchair. In one version the woman is flat-chested. In the second she is wearing falsies. Respondents of both sexes pronounced the latter version more mature, and whereas the woman was frequently seen as a daughter in version one, she was as frequently described as a nurse in version two—that is, as more independent and adequate.

It seems reasonable to conclude that there are two aspects to the signal function of breasts—sexuality and maturity. Even in cultures in which women are bare, as in Melanesia, breasts are fondled and stroked in lovemaking (Davenport, 1965; Ford and Beach, 1951), and no culture has been described in which breasts are specifically noted as *not* an integral part of female beauty (Ford and Beach, 1951). Even in aristocratic Japan and China, where until recently breasts were bound tightly to flatten them out, it was acknowledged that this practice attempted to deanimalize the woman and to make her less obviously an object of lust.

A highly imaginative ethologist, Wolfgang Wickler, has had the courage to print what others might say only after cocktails. One of Wickler's conjectures involves a hypothesized signal relationship between breasts and buttocks. For the nonhuman primates, including the great apes, presentation of a female's hindquarters during estrus is straightforward sexual solicitation. Wickler (1972) believes that we are not so different, and indeed men ogle female buttocks with at least as much interest as they do breasts. Wickler suggests that in the human, as we became upright, prominent breasts evolved to take on the formerly exclusive signal function of the extended buttocks—a sort of behind brought forward. Actually, Julian Huxley is reported to have conjectured in exactly the same way (Darlington, 1969).

In an admittedly weak attempt to deal with such issues experimentally, a series of cards were drawn in which we varied a female's hair length, the extension and prominence of her buttocks, and the prominence of her breasts (see p. 108). These cards were presented to several classes, and male judgments of relative "sexuality" were requested. The relevant factors, in order of "impor-

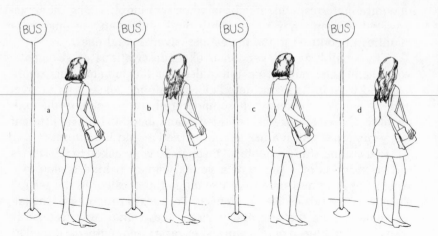

Male respondents judged sexuality of these figures in the order: *d, c, b, a.*

tance," were prominence of the buttocks, prominence of the breasts, and presence of long hair. That is, despite our supposedly breastoriented society, the buttocks (presenting hindquarter?) still get first place.

There appear to be cultural variations in male interest in and female exhibition of hindquarters and, naturally enough, these variations seem to follow the natural physical endowments in a particular culture area. For example, Japanese women, on the average, have very flat hindquarters compared, say, to Yoruba women in Nigeria. It is therefore not surprising that the shape of the hindquarter is hidden by traditional female garb in Japan, whereas among the Yoruba cloth is wound tightly over the hips to emphasize them. Sub-Saharan Africans in general tend to consider well-formed hindquarters an integral part of female beauty (LeVine, 1969). This seems less true in Asia, where the emphasis is more on the studied exhibition of subdominant femininity—walk, mannerisms, and the ideal of the delicate, willowy figure. I shall discuss this insistence on subtlety and the eschewal of raw sensuality among Japanese and Chinese in Chapter 9.

It is perhaps worth repeating here that such cultural variations are not to be taken as evidence that biology is out of the picture. After all, we have been talking about basic biological events, the signals that lead to sexual arousal. Once again, our species is biocultural—100% biological and 100% cultural. To argue over which behavior is cultural and which biological is to reenter the insoluble dilemma inherent in a dualistic view of nature.

GOOD LOOKS

Although it is completely appropriate to bring up the subject of good looks in a discussion of status, there is precious little data available. In the study with which I opened Chapter 4, the development of status hierarchies among adolescents in a summer camp (Savin-Williams, 1977), the very best single indicator of social rank among the male campers was *facial good looks* (Appendix Study 17). In the same study, however, girls did not use good looks in ranking one another's relative status, even though boys clearly rank girls on such a basis.

We all know that beauty and good looks are venerated so that it is perhaps too obvious a question to investigate, and thus the sparse data. No modern psychologist, for example, has yet bothered to launch a major study of the social consequences of having been born beautiful, plain, or ugly, nor do I know of any major psychoanalytic writing along these lines. All the studies that are available point in the same direction: If one is born with good looks, he or she is at an advantage thereafter (see Dion et al., 1972; Farina et al., 1977; Kirkpatrick and Cotton, 1961; Sigall and Landy, 1973). Sorokin arrived at the same conclusion:

> Other things being equal, beauty, especially for the female, is a condition which facilitates her upward promotion in the social pyramid. . . . A similar process takes place in regard to males as well. Other conditions being equal, from two candidates for a position, the one who appears handsomer is likely to be preferred, and from two lovers or rivals, the more handsome is likely to be preferred as a husband or lover. . . . Since this process of recruiting handsome males and females into higher social strata, and leaving the less handsome in the lower classes, is a permanent one, it is natural that in the long course of time it has greatly contributed to the handsomeness of the upper classes. (Sorokin, 1959, p. 246)

It is perhaps unnecessary to belabor this point. If it is better to be rich than to be poor, then it is equally safe to assume that it is better to be beautiful or handsome than plain or ugly. It is likely that U.S. senators are, on average, better looking than members of the House of Representatives, who probably are, on average, better looking than state legislators. But we have no data. It is obviously a difficult area to study because of the elusiveness of "beauty." Yet, however reluctantly, most of us share the feeling that Sorokin is right.

As for the frequent remark that beauty is relative and that standards vary considerably around the world, it has been my experience that persons I have considered beautiful or handsome, whether in Asia, Africa, Europe, or Australia are similarly regarded by their contemporaries. Darwin (1871) had much to do with this notion of relativity, having reported, for example, that Hottentot men prefer women with grotesquely large buttocks. However, this condition, known as steatopygia, affects only older Hottentot women (see figure). The nubile Hottentot women are attractive by almost anyone's standards (Singer, 1968). Similarly, Ford and Beach (1951) reported on the great variation around the world in what men consider beautiful in women, noting, for example, that the Masai prefer tall, thin women, whereas the Yoruba prefer plump females. These data, however, were presented out of context and it has to be understood that the Masai, on average, are tall and thin; the Yoruba, on average, are full-bodied.

In general, the selection for facial good looks can be thought of at two levels: the group and the individual. As a group phenomenon status and handsomeness (or beauty) tend to be closely related; and in the absence of other criteria, good looks provide a ready means of sorting out relative position in the social hierarchy. In addition, physical attractiveness clearly plays a role in the formation of bonds of love, a homily that I include only because it has to be stated. Both levels are phylogenetically adaptive and, as I have maintained right along, neither the group nor the mating couple should or need be considered the "more basic."

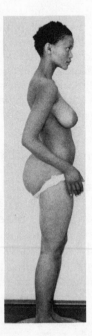

Sixteen-year-old Hottentot mother. With age, steatopygia increases, possibly because of increased fibrous deposits (Krut and Singer, 1963). Courtesy of and copyright reserved by Professor Ronald Singer, The University of Chicago.

GRAYBEARDS AND BALD HEADS

Men and women of all races become gray with age, as indeed do many other mammals. What is the point of advertising advancing age and declining sexuality in this way? There appears to be no physiological necessity for grayness. Is there an adaptive function here? In humans, at least, it appears that there is. Sherwood Washburn, a highly respected evolutionary scholar, even as he approaches retirement is a most youthful appearing man. In his late thirties he looked younger than many of his graduate students, who called him Sherry, despite his eminence, for "Professor" seemed inappropriate. Then, over a short time span, his blonde hair turned to silver gray, whereupon students began addressing him as Professor Washburn. Gray hair had created a sense of social distance and awe among his younger colleagues though eminence had not (Washburn, 1968).

That, in brief, appears to be the evolutionary function of graying. Our empirical work (again, with TAT cards) consistently has yielded the same message. Furthermore, the contrast of gray and blonde, in Washburn's case, was particularly telling in that blondness in Caucasians is a signal of youth (see Appendix Study 45). Although the evidence is not completely clear, it appears that circulating testosterone tends to darken blonde hair; thus, prepubertal Caucasian boys, as well as female Caucasians, tend to be more fully blonde than are postpubescent males.

Balding appears to have a function similar to that of graying when it is age appropriate and accompanied by other signals of dominance. In our youth oriented West, however, baldness is frequently experienced as a personal disaster. In contrast, in eighteenth-century Japan the Samurai shaved their heads in simulation of the normal balding pattern, and we see that at least in other ages and other places the positive meaning of baldness was apparent.

Although it is perhaps a digression, I cannot resist concluding this chapter with a few thoughts on our extreme youth orientation, and I shall start with a paradigm borrowed from evolutionary botanists. They have demonstrated that in rapidly changing environments novel genetic combinations are most adaptive, whereas in stable, nonchanging environments tried-and-true combinations are best. Some plants are particularly good examples of this phenomenon in that they produce asexually in stable conditions, the tried and true, but under changing conditions they begin to reproduce sexually, thereby creating new gametic combinations (Stebbins, 1950).

If we substitute novel ideas for novel genetic combinations, the analogy seems to hold at the cultural level. We live in such changing times that man tends to focus on the new rather than the old, on youthfulness rather than wisdom, and new ideas appear at such a rate that scientific books are outdated before they are printed. But Carl Jung pointed out that deep within us, in what he labeled the "collective unconscious," there is a need to find an old, wise one as a guide for one's life. And insofar as this need is not fulfilled, in our deference to youth and the new, we have a sense that something is missing.

I had a teacher, Kurt Goldstein, whom I always think of as "my teacher." He was wise, gray, and balding when I knew him, and I still venerate him and try to follow his guidelines. I notice today that our more serious students are looking for such a teacher and are happy only when they believe they have found one. I must conclude that part of human fulfillment comes from such a venerating relationship. Furthermore, it seems that many if not most successful scientists have themselves had such a relationship with a teacher and that scientific advance is often passed from one generation to another via such relationships (Roe, 1953).

Again, in my experience with the Navajo and Hopi of America's Southwest, it is clear that whatever stability these cultures have lies in their adherence to tradition, including the spoken language and the veneration of old people. As a result, these cultures always seem somewhat behind the times, even to many Navajo and Hopi. Fortunately, most still also feel the beauty of the old ways, and few are as happy away from the reservation as on it. Indian tribes thus symbolize life as it once was and may again become and therein, I believe, lies the anthropologist's and the public's romantic attraction to traditional peoples (Horton, 1967). They have managed to retain a part of themselves that we have let go in our devotion to individuality, to progress, and to the future.

7

Blood Is Thicker
than Water

I am your father and you are my son;
and there is nothing we can do about it.

Y. F.

At the heart of selfish-gene theory lies kinship genetics
and its corollary, biological altruism. According to these notions, the
motive-force of life and evolution is to pass on one's genetic material
to subsequent generations in any way possible. Thus, since I and my
sister share about half our genes (as do all full siblings), if I gave my
life to save hers only 50% of my genes would be left to carry on
—not good evolutionary economics, and a biologist would bet
against my making such a sacrifice. But if I gave my life to save, say,
three siblings who otherwise would have died, my sacrifice would
leave 150% of what I gave up; hence, such an altruistic act is in
order. That, in a nutshell, is the logic of kinship genetics and the way
most sociobiologists view biological altruism.

This logic can lead to a host of predictions and explanations,
and it is the purpose of this chapter to see how far we can go with
them. Take sibling rivalry. From a parent's point of view, each child
has 50% of his or her genes, and therefore all children (save possibly
the sickly) should receive evenhanded treatment. The child's main
aim, however, is to make sure that his own genes survive and if a
sibling threatens his well-being, for example, if he thinks the parents
are playing favorites, we should not be surprised at his becoming
upset and vindictive. Of course, siblings are kept from actually
doing away with each other by their evenhanded parents and by the
fact that the sibs, on average, share 50% of their genes. It is assumed

that because they are related, mechanisms have developed whereby the ambivalence of sibling rivalry rarely turns to pure hatred. We have found that some 70% of respondents presented with the choice of throwing a life preserver to a brother or to a best friend (equally good swimmers being pulled out to sea by the tide) answer immediately that they would toss the preserver to the brother. Others refuse to answer (it is, after all, a tormenting decision), make a joke ("Cut it in half"), or invent some outlandish solution, but they tend not to leave the sib to be swept out to sea.

Now we have to extend our kinship equations. In the altruism model, saving one sib (50% shared genes) equals saving four cousins, two aunts or uncles, one parent, or two half sibs. Tom Borden, having these equations in mind, developed a test for such selective altruism and gave it to 93 high-school students (Borden, 1975). The respondents were asked to assess the chances of their putting themselves in jeopardy for someone else in a variety of fictional settings. The degree of relationship between the subject and the person she or he was supposed to aid was varied. Borden found that brothers would be helped when cousins might not, sisters before girlfriends, family before strangers, and one's own ethnic group before another's. (The latter finding will be discussed in detail in Chapter 8.) The results were stronger for boys, but this finding is not too surprising since many of the acts required imagined physical courage. Females may well have been more reluctant to put themselves in physical jeopardy, however imaginary, whereas risk taking and bravery are expected and characteristic of males.

In a study in which stealing rather than self-sacrifice was required, both male and female eighth graders were quite ready to steal for relatives but not for strangers. They felt stealing a lifesaving drug for a relative was morally justified, whereas a similar theft for a nonrelative was morally wrong (Appendix Study 46)! In this study, Irene Sebastian used a psychological test for determining six stages of altruism (Kohlberg, 1964). These stages range from "doing right out of simple fear" through "doing right from an abstract sense of justice." The test consists of such stories as the following:

> In Europe, a girl was near death from a special kind of cancer. There was one drug that the doctors thought might save her. It was a form of radium that a druggist in the same town had recently discovered. The drug was expensive to make, but the druggist was charging ten times what the drug cost him to make. The sick girl's father, Heinz, told the druggist that his daughter was dying, and asked him to sell it cheaper or let him pay later. But the druggist said "No, I discovered the drug, and I'm going to make money from it." So Heinz got desperate and broke into the

man's store to steal the drug for his daughter. (Adapted by Sebastian from Kohlberg, 1964)

Sebastian substituted different kin relationships between the principals and found corresponding shifts in the altruistic stage achieved. It turned out that 13-year-old subjects quite openly advocated stealing for close kin, approved less of stealing for distant kin, and not at all for nonkin.

The question of how this kin bias develops within individuals is most interesting and is being examined by a behavioral scientist at Southwest Texas State University, Harvey Ginsburg. He finds that three- and four-year olds, when given the hypothetical choice of saving either their playmates or their parents, invariably choose to rescue the playmate! By six and seven years, however, they begin showing the kin bias I have described. For the developmental psychologists reading this, such a finding sounds Piagetian. That is, this turnabout appears to be yet another instance of a switch in behavior between five and seven years of age (see White, 1967, for a long list of such switchovers). It probably goes hand in glove with the fact that youngsters under five rarely ask, "What am I?" in the sense of "What is my ethnic background?" By six years such questions often arise. In Piagetian terms, they have gone from egocentrism to a stage in which they can imagine the role of others. Apparently, the proper level of neurobehavioral growth must be achieved before kinship and other comparable abstractions can be dealt with.

Ginsburg (1977) tried the "Who would you save?" test on grandparents, asking them to choose between children (related at the 50% level) and grandchildren (related at the 25% level). He felt nearly certain, given the obvious joy grandparents find in their grandchildren, that the kinship rule would be broken. It was not. An exception were grandparents whose own children were beyond their reproductive years, and among them the tendency was to "save" the potentially reproductive grandchildren.

One problem with these studies is that all have been done within our own culture, and they may reflect a strong culture-specific bias. We know that siblings relate differently depending on cultural proscriptions (for example, whether the older daughter or the older son will inherit the family wealth), and it would indeed be necessary to expand such studies to groups radically different from our own. Furthermore, even within our culture, results do not always come out as predicted (see Appendix Study 47), and much research remains to be done before this becomes a convincing body of facts. Nevertheless, it looks as if an empirically based model is being developed out of the old saw "Blood is thicker than water."

SAHLINS'S CRITICISM OF SOCIOBIOLOGY

The major criticism of kinship genetics theory as applied to humans has come from the anthropologist Marshall Sahlins (1976) in his *Use and Abuse of Biology*, subtitled *An Anthropological Critique of Sociobiology*. This critique is so compelling that it is both an obligation and a challenge to answer it. Here is his precis of the sociobiological view of altruism:

> [The sociobiological view of altruism] consists of transforming social altruism into genetic egotism by the observation that the "kin" of the self-sacrificing animal, who share a certain amount of genetic substance with him, are often benefited by his act. Therefore, service to others can actually optimize ego's "inclusive fitness," the proportion of his genes . . . passed on to subsequent generations. This net advantage occurs in the measure that the benefit to the same genes as possessed by kinsmen is greater than the cost to one's own reproductive success. For sociobiologists, altruism is the spite of life. (1976, p. 20)

Sahlins then takes E. O. Wilson to task for such remarks as

> the coefficient of relationship, r, translates easily into "blood," and the human mind, already sophisticated in the intuitive calculus of blood ties and proportionate altruism, races to apply the concept of inclusive fitness to a revaluation of its own social impulses.

> True spite is a commonplace in human societies, undoubtedly because human beings are keenly aware of their own blood lines and have the intelligence to plot intrigues. (Wilson, 1975, p. 119)

Sahlins responds:

> We thus arrive at a point of argument where there is no appeal but to the facts. I have to insist from the outset—taking my stand on the whole of the ethnographic record—that the actual systems of kinship and concepts of heredity in human societies . . . never conform to biological coefficients of relationship. . . .

> My aim is to support the assertion that there is not a single system of marriage, postmarital residence, family organization, interpersonal kinship, or common descent in human societies that does not set up a different calculus of relationship and social action than is indicated by the principles of kin selection. (1976, pp. 25, 26)

Sahlins then points out that in patrilineal societies, one often loses sight of maternal blood ties, whereas in matrilocal societies, one often loses contact with paternal relatives. In each case one lives with and shows allegiance to some relatives who are mathematically more distant than others who live elsewhere and who are therefore often treated as strangers. He quotes Malinowski on the Mailu of New Guinea:

> Brothers living together, or a paternal uncle and his nephews liv-
> ing in the same house were, as far as my observation goes, on
> much closer terms with each other than relatives of similar
> degree living apart. This was evident whenever there was a ques-
> tion of borrowing things, or getting help, of accepting an obliga-
> tion, or of assuming responsibilities for each other. (1915, p. 532)

This criticism seems almost trivial if one considers that man, in his inventiveness, by observing matriarchal or patriarchal descent, is approximating a genetic lineage even if he is slighting half of his relatives. That is, allowing that there is an apparent arbitrariness in descent systems, *all* peoples nevertheless find it important to have a system. Why? Only the sociobiologists deal with this question of universality, and their answer, however shaky, is that the *need to trace and maintain kin ties* is biologically mediated although the channeling of that need is indeed variable. The sometimes over-powering desire to find biological kin felt by adopted children in our society (Pannor and Sorosky, 1976; Treseliotus, 1973) is perhaps evidence on this score.

Sahlins presents several examples of exogamous New Guinean tribes that exchange women of warring villages. Indeed, the Enga can say, "We fight the people we marry." This he cites as another glaring instance of culture overruling biology since in war an Enga may, for example, end up killing a sister's son. First of all, no one has yet observed whether Enga or similar groups do or do not avoid killing immediate kin in battle. Chagnon, in fact, tells me that he has heard Yanomamo discuss such issues before a battle, and it appears that they do indeed try to avoid harming near kin on the enemy side! Second of all, has any biologist ever reported on a species in which some steady outlet for gene flow is not present? As discussed earlier, in Japanese monkeys it is the males who leave the natal group, take up residence in another troop, and thereafter become the "enemy." I discuss this question in more detail in Chapter 8. Suffice it to say here that if the Enga, or any other people, were to marry within their villages, the inbreeding coefficient would soon be unity—everyone would be the genetic equivalent of everyone else—and that is simply not good evolutionary "planning." As far as we know, the whole point of sexual reproduction is to achieve a substantial level of heterozygosity—genetic variability—for only such a diversified population can adjust to environmental changes. The final point is that intratribal warfare in a patrilineal, polygynous people such as the Enga, or the Dani (Heider, 1970), or the Yanomamo (Chagnon, 1968) establishes the male dominance hierarchy and hence helps determine the apportionment of women. As I have pointed out several times, differential male mortality is the major means of within-group selection in a great variety of mammalian species.

In a major part of his argument, Sahlins points to Polynesia as a crucial test case:

> Polynesia offers us privileged sites for testing the theory of kin selection. It is something like Durkheim's one well-chosen experiment that can prove (or disprove) a scientific law. The case is privileged because to all appearances the Polynesian societies afford structural conditions that are favorable to the operation of kin selection. In these island societies, descent may be bilaterally reckoned ("cognatic"), rather than the kind of patriliny or matriliny that a priori renders the thesis of kin selection vulnerable. Analogously, residence is often optional, with either the mother's kin or the father's, and the people are notoriously mobile. They are also famous for the value they attach to genealogies, which in some instances range back forty generations and more. Finally, their own theory of heredity conforms to that of scientific biology, at least to the extent that children are equally of the "blood" of the mother and the father. (1976, p. 28)

Sahlins first criticism via Polynesian culture centers around the fact that Polynesians do not fractionalize relations as do biologists (sibs 50%, half-sibs 25%, cousins 12.5%, and so on) but use whole numbers instead (sibs a whole blood, cousins two bloods, and second cousins three bloods). However, since these fractions require knowledge of the science of genetics, I believe even Sahlins would consider such a point relatively trivial. The second problem for Sahlins concerns the prevalence of cognatic descent in Polynesia. That is, in the Polynesian opu system one traces descent from a common ancestor, often an arbitrary choice (opu means belly). Thus, two brothers can belong to different opu, drawing property rights and incurring obligations with persons less related. But Sahlins fails to deal with one crucial question. How is it that the Polynesians favor such a system over, say, unilineal descent (Fox, 1967)? This is a curiosity that, as far as I know, anthropologists have not yet tried to explain. Might it not be that, given inbred populations in which everyone is greatly related anyway, arbitrary, widely overlapping descent systems can exist? Although it is obviously true that Polynesians, like all peoples, achieve a balance between exogamy (marrying out) and endogamy (marrying in) (Webster, 1975) and that on the less isolated islands exogamous matings are more possible, the overall situation in widely spaced islands would appear to favor a higher rate of endogamous marriage than, say, would occur among Cantonese. In any event, this seems a reasonable hypothesis.

The same circumstance can also account for another Polynesian uniqueness, the high rate of adoption. Sahlins claims that neither adopted child nor adopting parents are concerned with identifying biological parents. If this is true anywhere, it would hold in inbred island populations. However, in the most recent and complete ethnographic report on a Polynesian people, the Tahitians, Levy (1973) makes it clear that although adoption is indeed common, blood ties are always known, they remain important, and most adoptions, as among all tribal peoples, occur between close kin. In an ongoing study among the Marquesans, another Polynesian people, Martini (1977) has found exactly the same situation. By the way, Scheffler (1965) reports similarly high adoption rates among the Melanesians, where some 41% of adult married males had a history of adoption or fosterage! As far as I know, comparable rates have not been found in any non-island population.

Sahlins also uses the common Polynesian practice of population control, infanticide, as another gun to the head of sociobiology. Why kill off one's own children only to adopt someone else's? In answer, he points out a number of culture-specific examples that he feels are particularly independent of biological channeling: "Human society is cultural, unique in virtue of its construction by symbolic means" (1976, p. 61). Accordingly, when offspring of parents of different rank, or of youthful liaisons, or of an irresponsible entertainer class are all more prone to being killed off, we are presumably witnessing nonbiological, strictly cultural mechanisms at work. But data such as these could as well fit a sociobiological schema. Recall that langur male monkeys kill the offspring of a previous head male after taking over a harem group or that in the United States children whose biological fathers do not live at home are much more prone to abuse by their mothers (Chapter 2). Another rather obvious reason for infanticide among relatively inbred groups is the elimination of defective children, nor can infanticide as a means of population control be overlooked (Ward, 1977). And then, of course, there is the tendency to eliminate infant girls, even in polygynous societies, ostensibly to make room for a boy, with his greater gametic potential (Chagnon, 1968). Thus, for any or each of these reasons, infanticide, even when coupled with widespread adoption, is indeed open to a biocultural interpretation.

In sum, the problem is not that the facts of ethnology contradict the predictions of sociobiology. Rather, as Sahlins himself suggests, the problem centers on ideological adherence to a reductionistic approach from below. The critique Sahlins developed with ethnological data could as well be offered by a primatologist working with rhesus monkeys. As indicated in Chapter 3, data such as group cohesion in the face of attack are especially resistant to selfish-gene theory. It is not the uniqueness of man that is at issue but the logical defect inherent in a strict mechanistic approach—at any phyletic level.

At the risk of retreading ground already covered, there is no monolithic biological theory within which selfish organisms vie for their place in tomorrow's sun. There are instead a substantial number of biologists who admit to supraindividual phenomena (see review by Wade, 1978c), and some who suggest that evolution (differential selection) with regard to altruism must have occurred at the level of populations (or families) *not* individuals. As Wade (1978a) has put it, "Individual selection within families *always* favors nonaltruistic individuals whereas selection between families favors the evolution of altruism." A good example is the nine-banded armadillo, who always has litters of identical quadruplets. According to Dawkins (1976) they are ideally suited for the evolution of strong altruism by kin selection. But, as Wade points out,

> since nine-banded armadillos are born in litters of genetically identical quadruplets, there is no genetic variation *within* families. Therefore, there can be no selection within families as a result of interaction between sibs. The hypothetical evolution of a strong sib altruism in the nine-banded armadillo would have to occur by selection at the family level operating upon the between family variation for the appropriate behaviors. (1978a, p. 220)

In Sahlins's (1976) last chapter an interesting issue is raised. To what extent, he asks, does the economic and political climate influence science? Do Western scientists stress the competitive aspect of relationships and social structure in a mirror image of the marketplace? Contrariwise, one might ask whether Marxist scientists stress primacy of the group and cooperativeness. Sahlins rightfully says that such tendencies need in no way reflect on the scientists' honesty or sincerity for they are unknowingly caught up in their national paradigms. I would go further and note that each political system undoubtedly spawns its scientist-demagogues, and I do not doubt that Lysenko has had his capitalist counterparts. But the opposition between individual competition and group cooperation is not merely a political dilemma. It has appeared throughout this book as a dilemma for the entire field of biology, East or West, and I would not dismiss selfish-gene theorists as apologists for capitalism. I would rather point out that they have paid insufficient attention to processes that other Western, not necessarily Marxist, scientists have pointed out—(notably Wynne-Edwards, 1971)—that the group has a life of its own, that the group is as "primary" as is the individual, and that many phenomena simply make no sense when analyzed in terms of individuals in competition with one another.

THE EFFECTS OF INBREEDING ON ALTRUISM.

One process that has its primary effect at the group level involves the balance within a population between heterozygosity and homozygosity (genetic variation versus genetic homogeneity). This dynamic process makes all members of a breeding group kin to one another, the extent of that kinship depending on the rate of inbreeding. I believe many sociobiologists are as naive as laymen regarding the extent of inbreeding in an average population, and in order to give the reader an idea of how inbred modern human populations must be, let me relate an experience.

The occasion was a speech before a group of some 350 Jewish women on the topic of inheritance of behavior. In the question period that followed, I was asked whether there is anything to the notion that Jews as a group are genetically unique. By way of answer, I asked were any of the women present related. It turned out that no one was. We then calculated that on the basis of each of the 350 women having had four grandparents, eight great-grandparents, and 2^n ancestors n generations ago, each woman present would have 2^{40}, or approximately a million-million, ancestors 1,000 years ago, if we assume four generations every 100 years. Multiplying by the 350 individuals in the audience yielded an even more impossible figure. Since all were descendants of middle European immigrants, it is apparent that these women were far more related than they realized, as are the members of any relatively bounded breeding group and that they were indeed "unique." In island populations, where outbreeding is further limited, the degree of inbreeding has to be enormous and beyond our present means of assessment. The fractions of relationship (one-half for sibs, one-fourth for half sibs, and so on) thereby become diluted in their significance, and the lack of a ready method to assess the average degree of inbreeding in the population poses a major problem (Roberts, 1971).

At this point in the science one can only guess about the inbreeding history of an indigenous people. One might think that homozygosity of blood groups could provide the key, but blood groups are unusually conservative, monogenetic (single-gene) traits and tend not to change as readily as do polygenic traits. Tallness, smartness, skin color, eye color, fat deposit, and muscle mass are polygenic—determined by many genes—and rather susceptible to pressures toward change. Single-gene traits are either present or lost, and their adaptive value is rarely clear (Mourant et al., 1976). Thus, single-gene blood groups and blood proteins indicate that we and the chimps had a common ancestor but four million years ago (Sarich, 1968). The archeological record, however, brings the figure to a minimum of fifteen million years. In comparing a chimp's blood factors with ours, we might conclude the two species were mating cousins—instead of merely playful friends. Can we, then, assess the degree of inbreeding in any natural population on the basis of single-gene traits? Apparently not, and we are probably more accurate to use gross measures such as skin color, stature, and facial features in assessing human inbreeding.

In studies of short-lived animal species, comparative techniques for assessing inbreeding are available, and the model for such studies is Jerram Brown's (1974). Brown quietly made a new ball game out of sociobiology by demonstrating the close relationship between rate of inbreeding and social behavior. Comparing different species of jays, he noted that there is an apparent progression from species in which the young disperse on their own and in which competition is maximized, to species in which the young remain for a while and help feed the next generation, to the most communal species, the Mexican jay:

> In the Mexican jay the young continue to remain with their parents; when mature they breed in pairs in their home flock at separate nests and most individuals probably live their entire lives within their home flock territory. Young do not attempt to pair and breed until the age of three years or more. (1974, p. 72)

In this remarkably cooperative species, the young help with the care and feeding of nestlings until they themselves breed and, as in the social insects, the key to such selfless behavior seems to be a high degree of genetic relatedness:

> Hamilton (1963, 1964) has pointed out a relationship between genes conferring altruistic or helping behavior and the degree of genetic relationship, r, between the helper and the recipient. If closeness of relationship has been an important factor in the evolution of actual examples of communal breeding, we should expect to find a high r among members of a communal group. (1974, p. 74)

Brown then calculated the degree of relationship in a particular flock and concluded that a Mexican jay, given the amount of inbreeding, would be more closely related to *any* of the young in the home flock, no matter who the parents were, than to his own young if he were to mate at random outside the flock. This degree of inbreeding, then, goes hand in glove with a social organization in which the maturity of young is delayed, in which fewer young are better cared for, in which juveniles help in caring for nestlings, in which the same territory is occupied year after year, in which there is no territorial fighting within the flock, and in which all aggression is directed outward toward other territorial communal flocks. This is not to say that communal jays are a high point of evolutionary development, only that they fit very well certain ecological conditions; whereas those species that disperse and compete as individuals do better in others.

It is as if there are species of jays particularly suited to selfish-gene theory and other species better suited to group selection theory. Again, we cannot reasonably assume that Mexican jays were derived from a dispersing group (as Brown himself assumes) for it is just as logical to assume that the communal jays came first and that dispersing jays derived from them. All we can say with certainty about the Brown (1974) study is that the degree of cooperation within a group varies with the amount of inbreeding.

Since the focus of this book is our own species, the question to raise is, Are inbred human populations more altruistic and less conflict ridden than outbred groups? Does care in the former extend to all young, no matter who the parents are? To answer these questions, we might compare isolated human island populations, which by definition are highly inbred, with obviously heterozygous populations, like the Bantu of the Congo or the Anglo-Saxons. I have already spoken of the relative unimportance of kin distinction in Polynesia and the ease with which adoptions occur. The parallels with the communal jays are perhaps too compelling for they may lead us down a garden path we may be better off not following. However, I am going to venture down that path although the data are thin to absent and although I must, too often, rely on anecdote and personal observation.

The population I have in mind is the Japanese. Japan has long struck me as an excellent example of a sizable but isolated population, apparently substantially inbred. Although hominid occupation probably goes back some 50,000 years (Bleed, 1977), as best as can be reconstructed, modern Japanese derive mainly from proto-Korean-speaking peoples who came in several waves from the Korean peninsula. Using a lexico-statistical technique, Hattori (reported in Befu, 1971) found that the separation of the Korean and the Japanese language occurred some 6,700 years ago, and we can assume that at least an incomplete isolation of the Japanese started then; the final wave of immigration seems to have occurred in about A.D. 300, and exchanges after that time have been largely cultural rather than genetic (Befu, 1971).

Japan has been described by geneticists as having the highest rate of consanguineous marriage in the world (Fujiki et al., 1968), and cousin marriages, for example, are about as common in Toyko as in the smallest hamlets (Schull and Neel, 1965). The picture, then, is one of many inbreeding family lines contributing to an overall "genetic homogeneity" (Fujiki et al., 1968). A theoretical problem here, pointed out by W. D. Hamilton (1978), is that overall homozygosity in any breeding group is better achieved if there is generalized random mating than if there are such samples of inbreeding subgroups; the subsamples will tend to achieve different genetic frequencies and some genes actually will be lost. Thus, it must be made clear that genetic homogeneity is a relative term, and given the enormous population of Japan one must be cautious about making comparisons with, say, genetic homogeneity among the Yanomamo (Chagnon, 1972). Although the latter exhibit the same pattern of highly inbred village populations, the smaller overall population would clearly lead to greater genetic homogeneity. Few would argue, however, that Japan is not considerably more homozygous than that other set of islands off a major continental area, the British Isles.

In Japan, for example, recent immigrants from Korea as well as the so-called untouchable class (*burakumin*) have been forced to marry among themselves and have been prevented from entering the mainstream (Reischauer, 1977). The Ainu, too, have been maintained as an isolated population, and although they have been somewhat infiltrated culturally and genetically by the surrounding Mongoloid population, they seem to have had little influence on their neighbors (Befu, 1971). It thus appears that there has been no major gene mixing among the central Japanese for some 1,700 years.

While it is true that Japan was and is socially stratified and profoundly hierarchical and that, like any substantial population, it has a history of splintering groups (often along familial lines), followed by bloody rivalries for power (De Bary, 1958), Japan is today nevertheless strikingly homogeneous to outsiders. Furthermore, it seems likely that once Japan opened its doors to the West, their country's homogeneity was recognized by the Japanese themselves, which helped Japan achieve internal amity and true nationhood.

This, in turn, may help explain a lot about Japan and the Japanese, particularly in the areas of general cooperation and altruism. Western foreigners, for example, are struck by Japanese honesty, even in the largest cities. True, there is corruption, but it is rare, and once discovered, not only is the culprit expected to do away with himself but often he does.*

Japan is probably the only free enterprise democracy in which a delegation of workers in nondepression times has voluntarily asked their boss for a cut in pay so that the company might better survive. In Japan every school child knows the meaning of gross national product (G.N.P.), and everyone considers the raising of the GNP a personal as well as a national goal. There are no national unions in Japan, only organizations of lower echelon workers within a company, and they do indeed bargain over wages. But each company, no matter its size, is a family, and each boss the family head. On holidays, the "father" takes his employees on a picnic, and it is important that he and not an underling preside over the festivities. As Reischauer points out, Japanese business is at once typified by strongly hierarchical organization and close personal affiliation: "Leaders are not expected to be forceful and domineering, but sensitive to the feelings of others. Their qualities of leadership should be shown by the warmth of their personalities and the admiration and confidence they inspire, rather than by the sharpness or vigor of their decisions" (1977, p. 165).

A Japanese wife prides herself on knowing what is on her husband's mind before he has spoken, and, in general, much is unsaid but understood in Japan (again, see Reischauer, 1977). This common baseline of understanding is certainly in part the result of the highly homogeneous culture of Japan, but I surmise that it comes, as well, from the apparent parallel fact that Japan is also highly homozygous.

Even student riots and marches against the government usually have gone according to protocol in Japan, and such protests have far outnumbered the more publicized bloody ones. Father J. E. Frisch (1975), who is now a Japanese citizen teaching in Tokyo's Sophia College, confirms that the student riots of the early 1970s were well scripted. Both sides wore riot helmets, the exact location of each demonstration was known in advance, and police tended to use their truncheons on those students who were properly protected. In Kyoto in 1972 I witnessed a left-wing demonstration against the government in which the demonstrators received official permission to march on one-third of the main street so as not to impede traffic. The entire protest went without a hitch, and the contrast between anarchic slogans and actual behavior was remarkable. Again, much of

---

* Nonetheless, foreign scholars tend to overemphasize harmony and selflessness in Japanese society. One could stress the self-serving aspects of Japanese social exchange or focus on labor or farmer unrest, as the Japanese themselves frequently do.

what I have said here is reinforced and elaborated in Reischauer's book *The Japanese.*

Finally, I should like to point out that adoption of nonrelatives is a widespread Japanese institution that goes back many centuries (Befu, 1971). In Japan it was and continues to be quite common for a family without a male heir to adopt a son-in-law so that he may eventually take over the headship of the family. Such a son (*yōshi*) changes his name to that of the new family, a fact I was confounded by when I first ran into it. One of Japan's foremost primatologists became a *yōshi* after he had established a substantial reputation under his original family name. When I was introduced to him, I naturally did not recognize the new name and found out only gradually, and to my embarrassment, who he was. There are some 140,000 *yōshi* adoptions in Japan each year, and Japan has probably the greatest rate of adoptions in any advanced nation in the world (Matsumoto, 1962). Although these adoptions are unique in that most are of adult males, the principle still appears to hold that only in homogeneous populations do we find adoption so widespread.

Ruth Benedict (1970), in lecturing on the Japanese and the Polynesians, used the concept of *synergy* to describe those populations in which one sees mutual identification and the mutual pooling of goals and energy. Japan also has been called a collateral society (Caudill and Scarr, 1962) insofar as each member implicitly assumes a relationship with the others around him. In our own linear society, comparable relationships travel up and down a narrow range, grandfather through grandchild, with little expectation of intimate involvement outside these boundaries.

It may be coincidence that national unity is most easily perceived in a country that appears to be genetically homozygous, or that cultural and genetic homogeneity seem closely to parallel one another. Kinship genetics nevertheless offers a rationale for such a state of affairs, and only future investigations will tell us whether the hypothesis is correct that more internal altruism will be observed within genetically related groups than within groups more genetically diverse.

On the one occasion when I dared utter these ideas in public, a fellow panelist, an expert in criminal statistics, agreed that Japan has very low crime rates, especially for crimes of violence. But he argued that the Kentucky mountains, where inbreeding is notorious, was a glaring contradiction to my thesis. However, violence there is largely *between* inbreeding groups, not within them. He was referring to the Hatfields and McCoys and other famous feuding families and, if anything, this is but another case illustrating my point: an insult to one member of such an extended family is taken as an insult to all.

A more serious contradiction to the kinship hypothesis is the fact that visitors to an area are often immune from its violence. In Japan, for example, the equivalent of "teddy" boys may rob a Japanese drunk but almost never an intoxicated non-Japanese. Or consider that black violence in urban America is almost always directed at other blacks. For that matter, murder within all ethnic groups usually involves ex-lovers or members of the same family. Certainly nothing I have said about the dominance-submission order *within* groups, or about male and female jealousy, would lead one to be surprised at such intragroup violence. The fact that a father can both beat and love his son exemplifies the two-edged aspect of all relationships. Even identical twins, who are, after all, related 100% to each other, often squabble. Love and hate are first cousins, and a family or group often forgets its unity until an external threat occurs.

In general, we know that kinship and societal traits such as belligerence versus pacifism go together. Robert LeVine has shown that where family ties are geographically extended (for example, Kipsigis, Mundurucú), on the one hand, or localized (for example, Bedouin, Gusii), on the other, there will be a tendency to tribal cohesion or intratribal bickering, respectively (LeVine, 1965). That is, if one has relatives throughout the tribal lands, there is less likelihood of regional rivalries within a tribe. LeVine goes on to point out that such socially integrated tribes, insofar as they can act as a trusting union, are more prone to wage war than are the socially divided tribal groups that have largely localized blood ties. Furthermore, they are more likely to do so successfully.

Similarly, among the Navajo cultural cohesion and kinship are one and the same process. The Navajo accomplish this identity by a kinship system that is confusing to their Anglo neighbors. There is no Navajo word for cousin, aunt, or uncle. These individuals are, instead, called brothers, sisters, mothers, and fathers, and every effort is made *not* to make a distinction between, say, a true sister and what we call a cousin. As a consequence, and given larger families, Navajos have brothers, sisters, and parents everywhere they go. In addition, they are born into two clans, their mother's and their father's, and thus have clan brothers and sisters as well. When in their territory, Navajo are never without a place to stay and a meal to eat, and although a notoriously independent people they are bound together in this effective network of kinship.

To summarize, systems of kinship vary from culture to culture, but with rare exception special privileges are everywhere reserved for kin, and culturally defined and genetically defined kin usually converge. It is perhaps not cricket to use a man's own words against him, but in the old days, before the "menace" of sociobiology, Marshall Sahlins said similar things:

> The span of social distance between those who exchange, conditions the mode of exchange. Kinship distance . . . is especially relevant to the form of reciprocity. Reciprocity is inclined toward the generalized pole by close kinship, toward the negative extreme in proportion to kinship distance. (1965, p. 149)

One might well ask, If kinship genetics indeed works this way and, furthermore, if greater inbreeding leads to greater altruism, what are the recognition mechanisms within the inbred group? A common language seems necessary and, of course, a common culture. Growing up in a culture is like an extended initiation ceremony and, as we have seen, man seems built to respond with tribal allegiance to others like himself. Perhaps, to the extent that the fine tuning is alike in sender and receiver, two may feel as one, and the two can consequently sacrifice for one another. That is, the closer we are to being identical twins with identical backgrounds, the closer we are, theoretically, to the case of pure biological altruism. Is this, in fact, the way it works with twins?

No one has yet compared relative altruism in identical (always 100% identity of genes) and fraternal twins (an average of 50% identity of genes). But, as usual, there are anecdotes and incidental observations that reveal that identicals are much closer to one another, spend considerably more time together, and, despite the many fights, are often described as sharing a common ego. It may be said of many identical pairs that the twinship itself constitutes their central identity, so that where you and I say "me" they tend to use "we" (Leonard, 1961).*

It often happens that in individual psychotherapy with an identical twin, the patient tries to re-create his or her relationship with the twin within the patient-therapist relationship (Leonard, 1961). Unfortunately, since the doctor is never as attuned as is the twin, the patient is usually disappointed. A psychiatric colleague once described to me a patient's long silences, which he found to be tests of whether he, the doctor, was as in touch with her thoughts as was her twin sister. This discovery and the subsequent working through of the insight was the major factor in the patient's recovery.

Thornton Wilder, who had uncanny insight into people anyway, was an identical twin. If you recall his *Bridge at San Luis Rey*, an identical twin, Sebastian, died with the fall of the bridge, whereupon

---

* Over the course of psychological treatment of a pair of identical twin boys, I became aware that, despite an inordinate amount of intratwin aggression (the presenting problem), the twins' similarity in outlook and taste on a variety of issues, their similar physical abilities and responsivity, even their shared understanding of what it is like to be so competitive, helped envelope both with a sense of inseparability. For me, this case illustrated some of the subtler aspects of altruistic relationships and the fact that aggression and altruism are not mutually exclusive.

his grieving brother, who thereby felt partly dead himself, had no recourse but suicide. Indeed, the breakup of identical pairs in wartime brought to light examples of similarly strong attachments. I knew of one such case, during World War II, in which both twins felt not quite whole over the entire duration of the war. Their subsequent reunion was described to me by one of them as the most emotion-filled event of their entire lives.

Is it, then, something like this attachment, in less intense form to be sure, that underlies tribal unity? Is there an ever so subtle sense of "we" between ourselves and our fellow tribesmen that renders self-sacrifice not unthinkable? I believe the answer is yes. Recognition of this sense triggers a series of emotions whose net effect is tribal unity and the increased chance for altruism (Appendix Studies 48 and 49 try to deal with this issue).

In general, the implications of kinship genetics and inbreeding have hardly been tapped by social scientists, but they must be enormous. The in-group/out-group phenomenon, or ethnocentrism, a major issue in the social sciences, has to my knowledge never been examined in light of inbreeding and kinship, and that will be our next concern.

8

Breeding-out and Breeding-in

The evolutionary purpose of sex is to create genetic variation. Why variation? Because, as Darwin discovered, it alone makes possible evolutionary change via selection of optimal variants. There are asexual forms, usually very simple, one-celled animals, but it seems clear that without sex there would be very few forms of life.

Nevertheless, too much variation will create problems. If mating is to proceed between any two animals, they must be able to recognize each other, behaviorally and physiologically, as members of the same species. Just a 12% difference in the genes of any two organisms may mark them as separate species and unmatable, although some matable organisms show considerably more difference than that (Lewontin, 1974). To maintain species integrity, however, variation must be kept in check.

There is, then, a corresponding tendency for living things to breed with others like themselves, and subspecies tend to mate with one another, even as subpopulations within subspecies do so, too. Recognition mechanisms of all sorts have evolved to help in this sorting out process, so that in ants local groups recognize one another by smell; in birds, by song or coloration.

Humans, too, can recognize members of their local mating group by such mechanisms although many others have been devised by local groups, for instance, facial scarification, unique clothing, and language variants. But, in addition, local mating groups take on a unique look, so that, for example, Kikuyu and Masai can recognize fellow tribesmen on a Nairobi street though they are wearing Western dress and lack facial scars. As already pointed out, we are much more highly inbred than we usually realize. And when Irish marries Irish or Navajo marries Navajo, although the betrothed belong to different clans, they are marrying a relative of some degree.

We have not yet devised a foolproof way to tell how great the relatedness is in such a marriage, nor can we estimate average degrees of relatedness in, say, Japan versus the United States. Practically speaking, we know that average relatedness is much higher in Japan because the United States is a nation of immigrants, but we lack the methods to determine *how much* higher.

We can calculate a relative number based on the frequency of cousin marriages occurring now or, via registration records, in the recorded past, and Japan is indeed higher on this measure (Schull and Neel, 1965). But this tells us only about current or recent rates of inbreeding; it does not take into account the inbreeding that did or did not occur before those records started—so that at present cousins in Japan may be more related than cousins in a less isolated area such as Korea or Canton (Roberts, 1971).

The key point to make right now is that inbreeding, which leads to genetic similarity (homozygosity), is every bit as important for evolutionary success as is the achievement of genetic variation (heterozygosity), and that the two are always in dynamic balance. There is a tendency in animals and man to form small, local breeding groups, just as there is a tendency to break out of them. In this chapter our job is to see how these contrasting forces affect human populations and cultures.

MECHANISMS THAT ASSURE OUTBREEDING

Incest Taboo

The universal institution for assuring some measure of outbreeding is the incest taboo. It is one of the few acknowledged universals in anthropology, and reams have been written on it. It is generally agreed that father-daughter incest is the most common form of it, followed by brother-sister incest, with mother-son incest rare and universally judged as the most pathological (Masters, 1963). Why people in every nook and cranny of the world have decided incest is bad is a recurrent question and the argument that there is an innate "heterozygous drive" has often been made. Do we have a built-in distaste for incestuous sex? As Lorenz (1966) has said, if a behavior is not innate but yet universal, there must be an innate teacher built into all of us.

Donald Sade, working with rhesus monkeys on Cayo Santiago Island near Puerto Rico, has found that rhesus, too, appear to respect the mother-son incest taboo and to some degree the brother-sister one as well (Sade, 1968). Sometimes exceptions are most illuminating, and Sade found one case in which a rhesus did copulate with his mother. Careful notes seemed to explain why. Just prior to the copulation, mother and son had had a squabble over food, and the angry son had beaten her decisively. Then, within 45 minutes, he mounted her for the first time and copulated successfully. Sade's conclusion? Mother-son incest in rhesus is prevented by the dominance differential, and when the dominance-submission order is reversed, as happens only occasionally, the stage is set for normal sexual mounting. If this explanation is sufficient (I doubt that it is), it is as if evolution has made use of the dominance-submission hierarchy to avoid mother-son incest and thereby to promulgate heterozygosity.

Does this mechanism work the same way in humans? Possibly. Take the most common form of incest, the one with the least guilt involved, father-daughter incest. The father is naturally dominant over the daughter, and only legalisms, traditions, and maternal objections would stand in the way of a sexual liaison. Needless to say, father-stepdaughter incest is even more common. In interviews with both incestuous fathers and daughters there is an astounding *lack* of guilt although there is a sense that it was "wrong" to have had intercourse (Masters, 1963). It therefore appears that only mother-son incest is universally considered "sick," yet the genetic damage is equal to that in the other forms of incest (all involve persons with 50% genetic relatedness). Is it, then, merely dominance reversal that causes in cases of incest extreme disgust, punishment such as stoning to death, and oedipal self-mutilation? Not likely. It is difficult to escape the conclusion that somewhere within us lies a reflex, or at least a low threshold for disgust, not unlike our reaction to putrefaction but geared to the idea of mother-son copulation. Others have examined this issue in great detail only to reach the same conclusion (Westermarck, 1891; Wolf, 1970).

It is possible, too, that something of this order, but more subtle, is working at the level of brother-sister incest. It has long been known that nonrelated Israeli children raised together in kibbutzim (cooperative communities) rarely, if ever, pair off or marry one another (Tiger and Shepher, 1975). Israelis questioned about this phenomenon indicate that no conscious decision is involved but that they experience a vague discomfort with the idea. Somehow, being brought up together reduces sexual interest in one another, and the result is complete exogamy in the kibbutz system. Similarly, Wolf (1970), in his lovely study of "major" and "minor" marriages in Taiwan, found that minor marriages, in which betrothal and life together start in childhood, rarely last long after the partners reach maturity, nor are they as fruitful as major marriages (arranged marriages between sexually mature partners). It appears clear that childhood familiarity makes for sexual contempt.

Whereas all cultures frown on father-daughter, mother-son, and sibling incest, only at the level of cousin marriage is there diversity of custom (Alexander, 1974), ranging from taboo to preference for such marriages, as among some Australian Aboriginal tribes (Meggitt, 1962). It would appear that cousins are at or near the breakpoint—the maximum level of inbreeding allowed and, in some cases, the balance preferred.

I already have spoken of the special mating system each culture develops, always in the service of outbreeding; among the Dani of New Guinea, all married women come from other villages, among the Navajo one may not marry someone of the mother's clan, in China one may not marry someone with the same patronymic, and so on. No one of these groups will specify outbreeding as the function of such constraints but the practice of setting limits on whom one may marry is present everywhere.

Migration and Migrant Advantage

Another related means of maintaining heterozygosity involves migration. Sometimes migration is semiinstitutionalized, as among the Navajo, who are spread over greater distances than are most Indian groups. A young man who comes to a squaw dance from across the reservation draws an unusual amount of attention from the girls, and according to my informant he probably will have easier access to them than locals of the same clan. That the young visitor has a certain glamour is an observation that seems intuitively correct, but it has not been noted in anthropological literature, probably because it has always seemed so obvious. Of course, if the young man is not of the same tribe or of the proper clan, this advantage is often lost, and the attraction has to be quite strong to break such traditional boundaries.

Wilson reports on the same effect, which he calls "migrant selection," among *Drosophila* and other animals: "As males become rare relative to males of other genotypes, their mating success increases. Thus, immigrants arriving in a population genetically different from their own enjoy an initial advantage" (1975, p. 104). I would rewrite the last sentence, substituting "a population *phenotypically* different" in that animals necessarily react to phenotypes not to genotypes (Leonard and Ehrman, 1976). In this way, too, we can include our Navajo example and other examples in which familiarity versus nonfamiliarity is more appropriate than genotypical similarity versus dissimilarity.

Migration is not a chance event among primates and just about every male Japanese monkey wanders from his natal troop to another upon reaching maturity (Nozawa, 1972). Among chimpanzees at the Gombe Stream in Tanzania, both sexes become extraordinarily nomadic at pubescence, and the chances are high that the female will become pregnant away from her home range. She does, however, then return home, whereas males may never return (Pusey, 1971).

As pointed out in Chapter 4 human males, too, exhibit a tendency to wander rather far from the hearth, even as prepubescents. With puberty, especially in the spring, those trips can become institutionalized, as in the Australian "walkabout," the Nuer young men's tour of the tribal villages, or in coast to coast motoring and hitchhiking in the United States (see such American works as Kerouac's *On the Road*). Given recent social changes, females of the same age are more and more mobile and it appears that, economics aside, the urge to see new or strange places is widespread and deep-seated.

Migration always increases during environmental chaos, and consequently so does heterozygosity. Among humans, economic disasters, such as the Irish potato famine of 1846, have led to mass emigration. Some two million left Ireland over a five-year period, mostly males, and Irish surnames now abound in North and South America. In Africa, as the Sahara continues its spread southward and as resources become scarcer, tribes that formerly never mingled now meet at food distribution centers (MacDougall, 1973). As described by Turnbull (1972) in his study of the Ik, the breakdown of group pride under these circumstances can be devastating and the erosion of traditional mating patterns is one consequence. It stands to reason that unrecorded instances of widespread migration have occurred over man's history and that disasters, plagues, and droughts have, ironically, served to increase heterozygosity.

This general phenomenon has been documented in several nonhuman primate species as well. Yellow baboon troops in the Amboselli Reserve of Kenya have been seen to break up into wide-ranging groups of one male with several females during periods of desiccation; this social organization, in fact, mimics the harem system of the hamadryas baboons, who normally exist in the nonlush, arid plateaus of Ethiopia (Hausfater, 1973). Chimpanzees, too, scatter widely when food is scarce (Izawa, 1970) as does the small South American monkey the marmoset (Herschkovitz, 1977). When there is plenty of food, marmosets tend to stick to certain forest areas in one- or two-family groups and inbreeding levels are relatively high. So high, in fact, that the marmosets in one area are clearly distinguishable from those of another by color, size, noisiness, and many more characteristics. However, when food is scarce the cruising area increases and animals normally found on one side of a river may now be seen on the other side. Mating may then take place between differently colored animals, resulting in hybrid offspring.

Such outbreeding at times of environmental instability is a universal phenomenon that is perhaps most dramatic in plants (Stebbins, 1950). Certain plants have asexual phases and reproduce themselves exactly when the environment is stable and conditions good (we call such seeds haploid in that there is but a single set of chromosomes); under unstable conditions, such as drought or excessive rain, these same plants will switch to sexual reproduction (diploid seeds) in the "hope" that some new combination will better withstand essentially unpredictable conditions.

By way of summary to this point, inbreeding leads to genetic similarity (homozygosity) and outbreeding leads to genetic diversity (heterozygosity). Both vectors if carried to extremes will be nonadaptive and in all populations the two are in dynamic balance. All cultures acknowledge this situation, however unconsciously, since all insist on a certain degree of exogamy via the incest taboo and via clan and moiety rules that prevent certain matings and permit others. At an informal level, and serving the same end, migrants are often found to have a mating advantage.

At the same time, all groups are ethnocentric and insist that marriages occur within defined ethnic boundaries. Ethnocentrism is rarely discussed as a genetic mechanism, but it is very like troop allegiance, seen in all the terrestrial monkeys and it may well be a homologous behavioral pattern. It is our next concern.

MECHANISMS THAT ASSURE INBREEDING

Tribalism and Ethnocentrism

If first cousin marriage is as far as one can go in breeding-in, what is the comparable point of transgression in breeding-out? In other words, are there rules at the heterozygous end that are as powerful as incest rules at the homozygous end?

Ever since the publication of William Graham Sumner's *Folkways* in 1906, in which he coined the word "ethnocentrism," social scientists have been aware of the universality of the in-group/out-group distinction. It appears that all people, most particularly tribal people, have tended to consider only themselves as human and invariably have given derogatory names to their neighbors. Thus, the term "Navajo" comes from the Spanish and means "Apache who till soil." The Navajo call themselves Diné,

which means, simply, "the People" and apply a series of comic ap-
pellations to their neighbors the Hopi, who in turn think of
themselves as "the Peaceful People," compared to their thieving
neighbors the Navajo.

Each tribe has established separate customs and a unique
language, which give its members a sense of specialness and unity.
Whatever mating customs a group has devised, the outer boundaries
of permissible mating—the usual limit of heterozygosity—is
membership in the tribe. True, slavery and wife stealing bring new
genes to a group, and groups vary considerably in willingness to incorporate strangers. But by far the bulk of consummated sexual relationships have been intratribal.

Does this reasoning mean anything in present-day nontribal
states such as Japan, America, or Germany? Members of such
Western and Eastern nations, of course, feel superior to those
backward tribal folks in Africa, the Americas, New Guinea, or Asia.
After all, we have left that stage for modern, supratribal combinations. But when we look somewhat carefully within each nation, we
see that regionalism and centuries-old affiliations continue to play
an important role in individual self-definition and in mating networks (Darlington, 1969).

It would appear that the tendency to close ranks within a unique
group still permeates the great nations, and in all modern countries
homogamous mating patterns (like mating with like) far exceed random, *heterogamous* ones (Spuhler, 1967). In other words, like still
tends to seek out like, so that in the United States, although ethnic
group boundaries are rather permeable, religious boundaries are
less so, and racial boundaries least of all. Within the science of
population genetics, such events are known as "assortative mating."
As for the effects of capitalism versus Marxism, my impressions are
that in the Soviet Union assortative mating patterns are just as persistent, save that religious boundaries are less significant. Why is
there, despite the avowed ideal of an American (or Soviet) "melting
pot," a mix of identifiable, somewhat mutually antagonistic groups?

Clearly, primary identification as an "American" has become
too complex to carry off easily. I was recently at a Navajo curing
ceremony and was rather belligerantly asked by an inebriated Navajo, "What are you?" I realized that he was asking about my tribal affiliation, and I answered that I belong to the Hebrew tribe,
whereupon he went off, apparently satisfied. This simple question is
the first that most people want answered about strangers, and it is
clear that many of us still use another's tribal affiliation in our initial
assessment of him.

The interesting thing in the United States is that even as formal
methods of induction into a tribe disappear, adolescents proceed to
invent comparable ceremonies. We have started to research this

area, and we find that preadolescent children wonder about what they are, but by adolescence they need to act on it. In San Francisco one can see preadolescent children of all races and ethnic backgrounds, often arm in arm, talking, laughing, and playing together on their way to school. But as adolescence approaches, such scenes decrease, and by adolescence, they are almost nonexistent. All have sorted themselves out. Chinese with Chinese, black with black, Italian with Italian, Chicano with Chicano, and so on.

Given that group identification is a strong force, a number of questions arise. Is there any genetic disadvantage to true miscegenation? That is, is tribalism a trait we should nurture in that it assures a correct amount of homozygosity? Can a population of humans become *too* heterozygous?

The answer seems to be yes, and the genetic logic need only be repeated. Recall that evolution is completely dependent on the existence of small, scattered samples of a species. Sewall Wright (1940) has estimated that semiisolated breeding populations on the order of 500 individuals would be the best size to insure overall species adaptation. It is interesting that that was about the average size of Australian Aboriginal and New Guinean tribes when Westerners first came on the scene (Elkin, 1964). The assumption is that as each group grew too large, there was a split, and the many tribes seen today were formed over time by some process of subdividing. If we assume that most of our evolutionary past was spent as members of small breeding groups, we may well have evolved a set of emotions that literally demands of us tribal affiliations.

Certainly a world without tribalism would be a far less colorful and interesting place. But mass culture is on the drawing boards, and perhaps such current events as the Basque rebellion are but a last hurrah. On the other hand, the continuously reappearing conflicts at tribal or ethnic levels in nations of geographically proximate peoples may be the major message: mass culture and supratribal unity is not working. Catholic and Protestant are at one another in Northern Ireland; Lebanese Muslims and Christians are fighting to the death; Flemish Walloons are not now rioting, but they and the Belge French do not speak; the Basque want independence from Spain and are dying for that cause; Greek and Turk, after millennia, are still bitter enemies; a few years ago, on the shores of Lake Tanganyika, I saw Wahutu refugees fleeing Burundi and possible massacre by the Watusi; in Northern Nigeria, some six years ago, Ibo bodies were stacked ten high as the Hausa rampaged; seven years ago, in Bali, "nonbelievers" and "communists" were garroted by the thousands (these were, in fact, merely an educated minority who had set themselves apart). What about those tribes whose conflicts are never reported in the world press? True, in each conflict, one group often is better off economically than the other and often the primary language is different. But to attribute such murderous, groupwide jealousies to either economic or linguistic factors is far too facile (see especially Shumpeter, 1951, on this issue).

Before closing this chapter, I must, out of conscience, give my personal view. I am all for outbreeding. I find it continuously exciting to be married to a Chinese woman who, in most other respects, is much like my mother. Such a marriage is clearly exogamous, and therefore nonincestuous, and yet it is the realization of almost every boy's secret, incestuous wish. At a more conscious level, outbreeding obviously involves a touch of antiestablishmentarianism as well as a vote for human brotherhood.

I also have a sister-in-law who is Egyptian. Our immediate families, especially our children, are deeply bound to one another. How can I, a Jew, then hate Egyptians? I would thereby be hating what is now part of myself, and here at once is the point of both having and not having blood alliances. If a fight occurs between two groups to whom you are tied, you are in perpetual conflict since you cannot take a firm stand, and indecision in wartime may be fatal. On the other hand, in such kinship, and the resulting reluctance to hate, lies the hope for peace. Half-breeds, scorned as they may be by both sides in any tribal conflict, are nevertheless the hope for turning enmity to amity. They are the bridge between black and white, Hopi and Navajo, Arab and Jew, particularly if they come from intact bicultural families.

We know that the promise of economic success has, on occasion, forced persons and families to relinquish ethnic and racial ties in favor of ties to a socioeconomic class (see Patterson, 1975), but I am afraid most of the world still believes, nay, violently insists, that tribal boundaries are inviolate and that all legitimate breeding must occur within them. Maybe the problem is cognitive: most people simply cannot cope with an abstraction beyond the tribe. Certainly, Trotsky's hope for worldwide unity of the workers won over only a relative handful of equally cerebral followers; as Stalin insisted, the notion of nation already taxes men's limits, and loyalty is best demanded at that level, lest defection or fragmentation into tribes occur (Trotsky, 1930). Nations obviously were formed out of economic and military necessity and they seem to work all right, especially vis-à-vis other nations; but look carefully at even the oldest national confederations of Europe, and regionalism and the remnants of tribalism soon become apparent. Perhaps, as many have by now said, it will take an invasion from outer space before we trade our tribalism, regionalism, and nationalism for the abstraction we call *mankind*.

9

Biology or Culture?

INNATE OR ACQUIRED?

I have saved this chapter for last because it is the most controversial. I shall show that within hours of birth, babies of different ethnic groups and different races show substantial behavioral differences. Furthermore, these differences seem best explained on the basis of gene pool variations.

My position on this issue is a very simple monistic one. It is identical with the Zen view that we are totally biological, totally environmental, that the two are as inseparable as an object and its shadow. Or, as Hebb (1959) put it, we are 100% innate, 100% acquired; one might add, 100% biological, 100% cultural. I believe this chapter will make clear what Hebb had in mind.

At the 1964 meeting of the International Ethological Society in Zurich, I tried to convince ethologists of the propriety of the monistic position with a paper called "Evolved Behavior: A Term to Replace Innate versus Acquired." My argument follows:

> There have been a number of attempted solutions to the innate versus acquired controversy: One can say both innate and acquired components always play a role, but with unease, since this solution implies the two parties somehow exist, independently, but that they can never be separated from each other. This view is then open to the 60–40 solution, the one commonly used by behavior geneticists who deal with polygenic systems. They speak of the relative variance contributed by each, e.g., 60% heredity (or environment) and 40% environment (or heredity). This is an unstable solution since it produces the observation, "60–40 in this environment, but possibly 40–60 in that environment and 49–51 in another, etc." Because of this instability problem, Hebb (1959) has resorted to the 100%–100% solution, i.e., it is always 100% of each. This solution satisfies

few scientists, but it has served to temporarily alleviate a growing discomfort with the 60–40 solution.

What is then left? There is the American empirical tradition which instructs us not to meddle with problems of innate versus acquired, but rather to roll up our sleeves and gather data (for example, Beach, 1955). Alas, this is a non-solution.

As for the ethological position, it has been well chastised by Lehrman, who, despite a number of mistakes in his critique (Schaffner, 1954), showed that the term "innate behavior" as used by ethologists cannot withstand the test of logical or experimental analysis. However, no solution being offered, none was adopted. As far as I can see, although Tinbergen and Lorenz have agreed that the logic of "I" in I. R. M. (Innate Releasing Mechanism) is tenuous, the term is very much in use by ethologists and is still open to the criticisms leveled by Lehrman in 1954. Actually, it can usually be shown that "innate" means only that the behavioral unit under discussion appears to have evolutionary meaning and/or that it appears to be a reflection of the organism's genotype.

For those, like myself, working within an evolutionary framework, but with higher mammals (including humans) rather than with fish or birds, the interchangeability of "innate" and "unlearned" is particularly touchy. Few scientists would object to the principles that a healthy organism is one which is totally organized, and that in an organism in which learning has a major adaptive role, no important behavior is immune from learning, i.e., is purely "unlearned."

But this is not to say that behavior in such organisms is unevolved. The smile of a baby, for example, clearly has learned aspects, but just as clearly has a genetic component and obvious evolutionary significance (Freedman, 1964). To term the smile "innate" in the sense of "unlearned" is sufficiently inaccurate to result in insoluble and fruitless debate. It seems preferable, then, to simply speak of the smile as *evolved* or phylogenetically adaptive behavior.

The problem with the term "innate" at the level of higher mammals exaggerates similar difficulties at the level of lower vertebrates. For example, the incomplete embryological study of a chick egg by Kuo (1932) is often cited to illustrate anti-instinctual arguments. The point is made that pecking in chicks is not an innate response but is dependent on the physical juxtaposition of head and heart in the egg. It was postulated by Kuo that the beating heart initiates the head movements which later become pecking. If we assume this interpretation is correct, although apparently it is not (Gottlieb and Kuo, 1965), there would be no alternative but to assume further that the position of the fetal head and heart have been channeled by evolutionary changes which must be reflected in changes at the genetic level.

Thus, if we call pecking phylogenetically adaptive rather than innate, the mechanisms, no matter what they are hypothesized to be, may be dealt with directly and logically and with a minimum of polemics.

In conclusion, then, it is suggested that the obfuscating term "innate" no longer be used in any serious description of behavior. Since instinctive, inborn, unlearned, and innate are functionally synonymous, the former terms should also be dropped in favor of *evolved* or *phylogenetically adaptive*. Such a terminological change will have the secondary advantage of bringing evolution into the forefront of our thinking where it belongs.

As a young scientist uncertain about my rank, I was staggered by the negative response. For example, the eminent British ornithologist Robert Thorpe said sharply, "If we deny that innate and acquired are separable, all of our plans for ethological research will have to be shelved."

Indeed, with songbirds, Thorpe's specialty (Thorpe, 1963), it does appear possible to analyze behavior into innate and acquired components because complex learning rarely plays a role. A canary, for example, will start all over again if you block some aspect of its nest building by removing its usual nesting materials. It simply does not have the capacity to modify its behavior—to roll with the punch —and acts as if there were a built-in chain of commands (Hinde, 1965). This chain, then, is what either-or scientists then analyze into fixed and modifiable components.

What is usually required for this kind of work is a relatively stupid bird. Ravens, for example, are too smart to be used in such analytic work. If necessary, they will use substitute materials for nests, and in general, they can modify their behavior depending on what is currently happening around them. The European cuckoo has come to "know" this difference between songbirds and the smarter Corvidae (crows and ravens) and will drop its eggs only into the nests of songbirds; unfortunately for these musical little creatures, with their machinelike mentalities, they cannot distinguish their own eggs or even their own young from the cuckoo's. A cuckoo's egg would not last a minute in a raven's nest. Similarly, when food is stolen from a songbird's cache, the bird nevertheless continues to use the same hiding place. Not so a raven (Lorenz, 1957).

Innate and acquired also fall apart as a meaningful separation if we look just at the acquired, or learned, side. Take the phenomenon we call "imprinting." As Konrad Lorenz (1957) and his teacher Oscar Heiroth demonstrated, ducklings will follow any moving object soon after hatching, and thus they may become as attached to a human being as to their true parents. In other words, ducks learn who their parents are by following the first animate object they see.

But not all species of birds do this, and even among ducks there are differences in the duration of the "critical" learning period (the range is several hours to several days according to Hess, 1959). In other words, since it differs from species to species, "imprinting" itself must be genetically encoded, and we have the apparent irony of a genetically encoded ability to learn.

There is no way to separate the genetic and the learned for they are permanently glued together, and that is true everywhere in nature, including man. Logically, anything we do is gene related. If I think, it is my genetically derived brain that is thinking and not some disembodied mind. But, many Western scientists do believe that mind is nonbody. Nobel prize-winning neurologist Sir John Eccles, for example, has clearly stated such a dualistic position (Eccles, 1966). Whether this view is Christian or pre-Christian, I have no idea; but as a Zen sympathizer and perhaps more to the point as a Jew with a strongly monistic tradition, I see no merit in even temporarily tearing asunder mind and body or, for that matter, culture and biology. Certainly, as you and I negotiate life, we do not have separate cultural and biological experiences, for experience is marvelously unitary. Curiously, it takes an added intellectual step for modern Western man to return to this simple view.

GROUP DIFFERENCES IN NEWBORN BEHAVIOR

These ideas, then, provide the setting for our work on interethnic newborn differences. The first study was conceived when my wife who is Chinese, and I, in the course of learning about each other and our respective families, began to suspect that some character differences might well be related to differences in genetic backgrounds.

These notions were already near the surface as a result of my doctoral thesis, finished some years before. I had worked with different breeds of dogs and I had been struck by how predictable was the behavior of each breed. A *breed* of dog is a construct zoologically and genetically equivalent to a *race* of man. To look at us, my wife and I were clearly of two different breeds. Were some of our behavioral differences determined by breed?

How does one answer this question with humans? Adoption studies might be one way—Chinese raised by Caucasians and vice versa. Yet such an approach is fraught with complications at both the practical and the theoretical level. Instead, we modeled our study after my work with puppies.

In my thesis work, I had raised four breeds of dog from two through twelve weeks of age, spending all my days and evenings with them. It became clear, as the ears and eyes opened, that the breeds already differed in behavior. Little beagles were irrepressibly friendly from the moment they could detect me, whereas Shetland sheepdogs were most sensitive to a loud voice or the slightest punishment; wire-haired terriers were so tough and aggressive, even as clumsy three-week olds, that I had to wear gloves in playing with them; and, finally, basenjis, barkless dogs originating in central Africa, were aloof and independent.

With this background, then, we decided we could get at comparable, precultural differences in humans by carefully watching newborns and very young infants of different ethnic backgrounds. If we could detect differences right at the start, we could speak of "breed" differences here, too. Fortunately, Berry Brazelton, the well-known Harvard pediatrician, came through Chicago at this time to attend a convention. We were introduced and in a short time had developed the Cambridge Behavioral and Neurological Assessment Scale (Brazelton and Freedman, 1971). A later, more elaborate version of the test is known simply as the "Brazelton" (Brazelton, 1973).

The test provided for the first time a scheme of infant assessment that went beyond just reflexes and tapped early forms of social and emotional behavior: How easily did the baby quiet? Was it able to quiet itself or did it have to be carried and consoled? Did the baby turn to the examiner's face and voice? Did it prefer face over voice or voice over face? How did interest in the voice compare with interest in a ball or a rattle? Was the baby very active or did it just lie quietly? Did it fit comfortably in the examiner's arms or did it fight being held? Did it generally resist or accept our testing? Was it floppy or stiff? And then there were all the reflexes: were they crisp or just barely elicited?

Considerable hokum appeared in pediatric textbooks on what newborns can and cannot do. We know now that they can focus on a face, follow it from side to side, and turn in the direction of a voice even if the speaker is out of sight. Also, they prefer a high-pitched voice to any other sound. In fact, the more we study newborns, the smarter they seem to get (see Freedman, 1974).

Now, armed with our baby test, my wife, Nina, and I went in San Francisco to the hospital where our first child was born. A substantial number of Chinese babies are born there, and we were able to examine both Chinese and Caucasian newborns. To keep things neat, we made sure that all the Chinese were of Cantonese (south Chinese) background, the Caucasians of northern European origin; that the division of sexes in both groups were the same; that the mothers were the same age; that they had about the same number of previous children; and that both groups were administered the same drugs in the same amounts during labor. Additionally, all families were members of the same health plan and all mothers had had about the same number of prenatal visits to the doctor and were of the same, middle-income bracket.

It was almost immediately clear that Chinese and Caucasian babies were indeed like two different breeds. Caucasian babies started to cry more easily, and once they started, they were more difficult to console. Chinese babies adapted to almost any position in which they were placed; for example, when placed face down in their cribs, they tended to keep their faces buried in the sheets rather than immediately turning to one side, as did the Caucasians. In a similar maneuver (called the "defense reaction" by neurologists), we briefly pressed the baby's nose with a cloth, forcing him to breathe with his mouth. Most Caucasian and black babies fight this maneuver by immediately turning away or swiping at the cloth with the hands, and this is reported in Western pediatric textbooks as the normal, expected response. However, not so the average Chinese baby in our study. He simply lay on his back, breathing from the mouth, "accepting" the cloth without a fight. I must say that this finding is most impressive on film, and audiences have been awed by the intergroup differences.

Other, more subtle differences are equally important. For example, both Chinese and Caucasian infants would start to cry at about the same point in the examination, especially when they were undressed, but the Chinese would stop sooner. Furthermore, if picked up and cuddled, Chinese babies would stop crying immediately, as if a light switch had been flipped, whereas the crying of Caucasian babies only gradually subsided.

In another item, we repeatedly shone a light in the baby's eyes and counted the number of blinks until he "adapted" and no longer blinked. It should now not be surprising that the Caucasian babies continued to blink long after the Chinese babies had stopped.

It began to look as if Chinese babies were simply more amenable and adaptable to the machinations of the examiners, whereas the Caucasian babies were likely to register annoyance and to complain.

However, we hardly had enough evidence for so general a conclusion, and we set out to look at other newborns in other places. A good friend of mine, Dr. Norbett Mintz, was working among the Navajo at Tuba City, Arizona, and he arranged for a trip to the reservation in the spring of 1969. We ended our two-month stay with 36 Navajo newborns tested, and the results, since duplicated by other workers (Chisholm, 1977; Nisselius, 1976), paralleled the stereotype of the stoical, impassive Indian. These babies outdid the Chinese, showing even more calmness and adaptability (Freedman, 1974).

Subsequently I have spent considerable time among the Navajo, and it is now absolutely clear that the practice of tying the wrapped

Three-month-old Navajo infant and his mother getting ready for a trip. Cradleboard is typically Navajo, with safety head guard. Baby is often propped at this angle.

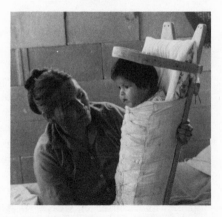

infant on a cradleboard (currently practiced only sporadically on the reservation) has in no way induced stoicism in the Navajo—a popular conjecture in the halcyon days of anthropological environmentalism. On the contrary, not all babies take to the cradleboard, and those Navajo babies who complain about it are simply taken off. Most Navajo infants, however, calmly accept the board, and, in fact, many begin to demand it by showing signs of unrest when off. However, by about six months, Navajo babies do start complaining when tied in, and at that time "weaning" from the board begins, the baby taking the lead. The Navajo, in fact, are the most "in touch" group of mothers we have yet seen, and the term "mother-infant unit" aptly describes what we saw among them.

James Chisholm of Rutgers University, who, in the course of his dissertation work (1977), studied infancy and cradleboarding among the Navajo, has written me that his observations are much like my

Testing of "automatic walk" in newborns at Fort Defiance, Arizona. Navajo infants' legs usually collapsed; 75% of Caucasian infants hold up weight and take several steps.

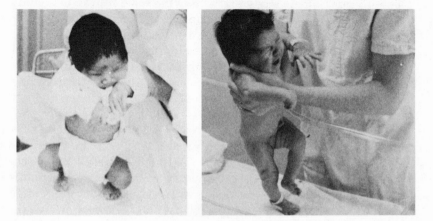

own (Chisholm, 1978; Chisholm and Richards, 1978). In addition, he followed a group of young Caucasian mothers in Flagstaff (some 80 miles south of the reservation) who had decided to use the cradleboard. However, their babies complained so persistently that they were off the board in a matter of weeks, a result that should not surprise us given the differences observed at birth.

Why are Navajo and Chinese newborns so much alike? We know that the Navajo were part of a relatively recent emigration from Asia. Their language belongs to the Athabaskan group, named after a lake in Canada, and whereas most Athabaskan peoples from Asia settled along the Canadian Pacific coast, the Navajo and the Apache went on to their present location about A. D. 1500. Even today, a significant number of words in Athabaskan and Chinese have the same meaning and, if one goes back several thousand years via written records of primitive Sino-Tibetan, the number of similar words makes clear the common origin of these widely separated peoples (Shafer, 1952).

Japanese babies, too, are much like Chinese and Navajo babies, although it must be admitted they were also unique in some ways (as were all the groups we looked at). We made observations on two Japanese groups, one in Hawaii and the second in Kobe, Japan, and it was clear that the Japanese babies in both places tended to be more irritable than either Navajo or Chinese but not to the level seen in Caucasians. As an example of another unique difference, the Navajo's skin reddened much more when the baby was disturbed, and their legs were unusually limber and pliable compared to those of other babies. Nevertheless, the test profiles of Chinese, Japanese, and Navajo infants were very much alike, and the baby test began to look like a fairly sensitive measure of genetic affinity (Freedman, 1974).

While we were doing these studies, other investigators were repeating our Chinese study and getting the same results. One study was performed in a Chinese community in Malaysia by someone who had read about our findings in the British journal *Nature* (Blurton-Jones, 1976). A second (to be reported on subsequently) was performed in the United States with infants of northern Chinese rather than Cantonese background (Kuchner, 1977). It was certainly gratifying to receive such confirmation, especially since the findings seemed so controversial.

Our first inkling of controversy came when my wife and I submitted our report to the American journal *Science*; the two reviewers could not agree. One wanted to see the findings published, the second did not since so important a claim as inborn behavioral differences across the races needed further confirmation. The editor therefore submitted our report to a second pair reviewers, who again

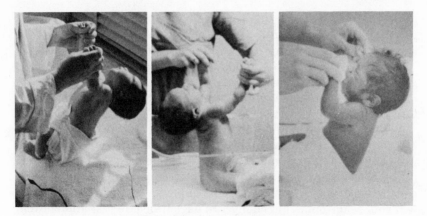

Japanese, Caucasian, and Australian Aboriginal newborns pulled to a sitting position. The head lag of the Japanese and Caucasian babies and the relatively erect head of the Aboriginal are typical. Navajo and Chinese newborns were much like Japanese.

split, apparently over the same issue. I then sent the report to *Nature*, the equally prestigious voice of British and European science, where again there was a split decision. But this time, the editor decided in favor of publication.

When we first presented these findings on Chinese and Caucasians, attempts were made to explain away the genetic implications by posing differential prenatal diets as a more obvious cause of differences in behavior among infants. But with the Navajo study that explanation had to be dropped for the Navajo diet is quite different from that of the Chinese, yet newborn behavior was strikingly similar. The only reasonable conclusion at present is that there are biological affinities between Navajo and Chinese, as well as biological differences between Orientals and Caucasians, that mediate the predominant temperaments of these two populations.

A GENETICIST'S INTERPRETATION

If a behavioral trait is at all interesting— for example, smiling, anger, ease of sexual arousal, and so on— it is most probable that many genes participate in its eventuation. Furthermore, there is no way to count the exact number of genes involved in polygenic systems because, as Crow (1960) has summarized the field, biological traits are controlled by one, two, or *many* genes.

A human polygenic trait often studied is *standing height*, which can be easily quantified and is also notoriously open to environmental influence. Thus, this variable has been frequently used as a paradigm for behavioral traits, which although genetically influenced are even more prone to change with the environment.

Geneticists speak of a *reaction range*, a range imposed by the genes within which a trait can vary. Irving Gottesman (1974) has drawn up a series of semihypothetical graphs on human height, illustrating how this process works:

Each genotype represents a relatively inbred human group. It can be seen that for genotype A, even the most favorable environment produces little change in height, whereas for genotype D a vast difference is seen as nutrition improves. Similarly, in conducting genetic experiments with mice, one can choose either a strain that will show environmental changes to have little effect or another that will show those same environmental changes to be highly influential (Fuller and Thompson, 1960).

Thus, when I speak of potential genetic differences in human behaviors, I do so with these notions in mind: there is overlap between most populations and the overlap can become rather complete under changing conditions, as in Gottesman's genotypes D and C; some genotypes, however, show no overlap and remain remote from the others over the entire reaction range as in genotype A.

Reaction range curves. From Gottesman, 1974.

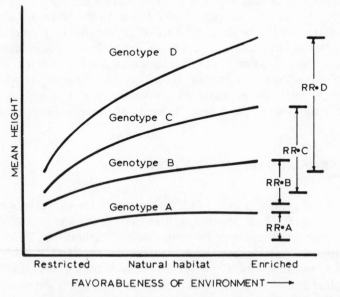

The reaction range concept applied to adolescent height (units for both X and Y axes are only ordinal and are not to scale).

MOTHER-INFANT INTERACTIONS

Before leaving Oriental-Caucasian differences, I must mention our experiences with Japanese babies. On our arrival in Hawaii in the summer of 1970, we met a well-known Honolulu pediatrician who, upon learning of our interests, volunteered that there were striking and consistent differences between Japanese and Polynesian babies in his practice. The Japanese babies consistently reacted more violently to their three-month immunization injections than did the Polynesians. Then, on subsequent visits, the Japanese gave every indication of remembering the last visit by crying; one mother said that her baby cried each time she drove past the clinic!

We then tested a series of Japanese newborns, and, as already mentioned, they were indeed more sensitive and irritable than were the Chinese and Navajo babies. In other respects, though, they were very much like them, being easy to console and quick to adapt to a light focused on the eyes or a cloth held over the nose. It is interesting, however, that prior to our work, the social anthropologist William Caudill (Caudill and Weinstein, 1969) had performed an extensive and thorough study of Japanese infants. He made careful observations of Japanese mothers and infants in Tokyo and of Caucasian mother-infant pairs in Baltimore, from the third to the twelfth month of life. Having noted that both the Japanese infants and their mothers vocalized much less to one another, Caudill assumed the Japanese mothers were conditioning their babies toward quietude, from a universal baseline at which all babies everywhere start. Caudill, of course, was in the American environmentalist tradition and, until our publication, did not consider a biological alternative. Now we can state that mother and baby were, in all probability, conditioning each other.

Joan Kuchner (1979), with this new interactive hypothesis in mind, examined mother-infant interactions among ten first generation Chinese and ten Caucasian mother-infant pairs over the first three months of life in an attempt to bridge the Caudill findings and our newborn results. The study was done in Chicago, and this time the Chinese were of north Chinese rather than south Chinese (Cantonese) ancestry. Kuchner started her study with the birth of the babies, and found the two groups of babies were different from the start, much as in our study of newborns. Furthermore, it soon became apparent that Chinese mothers were less intent on eliciting responses from their infants, and by the third month Chinese infants and mothers were rarely engaged in interactive bouts of vocalizations, as were the Caucasian pairs, even as in Caudill's study.

Following our work, Caudill and Frost (1975) repeated Caudill's original work but with third generation Japanese-American mothers and their fourth generation infants. He found that these mothers had become "super" American and were actually vocalizing to their infants at twice the Caucasian rate; this change indeed brought the Japanese babies up to Caucasian rates of activity and to even greater rates of happy vocalization. Assuming these are sound and repeatable results, my tendency is to reconcile Caudill and Frost's and ours and Kuchner's findings via the reaction range concept. If Japanese height can change as dramatically as it has with emigration to the United States, why not mother-infant behavior? On a variety of other measures, by the way, Caudill and Frost were able to discern continuing similarities with old-country Japanese mothers and infants vis-à-vis Caucasian Americans: fourth generation Japanese babies, like babies in Japan, engaged in less sucking of fingers, they were less playful, and the third generation mothers did more lulling and holding in the arms.

John Callaghan (1977), following a method developed by Alan Fogel (1976), compared fifteen Navajo and nineteen Anglo mothers and their infants (all under six months). Each mother was asked to "get the attention of your baby," and the subsequent scene was videotaped and later analyzed. The differences in both babies and mothers were striking and, again, the most obvious ones involved greater verbal stimulation by Caucasian mothers and greater passivity among Navajo babies. Caucasian mothers spoke to their babies continuously, using linguistic forms appropriate to someone who understands language, and the babies responded by moving their arms and legs much more. The Navajo mothers were strikingly silent, using their eyes to attract the baby's attention, and the relatively immobile infants responded by gazing back. Nevertheless, both groups were equally successful in getting their baby's attention.

Caucasian mothers also tended to shift the baby's position radically, sometimes holding it close, sometimes at arm's length, as if conducting an experiment on the best focal distance. Most Navajo mothers used only subtle shifts on the lap, holding the baby at about the same distance throughout. As a result of the relative overstimulation by the Caucasian mothers, the babies frequently turned their heads away, as if to moderate the intensity of the encounter. Consequently, the duration of eye encounter in Caucasians was shorter (half that of the Navajo) but more frequent.

It was clear, then, that the Caucasian mothers sought the baby's attention with far greater verve and excitement, even as their babies tended to react to the stimulation with what can be described as ambivalence: they turned both toward and away from the mother with far greater frequency than did the Navajo infants. Navajo mothers and their infants were engaged in relatively quiet and steady en-

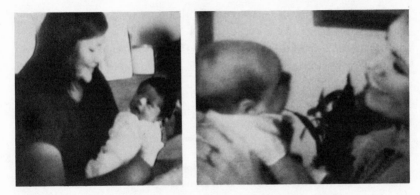

When asked to "get the attention of your baby," Navajo
mothers usually quietly watched their babies, who eventually
responded. The urban Caucasian mothers invariably spoke the
entire time, moving baby into varying positions. Both groups
were equally successful in getting their babies' attention.

counters. On viewing the films of these interactions, we indeed had
the feeling that we were watching biocultural differences in the making! (These and comparable data on the Hopi are summarized in Appendix Study 50.)

SOME IMPLICATIONS

The broader implications of these findings started creeping in on
me as we were testing the Chinese infants in San Francisco. At that
time, my wife and I made a number of visits to the Avery Brundage
Collection of Oriental Art at the De Young Museum, and I could not
resist the thought that only grown-up versions of our Chinese babies
could have produced art like this! There was, for example, the calm
quality of a Chinese jade horse, compared to the tempestuousness of
a Roman terra-cotta one. Since then, after reading such classics in
art history as *The Chinese Eye* (Chiang, 1960), it has become clear to
me that Eastern and Western art have had distinctive flavors:
Western art has consistently made its males heroic; whereas even the
military heroes of Chinese and Japanese art appear in sedate,
unemotional, and conventionalized pose. Furthermore, Chinese
landscape art, the most prevalent form of canvas painting, simply
never contained recognizable human figures. Human hubris was
kept below threshold, and the stick figures are a message that nature
is master, not man. There could be no Chinese Michelangelo.

Although noncommercial Navajo art is restricted to religious

sand painting, Oriental and Navajo philosophy are strikingly similar
in feeling. In trying to make this point, I recently tricked a group of
colleagues at a scientific meeting by purporting to read some lines of
a Navajo elder:

> Whenever someone sets out to remold the world, experience
> teaches
> That he is bound to fail.
> For Nature already is as good as it can be.
> It cannot be improved upon.
> He who tries to redesign it, spoils it.
> He who tries to redirect it, misleads it.

In fact, this is a translation of lines written by Lao-tze in the sixth
century B.C. (Lao-tze, 1958, verse 29), but anyone knowledgeable
about the Navajo knows the verse speaks for them. Some time after
these meetings, I received a letter from a well-known developmental
psychologist who was appalled at my apparent veneration of Lao-tze
and called the quote one of the most reactionary statements he had
ever heard.

What a beautiful and telling contrast in aims: to be one with
nature versus the treadmill of progress and improvement. Neither
side can quite believe the other. Not improve? Not advance? Unthinkable. Navajo elders, for their part, know that the holes sunk by
oil companies into the Tohatchi Mountains (near Fort Defiance) will
release monsters and evil spirits. And, in our new ecological
awareness, we know that they are at least symbolically right.

If you are sufficiently romantic or ecological to agree with them,
are you willing to give up your car? I shall answer for you and myself
and say, "No, not yet." Nor is the average Navajo, for we are all,
East and West, in this dilemma together. Each side may romanticize
or rudely stereotype the other, but there is power and weakness in
either camp, and a new world will have to come to terms with both.

That is, despite the fact that the East and the West have for a
long time each looked at the same world with quite another feeling
tone and emphasis, each has acquired much from the other. It would
seem logical, and this point has been made many times by both Oc-
cidental and Oriental scholars, that the best of each should be
merged in a new world outlook. However, that is usually easier said
than done, and, for example, Europeans who study Zen and seek
enlightenment in Japanese monasteries are notoriously unsuccessful
in their pursuits. They go so far in training, sometimes spending a
dozen or more years before they inevitably give up. Pirsig's (1974)
marvelous book *Zen and the Art of Motorcycle Maintenance* makes
a similar point, I believe, when the Western hero of the book
descends into the hell of psychosis while seeking Zen-like enlightenment.

On the other side of the coin, how deeply affected by Western thought are the Japanese exposed to it? The best discussion of this issue I know is by Endo (1969) in his novel *Silence*. There he questions whether Japanese Christians, including those martyred by the Tokugawa regime, ever "believed" in Christ in the same way as the European priests who converted them.

If genetic differences between populations are indeed at the root of ethnic contrasts in world view, it will remain for the handful of half-breed children to create the true bridge of understanding.

FURTHER DATA

At this point, in my mind's eye I can see an extremely skeptical reader. How can this so-called scientist leap from newborns to differences in East-West philosophy and art, blithely lumping Chinese and Navajo, throwing in some ecology for good measure, and then suggest a breeding program to achieve East-West understanding? I can try to support my position with more data and observations in hope of becoming a little more credible.

The fact is that studies of children beyond infancy bear out the theme of relative unexcitability and unemotionality in Chinese as compared to Anglos. In one such study, an independent research project at the University of Chicago, Nova Green, looked at a number of nursery schools, including one in Chicago's Chinatown. An excellent observer, she reported:

> Although the majority of the Chinese-American children were in the "high arousal age," between 3 and 5, they showed little intense emotional behavior. They ran and hopped, laughed and called to one another, rode bikes and roller-skated just as the children did in the other nursery schools, but the noise level stayed remarkably low, and the emotional atmosphere projected serenity instead of bedlam. The impassive facial expression certainly gave the children an air of dignity and self-possession, but this was only one element affecting the total impression. Physical movements seemed more coordinated, no tripping, falling, bumping, or bruising was observed, nor screams, crashes, or wailing was heard, not even that common sound in other nurseries, voices raised in highly indignant moralistic dispute! No property disputes were observed, and only the mildest version of "fighting behavior," some good-natured wrestling among the older boys. The adults evidently had different expectations about hostile or impulsive behavior; this was the only nursery school where it was observed that children were trusted to duel with sticks. Personal distance spacing seemed to be situational rather than compulsive or patterned, and the children appeared to make no effort to avoid physical contact. (1969, p. 9)

It is ironic that many recent visitors to nursery schools in the People's Republic of China have returned with ecstatic descriptions of the children, with the implication that the New Order knows something about child rearing that the West does not. As an example, a group of U.S. child psychologists (Kessen et. al., 1975) reported as follows on a visit to China:

> If our observations were at all representative, the outstanding feature of childhood in China, and that which raises the most basic problem, is the high level of concentration, orderliness, and competence of children. . . . The docility did not seem to us to be the docility of surrender and apathy; the Chinese children we saw were emotionally expressive, socially gracious, and adept.
>
> We talked a great deal to teachers about the control and restraint of children; . . . . We tried, not very successfully, to describe some of the behavior problems in American schools. By and large, Chinese teachers did not understand what we were talking about; they had never seen a hyperactive or disruptive child in school. . . .
>
> We left China convinced that we had seen radically different ways of thinking about and meeting children from the ways we knew as Americans. (pp. 216–217, 221)

Strikingly similar, is it not, to Green's 1969 description of a nursery school in Chicago's Chinatown? These psychologists obviously had in mind "American" classrooms with Caucasian or Afro-American children not Chinese Americans.

As they get older, Chinese and Caucasian children continue to differ in roughly the same ways that distinguish them in nursery school. San Francisco schoolteachers, for example, consider assignments in Chinatown plum jobs—the children are dutiful and study hard; classrooms are quiet. (Incidentally, since public schools operate on a seniority system, there is a perhaps unfortunate concentration of old-time teachers in Chinatown schools.)

I already have spoken of the phenomenon of adolescent tribalism, so it will come as no surprise that in high schools in the San Francisco Chinatown area, Chinese children tend to form their own groups and Caucasians (until recently, largely Italians from the neighboring North Beach area) tend to group together as well. When we asked Chinese high schoolers why they tended to keep together and away from whites, we got such answers as "Caucasians are too emotional" or "They tend too easily to fly off the handle" or "They change too much from day to day." Caucasian attitudes were 180 degrees around, and a typical answer was, "The Chinese are okay, but they're too clannish; you never know how they feel about anything!" As far as we could see, each was right about the other, and as always each thought the other's constellation of traits not quite as human as their own. It takes a third party to see that each is as good as the other, that each group has both decent citizens and gangsters, and that the difference is largely one of style and temperament.

I can appreciate a reader's accepting these data and yet having trouble imagining how such differences might have initially come about. The easier explanation involves a historical accident based on random variety in small founding populations. Peking man, some 500,000 years ago, already had shovel-shaped incisors, as do only Orientals today, including American Indians (Coon, 1962). Very modern looking skulls of about the same age found in England do not have similar grooving on the inside of the upper incisors. Given evidence like this, we can surmise that there has been substantial and long-standing isolation of East and West. Furthermore, it is likely that environmental demands and biocultural adaptations differed, so that this separation has certainly been meaningful.

AFRO-AMERICANS

Orientals and Caucasians are not the only newborn groups we examined. We have been to Nigeria, Kenya, Sweden, Italy, India, and Australia (Darwin), examining native newborns in each place. It would take me too far from the purpose of this book to examine each group in detail, so I shall focus on the favorite topic of urban America, sometimes called its most salient dilemma (Myrdal, 1944): black-white differences.

Some fifteen independent studies of infant behavior, including our own, have been made in various parts of East and West Africa (see Freedman, 1974; Warren, 1972). Although it is clear that African tribal groups vary considerably on any number of genetic markers, there nevertheless is a certain amount of genetic homogeneity in sub-Saharan Africa peoples when compared to other racial groups. Accordingly, it is not too surprising to find certain common features at birth, and the great majority of the studies reviewed by Warren (1972) show African infants advanced in physical coordination compared to Caucasians and Orientals. Many African newborns can hold their heads erect, and I have seen a Nigerian Hausa 24-hour old almost turn himself over. Black children

Many Australian Aboriginal and Afro-American babies could lift their heads immediately after birth, whereas few Japanese infant's could do so.

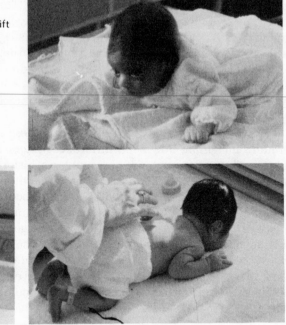

walk at an average age of eleven months, compared to twelve months in Caucasians and thirteen months in American Indians.*

Afro-Americans are just about as advanced although the newborn's abilities are somewhere between American Caucasian and black African. This pattern follows a genetic hypothesis very well since in the population we call Afro-American on average in Northern cities 27% of the genes are of European origin (Stern, 1973).

My conclusion? Africans and Afro-Americans are indeed exceedingly well coordinated in infancy—and, yes, thereafter, too. Any American sports buff knows that were it not for the Afro-American, our Olympic track record would be mediocre. Why else were blacks excluded from big league baseball for so long? They were simply too good to allow in, and the fear was they would "take over" baseball. American blacks do "own" basketball on both the college and the professional level, and as I understand it the entrepreneurial worry is that white fans will lose interest if teams become all-black, as they easily might. And where in the standings would an allwhite baseball

---

* Hallet (1975) has reported that pygmies of the Ituri Forest mature at astoundingly fast rates: they engage in social smiling by one month, sit and reach for objects by three months, walk and even run by six months, and say some 150 words by one year. Hallet reports that, in general, they develop at twice the rate of other people.

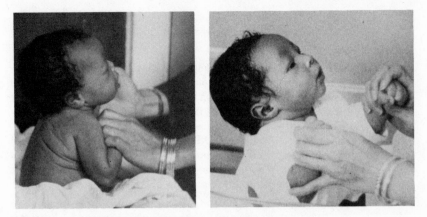

Kenyan (Kikuyu) and Afro-American newborns in sitting position, holding heads erect.

or football team end up today? As for boxing, are there any nonblacks on the heavyweight championship horizon?

I would like to quote from *Human Infancy* (Freedman, 1974), where I addressed this issue in some detail:

It should be acknowledged that the apparent genetically based motor precocity in African infants is a touchy issue to some and logical discussions have suffered as a result. Ainsworth (1967), for example, in an otherwise excellent study, first reported motor precocity at birth in her Ghanda (Uganda) sample and then explained the continued motor precocity with speculation about maternal permissiveness and "postural adjustment to being held and carried during the earliest months" (p. 328). At no time, did she seriously consider genetic differences as a possibility, although logic would immediately suggest such a hypothesis, given its early onset.

Similarly, Geber, who had been among the first to report relative motor precocity at birth among the Ghanda, somehow omitted these data in explaining a later study of older Ghanda infants. There she emphasized the availability, nurturance, and physical closeness of the mother to the infant (Geber, 1958) as the basis for the perceived differences. Geber and Dean (1958) went on to say, but presented no data, that African infants of the Europeanized middle class were less precocious than those of the lower class, implying that the difference was due to differences in rearing. Leiderman et al. (1973) do present data, and to the opposite effect. They report that middle-class Kikuyu infants in Kenya were more advanced in both the mental and motor scales of the Bayley Test than were lower-class infants. Such differences are understandable, given decisive differences in nutrition favoring the middle classes, and unlike Geber's claim, make considerable sense.

Warren (1972), in a most helpful review of infant testing in sub-Saharan Africa, found evidence for African motor precocity in 10 out of 12 studies which were adequately conducted. (Two other studies were deemed inadequate.) Despite this apparently decisive ratio, Warren chose to favor the results of the two studies which yielded no differences. We can only assume that these apparently illogical positions have been taken because of the taboo on genetic explanations of ethnic differences seen in recent decades and the related problems of racism.

Apparently one of the difficulties in the above findings involves the ill-intentioned hypothesis that human groups which exhibit motor precocity are "less sapient" in that the hominid line has been characterized by progressive infantilization. It is therefore important to report a recent study of Freedman and Stribey (unpublished data, 1973) using the Cambridge Neonatal Scales with 31 newborns of Punjabi extraction. The Punjabis are a Caucasian group of Northern India who have been highly successful economically in New Delhi, where the study was done. Our data indicate that this group is the most motorically precocious of any group yet seen, including African and Australian aboriginal newborns. They had the strongest neck muscling of any group as indicated by the highest average *pull-to-sit* and the best ability to support body weight as indicated by the highest average straightening-of-legs response. Thus, within the one race of Caucasians, differences wide enough to encompass the other groups have been found, and it would appear that motor precocity is related to localized adaptations rather than to broad phyletic trends. We hope these findings will help lay to rest unwarranted and mischievous speculation regarding the relative phyletic position of one or another group of mankind. (pp. 169–170)

With regard to this last point, Berry Brazelton, in his Cambridge pediatric practice, has encountered a number of middle-class black mothers who are bothered by their baby's motor precocity apparently because of the insidious logic referred to in the quoted passage. I must therefore emphasize that there is no genetic likelihood either that two such disparate systems as motor precocity and intelligence are controlled by neighboring genes or that the genes of one system play a major role in modifying the other. It is perfectly possible to be both smart and well coordinated. The work of Louis Terman (1925) at Stanford University resolved this issue long ago.

RACISM

Most biological scientists are in conflict over the issue of race. Although race is a reasonably useful term in discussing the distributions of plants and animals, its use in descriptions of human populations is too often pejorative and its history too often laden with evil. Some scientists have therefore set out to disprove the term's usefulness on biostatistical grounds.

In a very important study based on the relative frequency of blood groups and blood proteins around the world, Lewontin (1972) calculated that 85% of human genetic diversity is accounted for by individual variation within groups; 15%, by differences between groups. Now 15% is a sizable portion of human diversity and I am inclined to make much of that figure, especially since blood groups provide conservative estimates of group differences. Recall that serological comparisons between the chimpanzee and man show us to have been a single species a mere four million years ago—an impossibly small figure, the more usual estimate being on the order of twenty million years (Campbell, 1966). Blood factors are thus extremely conservative indicators of population differences and tend not to change with environmental pressures as do such polygenic traits as stature, nose form, or skin pigmentation (Nei and Roychoudbury, 1974).

Lewontin, however, chose to stress the finding that there is more diversity within races than between races and concluded his study as follows:

> Human racial classification is of no social value and is positively destructive of social and human relations. Since such racial classification is now seen to be of virtually no genetic or taxonomic significance either, no justification can be offered for its continuance. (1972, p. 397)

Although I agree with Lewontin's motives, he is in effect howling into the wind. If you are white, I am black, and my neighbor is Asian, we all know we belong to different races, and no professorial pronouncement will change that. Biostatistical data are simply not the answer to interethnic and interracial rivalry and suspicions.

If, as I claim, these antagonisms are more or less built into the species, what is there to do, say, in the U.S.? Frankly, I think the only sound solution lies in miscegenation.* The real heroes of America's

---

* In the long run (over thousands of years) it is clear that there has been an ebb and flow in the relative homozygosity of human groups; human history and

racial standoff are the intermarrieds and their children. It takes courage to break ethnic boundaries and hard work to maintain one's own ancestral ties while building new ones through a "strange" mate. A Marxist or Christian fellowship may serve to introduce the couple, but it is their union and their children, not rhetoric or preaching, that will help bridge racial divisions. And tolerant neighborhoods, such as Chicago's Hyde Park, are needed to support these families. The young people of today can be such heroes and help engineer these bridges if they have the courage and the desire to do so.

However, as I have said before, I am not so starryeyed as to believe that miscegenation will soon replace the general trend toward homogamy (marriage within ethnic or racial boundaries). Here is where my Jeffersonian-Marxism shows and where I certainly join forces with Lewontin. Unless we have a healthy economy and insure that everyone who wants to work can do so, and, conversely, as long as some groups suffer more when layoff time arrives, we will see intergroup enmities flourish. Our nation was founded by men and women of conscience, and it has been the continuous pressure by later Americans of conscience that has led to the progress in justice we have experienced. We know, too, that selfishness abounds, at all levels of life, but the United States has nevertheless always been a country that, at a basic level, knows right from wrong. That is, despite our selfish genes, a strong group morality persists. And it is this abstract fairness, or generalized altruism, that holds the promise for our and other nations.

---

prehistory has certainly been characterized by the miscegenation of formerly exclusive groups and their reconstitution into newly exclusive groups (e.g. Darlington, 1969).

Appendix

ABSTRACTS OF ORIGINAL STUDIES IN
HUMAN ETHOLOGY AND SOCIOBIOLOGY

Although I deem all these studies interesting, they clearly vary in quality. They range from the well thought out, closely supervised studies one expects in a Ph.D. thesis, to the somewhat less demanding M.A. thesis, down to generally inventive but nonrigorous term papers (the majority). The latter are included because of the hypotheses they tested and because their publication may indeed lead to more rigorous studies. The complete papers or theses are on file in my office at the Committee on Human Development, University of Chicago.

In these studies p, or probability level, refers to the probability that a result was obtained by chance alone. For example, $p < .001$ means that there is less than one chance in a thousand that the results are merely a sampling error and, therefore, that it is a significant result. NS means a result was not significant. The symbol r refers to a correlation from 0 (no correlation) to 1 (perfect correlation), and things may correlate either directly or inversely (negatively). S means subject of the experiment (children, infants, adults), E means experimenter, and N means number of subjects. Various statistical analyses were used, with Chi-square (X^2) the most common.

CHAPTER 2

Study 1   Koschmann, N. L. An application of sociobiological theory to the phenomenon of inter-racial adoption by fertile couples

CHAPTER 4

24   Lawrence, M. Sex differences in style and content in children's drawings

25   Costanzo, R. Sex differences in attention structure among sixth graders

26   Snow, R. B. Sex differences in parenting in the middle years

27   Weisfeld, G. E. A longitudinal study of dominance in boys

28   Post, H. Sense of humor: A study of male-female differences in children

29   Parker, R. Social hierarchies in same sex peer groups

CHAPTER 6

Study 30   Lang, F. Mate choice in the human female: A study of height preferences

31   Travis, M. Height differentials in male and female dyads

32   Laser, J. Infant reactions to adult and child strangers

33   Horowitz, S. Infants' fear of strangers: Reactions to a red or white mask

34   Dan, A. J. Aspects of visual interaction in human social life

35   Edelman, M. S. An evolutionary approach to staring encounters and to the development of dominance hierarchies

36   Goren, C. G. Form perception, innate form preferences, and visually mediated head turning in the human neonate

37   Magaziner, J. An ethological perspective on eye contact in newborns

38   Bare, J. Infants' reactions to dilated and constricted pupils of an adult stranger in a naturalistic setting: A preliminary investigation

39   Parker, R. An empirical investigation into the effects of beardedness on perception of social situations

40   Kubey, R. W. Dominance and submission in presidential politics: A sociobiological view

41   Hoard, S. Threat display

42   Whitaker, A. Baring one's chest: Ethological and evolutionary perspectives

43   Winstan, F. J. An inquiry into the adaptive significance of pubertal voice change

CHAPTER 7

CHAPTER 9

STUDY 1: An Application of Sociobiological Theory to the Phenomenon of Inter-racial Adoption by Fertile Couples

Nancy Lee Koschmann (1977)

Method

The data for this paper are limited. They were gleaned from responses on returned questionnaires ($N = 10$), notes from 20 adoptive parent meetings that I facilitated in Tokyo for International Social Service, and case records from four family therapies that involved interracial adoption conducted during 1973–1976. All the parents involved had both biological as well as adopted children with one exception: a couple who adopted four children and underwent voluntary sterilization. In every case, at least 50% of the child's racial endowment differed from that of the mother and usually from that of the father as well. Several of the families ($N = 4$) had adopted both interracially and intraracially.

The Individual

Most parents stated "concern over world population" as their reason for limiting their own reproduction and adopting children to fulfill their desire

for several children. One family forewent biological reproduction completely and adopted four black youngsters. Five couples limited themselves
to one biological offspring, but two of these later had accidental pregnancies
that they declined to terminate. The remaining couples had between two and
four biological children and became concerned over the population problem
after the birth of their last child.

Most calls made to the welfare agency requesting information on adoption are made by women. In the Tokyo parent groups, most wives had made
the suggestion to adopt and set about convincing their husbands of the
merits of the plan. Adoption may initially, then, be more directly satisfying
to women and hence motivate the female more than the male.

The implication for cross-racial adoption is that of a possible mismatch
between the child-raising practices of the adopting parents and the disposition of the adopted child. Such a mismatch could result in the child's being
labeled "difficult," "hyperactive," "unexpressive," or "passive." There is
evidence from the data that this in fact occurs. Three couples listed their
Japanese and Chinese children as "passive, easily swayed, and
unaggressive." Two couples who adopted black youngsters and one who
received an East Indian child described them as "hyperactive and
impulsive." A black woman who adopted a white Korean toddler found the
child so passive that she characterized him as "dull, unrewarding, and un-
challenging." Much has apparently to do with expectation. For example,
parents living in the country from which the adopted child comes accept differences in temperament with less surprise and difficulty than parents who
receive a foreign child at home. Two responding couples had adopted
Korean children in the United States and stated that they were "easy" and
"took less time" than their biological children. However, two of the four
therapy cases in Tokyo were American families who had adopted Korean
children in Japan and apparently expected Japanese-like infants. The Oriental stereotype of the Korean is that of a strong, stubborn, and competitive individual. Both of these American families lived and worked among the
Japanese and found that their adopted children encountered difficulties with
peers and at school because of their personalities. In neither case did the
community know that the children were of Korean nationality.

Exactly half the sample indicated experience with negative reactions
from relatives and the community. Even with adoption by sterile couples, the
act is looked upon with reservation, pity, and suspicion. First, most people
do assume that blood is important and there is a tendency to see sterile
adults as "handicapped" or abnormal. Unfortunately, the inability to produce offspring sometimes signifies a lack of masculinity on the part of the
male (as offspring are proof of the completed sex act). Adoption is therefore
seen as second best. Second, adopted children are assumed to be illegitimate
with all that that entails. Third, many physical and some mental conditions
are inherited, and there is constant fear that the child will at some time
manifest a dreaded symptom.

Most adopting parents reported that they felt their parents respected
and admired their decision and that the differences were over the value of
"blood." For instance, in one case pertinent to this paper in many ways, the
great-grandfather of the wife, who himself had raised four biological

children, one adopted child, and twenty-four foster children; the wife's parents, who had raised three biological children and one Chinese adopted daughter; and the husband's parents, who had raised four biological children and one Eskimo-Indian adopted child (both spouses had adopted cousins as well), all actively urged further biological reproduction while encouraging adoption. The reason they all gave was the same: "You owe the world your good genes."

STUDY 2:   Dominance-Submission Behaviors and Hierarchies in Young Adolescents in a Summer Camp

Richard C. Savin-Williams (1977)

This study is discussed in detail in Chapter 3. Here is a typology of "styles" found in the eight cabin groups. Not all types were represented in each cabin; neither did each cabin have only one of each type. Some individuals did not fit into any classification (10%).

Females

MATERNAL LEADERS (4 alphas)   Subtle when dominating others; frequently directed others, giving unsolicited advice in regard to proper dress, manners, grooming, etc.; perceived by peers as a source of security and support; described as confident, loyal, kindhearted, and manipulative.

Pubertally mature; older; heavy in weight; most popular with peers; liked by cabin counselor; intelligent; youngest child in the family; one of the lowest in cabin on socioeconomic status.

ANTAGONISTS (3 betas, 1 gamma, 1 delta)   Overt when dominating; frequently initiated counterdominance behaviors—and successful when so behaving; not successful in verbal exchanges (verbal control and verbal directives); most actively involved in cabin dominance-submission interactions; the mood setters; described as assertive and aggressive individuals who imposed themselves on others, frequently enticing others to break camp rules; charismatic and spirited individuals who were considered by counselors and administrators as problem campers; negative leadership.

Physically mature; in every cabin the best athlete was an antagonist; all returning campers; wealthy families; one of youngest in the family; all had older brothers; initially popular with peers but became unpopular as camp progressed; most disliked by cabin counselor.

AMORPHOUS MISS AVERAGE (1 beta, 2 gammas, 1 delta)   Distinguishing pattern was the lack of a pattern—average in most indices and settings; one of least involved in cabin dominance-submission interactions; fell in dominance as camp progressed; described as nondescript, placid, shy, neat, quiet, "just there," and "the most forgettable character"; superficially at peace with self.

Youngest; tallest; heaviest; three of four first-year campers; large families; all had sisters; liked by cabin counselor; perceived as having potential for leadership, but not manifested behaviorally.

COMPLIANT CLINGERS (2 deltas, 4 omegas) Frequently recognized the superior status of others; frequent givers of favors and compliments; behaved as if a hand servant; did best during verbal control; set self up to be picked on—a position of vulnerability; constantly monitored surrounds; described as friendly, talkative, and extroverted; cabinmates avoided her, considering her an embarrassment; a clinger (physically) if one shows affection or attention.

Males

LEADERS (3 alphas) Subtle when dominating; frequent initiator of verbal directives and receiver of recognition; most successful when displacing, least so when counterdominating; most dominant during athletic game; decreased in participation in cabin dominance-submission interactions over time; a leader during cabin discussions.

Pubertally mature, physically fittest; best or next best athlete in each cabin; most handsome; intelligent; wealthy families; had younger brothers; best or least liked by peers; most liked by cabin counselor; described by peers as dominant, the leader, rich, handsome, bully, athletic, popular, stubborn, and strong; they agreed with this assessment.

BULLIES (1 alpha, 2 gammas) Most successful when threatening or physically asserting self—but not during verbal exchanges (verbal control and ridicule) or discussions; overranked selves on dominance sociometrics; saw self as being more positive (handsome, masculine, smart, and strong) than peers saw them: stubborn, loud, bullish.

Physically mature; youngest; tallest; heaviest; physically fit; average to good athlete (due to physical size and not so much natural athletic ability); all from large families; all had older sisters; most disliked by peers.

FUNNY DUMMIES (1 beta, 1 delta, 1 gamma) Successful when ridiculing and during mealtimes—not during cabin activities; considered by peers to have leadership skills but not manifested in behavior; described by peers as funny, friendly, and "dumb."

Physically immature; shortest; lightest; second best athlete in cabin; from wealthy and large families; a middle child with a younger sister; most popular with peers but not with cabin counselor; lowest on intelligence (Wechsler Verbal Scale).

QUIET FOLLOWERS (2 deltas, 2 epsilons) All were omegas at one point during camp; successful at counterdominance; unsuccessful when directing others; infrequent participants in dominance-submission interactions; described as mature, quiet, "dumb."

Oldest; short; lightweight; poor athletes; least handsome; two were new campers; not popular among peers, becoming even less so as camp progressed.

WHIMPS (4 omegas) Most successful when verbally arguing; most subordinate during threats and recognition behaviors; ideas ignored by group during discussions; described as weak, submissive, poor, friendly, religious, and nonleaders; they agreed with this assessment.

Childlike pubertally; short; lightweight; least physically fit; last or next to last in athletic ability; lowest on socioeconomic status.

STUDY 3:   Sex Differences in Manipulation in Young Children

Suzanne Gaskins (1973)

Observed children (estimated ages: three to eight years) manipulating self-operated exhibits at the Museum of Science and Industry. More boys were observed manipulating the exhibits, but more boys passed each exhibit, too; so the proportion of children exposed to an exhibit who stopped to manipulate it did not show a sex difference.

| | Number of children manipulating | | Number exposed | |
	Male	Female	Male	Female
Exhibit 1	14	6	29	11
Exhibit 2	12	8	25	15
Exhibit 3	13	7	22	18

The number of boys and girls entering the museum was found to be about equal. Therefore, it was concluded that the boys must cover more ground in the museum than the girls, thus both passing and manipulating more exhibits.

STUDY 4:   Sexual Dimorphism of Children's Block Constructions

Lawrence J. Gianinno (1972)

This small-scale comparative study attempted to reassess Erik Erikson's 1951 study of genital modes and spatial modalities in block building play among children to determine whether the sexual dimorphism that Erikson found in 11-, 12-, and 13-year-olds held true for younger children.

Subjects were nine boys and nine girls, aged six to eight, in a middle-class, urban, private school. They were given wood blocks in a small room and instructed to build whatever they wanted on the table provided.

For both sexes, with increasing age, the time spent in block play decreased. Boys, in contrast to girls, spent more time in building ($p < .10$), used more blocks ($p < .05$), and utilized a greater variety of blocks, often building elaborate ornaments. Boys were more apt to build tunnels, lanes, and buildings— constructions expressing the concepts of transmission and structure.

STUDY 5: Sexual Differences in Scores on a Reading Test

Michael Long (1975)

The study demonstrated that it is possible to construct a reading test that by its design allows males to score higher than females.

Long's test parallels the embedded figures perceptual restructuring task. A moderately difficult magazine article was included among several article excerpts and short, one-page articles of completely unrelated material. After reading the material in the order presented, individuals were administered a true/false test, including 11 questions on the main article and 4 questions on the unrelated material. Six male and 6 female college students were tested. To score well, it was posited, an individual had to pick out and retain key concepts in the central article, while inhibiting or keeping separate the "noise" represented by the unrelated material. It was hypothesized males would score higher than females.

The mean score for males was found to be 20% higher than the mean score for females, representing a difference of over one standard deviation in the means. No differences in Ss' average scores between the article and the unrelated material were found. A biological theory by Broverman was discussed as one explanation for the findings of sex differences in cognitive performance (Broverman et al., 1968).

STUDY 6: Dimorphism in Seated Postures

Susan Blanck (1971)

Male and female differences in seated postures were observed in a college library. During seven days forty young adults were observed as they read in armchairs and in desk chairs.

Consistent sex differences were noted. Females tended to sit with rounded shoulders and chin tucked in, with the body bent forward at the waist; legs were held close to or curled under the body or were crossed at the knees; free hands and extra clothing (coats) were usually laid on the abdomen or in some manner close to or touching the body. Males, on the other hand, tended to hold their shoulders straight and head high with the torso comparatively straight; legs were either stretched out in front with little bend or crossed with knees apart; a free hand was usually placed on a table or chair away from the body, with extra clothing placed wherever convenient.

Further research should focus on the confirmation of sexual dimorphism in seating posture cross-culturally and developmentally, particularly on how early in life these sexual differences in body posture can be universally noted.

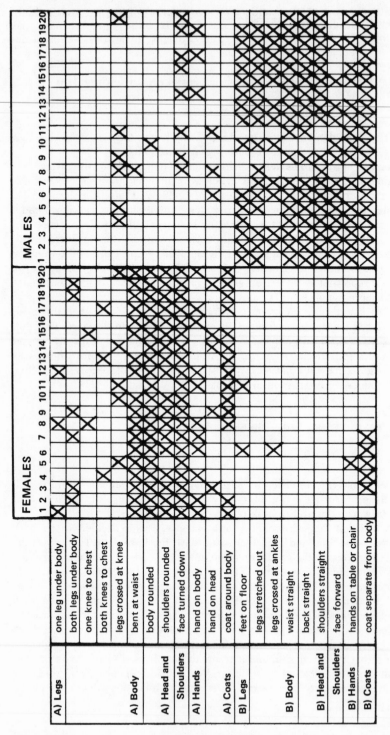

*N = 40 (20 females, 20 males).

STUDY 7: Sex Differences in the Sleep Postures of Three- and Four-Year Olds

Jeanne Kinnard (1973)

The paper hypothesized sexual dimorphism in the relaxed positions of sleeping children with females tending toward more closed, rounded positions and males toward more extended positions.

Ten males and ten females, aged three to four, were observed by the author while they slept in a Montessori school and in a day care center.

A composite picture of each child's body positioned during the thirty minutes of sleep revealed that the girls tended toward a rounded, closed position whereas boys showed no conclusive trend, indicating a possible developmental change from a rounded to a more extended sleeping posture. Females slept predominantly on their sides; males were more apt than females to sleep on their stomachs. This female body form was related to Blanck's (Appendix Study 6) study of the seating posture among college students.

STUDY 8: Dimorphism in Carrying Books

Linda Haraszti (1972)

The object of this project was to test the author's casual observation that males and females tended to carry their books in different ways. The hypothesis was that more females carried their books clutched to the chest than did males. The author tested her hypothesis by photographing a series of persons as they entered the University of Chicago library. Every person carrying books was photographed until a sufficient number of each sex was sampled. The Ss, 37 males and 36 females, were not aware they were being photographed.

Each picture was examined to determine whether the S was carrying books clutched to the chest. The operational definition of clutched to the chest was as follows: books had to be touching the ventral part of the trunk between waist and neck and the major part of the books had to be above the waist.

Of the 72 Ss sampled, 12 males and 33 females carried their books clutched to the chest; 25 males and 3 females did not. A Chi-square analysis of this difference in behavior by sex yielded a p of .001.

In seeking an evolutionary explanation for this difference, the author speculated that relatively greater size and strength in the male's hands may account for their tendency to carry books in the hand with the arm extended down against the body. The weaker females might need the extra support of the arms to carry the same load as comfortably. This explanation suggests that there might be correlation between the weight of the load and the manner of support, however, and apparently no such correlation was found.

The author also speculated that covering the breasts in nonsexual situations could be a female tendency—perhaps to prevent the attraction of males other than one's mate. It seems unlikely that this explanation accounts adequately for the degree of consistency observed in the behavior of the females sampled.

A final possibility could be that females, whose evolutionary history has involved carrying and nursing infants, have developed a greater tendency to cuddle, or cradle, carried objects to their chest. The author concluded that there may have evolved a generalized difference in the female's use of the hands and arms.

STUDY 9:   A Study of Left-Lateral Preference in the Holding of Infants

Rich Perline (1975)

The study examined the extent to which left-lateral preference, found to be a preferred mode among mothers, is differentially found among males and females aged six years to sexual maturity. Three hypotheses were examined: (1) mothers exhibit more left-lateral preference than any other group; (2) females of reproductive age display a degree of left-lateral preference intermediate between that shown by mothers and by males of reproductive age; (3) individuals at reproductive age show more left-lateral preference than individuals of their sex at prereproductive ages, with adolescents falling at an intermediate level.

Subjects formed four groups: group I: 83 F and 49 M, aged 6–12; group II: 47M and 30F, aged 13–17; group III: 57 M and 55 F single individuals over age 18; group IV: 13 mothers of newborns. A small doll was placed on a table. Each S, centered in front, was asked to lift the doll the way he would if it were a real baby. Lateral preference was determined by the side of the S's midline on which the lifted doll's head was placed. The handedness of each S was recorded.

The highest proportion of left-lateral preference was observed among mothers. Females in each group over the age of 13 were found to exhibit significantly more left preference than males at any age or the youngest group of females. Group I females had significantly lower preference than females of group II ($p < .05$) and group III ($p < .05$). Group I males also had significantly lower left preference than males of group II ($p < .01$) or group III ($p < .05$). No significant differences were observed for either sex in left preference between groups II and III. Left-lateral preference was shown to be independent of handedness, although the small sample of left-handed Ss precluded rigorous testing of this hypothesis.

STUDY 10:   Sex Differences in Infant Smiling

Marty DeBoer (1974)

In a study of sex differences in newborn (reflexive) smiling, the author observed 23 two-day-old infants. The 9 male and 14 female full-term infants were all normal, black, and bottlefed. A nurse delivered each infant swad-

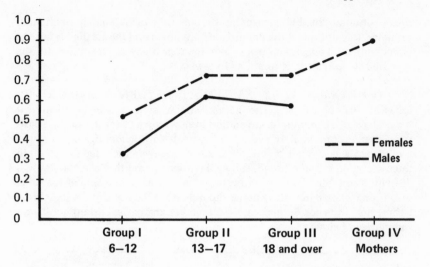

PROPORTIONS OF RIGHT-HANDED Ss HOLDING DOLL ON LEFT, BY AGE GROUP AND SEX

dled in its crib to the E so that the sex was not apparent. None of the males had as yet been circumcised. The observations were done within 90 minutes of the infants' last feed, and all infants were predominantly in a light sleep or drowsy state during the 10-minute observation period. During the observation, the author recorded any indications of smiling into one of three categories: full smiling (at least one second), assymetrical smiling, and fleeting smiles (short jerks of the corners of the mouth). The results are summarized in the table that follows. The female infants were observed to exhibit more smiling of all types, but especially fleeting smiles, where the difference was statistically significant ($p < .05$, two-tailed, Mann-Whitney U).

Ss	Frequency of Smiles		
	Full	Assymetrical	Fleeting
Female (N = 14)	27 $\overline{X} = 1.9$	25 $\overline{X} = 1.8$	169 $\overline{X} = 12.0$
Male (N = 9)	6 $\overline{X} = 0.7$	10 $\overline{X} = 1.1$	49 $\overline{X} = 5.4$
Difference by sex	NS	NS combined NS	Significant at .05 level

STUDY 11:   Human Smiling Behavior: Sex-Linked?

Constance Wolfe (1971)

The purpose of the study was to see whether women smile more than men in impersonal situations. The author hypothesized that an impersonal social situation might correspond to one in which, among nonhuman primates, the attitude of the dominant is unknown and the "smile" is used to deflect potential aggression from a dominant or unknown species mate. She specified three questions in all, as follows:

DO WOMEN, WHEN SMILED AT, RETURN A SMILE MORE OFTEN THAN MEN? The author and a male colleague positioned themselves at a commuter-train station in downtown Chicago during a post-rush hour. Approximately every tenth person with whom eye contact was established was given a broad smile. Responses were recorded on a zero to three scale: no smile to broad, full smile. It was found that eye contact was difficult to establish in this setting, especially so with members of the same sex. Young women in their twenties did not return the smile of the female experimenter. Data for 60 male and 60 female (largely Caucasian) adults are summarized below:

Rating of smile	Males				Females			
	Female *E*	Male *E*	*Total*		Female *E*	Male *E*	*Total*	
0	13	25	38	(63%)	9	18	27	(45%)
1	8	1	9		15	9	24	
2	5	2	7	(36%)	3	0	3	(55%)
3	4	2	6		3	3	6	

A Chi-square comparing frequency of men and women smilers and nonsmilers indicated that the difference in frequency was significant at the .05 level. That is, in impersonal situations women are apparently more likely to return a smile than are men. It is of interest to note that the male *E* received fewer smiles from both male and female Ss.

DO WOMEN, IN OTHER IMPERSONAL SITUATIONS, SMILE MORE THAN MEN? In this portion of the investigation, the author watched 10 males and 10 females at each of three different sales counters as they transacted their business. If more than one smile was observed, the one with the highest rating was recorded. Although the results varied somewhat across the three situations (a pastry counter, a train ticket window, and a short-order food counter), it seems likely that this could be accounted for by the age and sex of the salespersons at the particular location. Despite the variance in the proportion of men and women smilers, the women smiled more in each of these settings, and the results summarized across conditions were nearly identical to those reported in the preceding table. In the case of these 30 male and 30 female Ss, 37% of the males smiled, 53% of the females did so.

THE AUTHOR ASKED PEOPLE WHETHER, IN THEIR OPINION, MEN OR WOMEN DID MORE SMILING It was not surprising to discover that people's opinion supported the author's hypothesis that females do more smiling. The only part of the population sampled who felt that men smiled more than women were women aged 18 to 25—and such undoubtedly was their experience.

STUDY 12:   Sex-Linked Status Differentiation in Smiling
Sharon Rose (1972)

Rose hypothesized that smiling is an appeasement behavior. Relying on the assumptions that the smile occurs more frequently in individuals of low dominance and less so in high-ranking individuals and that "average females" perceive themselves and are perceived by others as relatively less dominant than males, the author predicted that smiling would occur more frequently in females.

Rose observed 382 Ss who walked by her on a street corner at the University of Chicago. The criteria for selection as a S were as follows: (1) the person was within a larger group of people while at the same time (2) the person was not engaged in conversation. These criteria were imposed with the idea that such persons would be exhibiting "essentially nondirected (but not nonsocial) smiles" and that smiles elicited from the context of conversations, for example, would be avoided.

Each individual who passed by and satisfied the criteria was classified and recorded as a smiling or nonsmiling male or female. Of the 158 females observed, 47 (29.7%) were classified as smiling. A total of 224 males was observed, with 36 (16.7%) of them smiling. A Chi-square value of 10.2 was computed, indicating that the sex difference in these frequencies was significant at the .01 level. The author interpreted smiling behavior in the context specified in the study "as a sort of generalized appeasement behavior" serving to prevent or forestall "any confrontation with a superordinate individual."

STUDY 13:   Sex-Correlated   Differences   in   Human   Smiling Behavior: A Preliminary Investigation
James Dickson McLean (1971)

McLean used yearbook photographs as his data in an investigation of sex correlated differences in human smiling behavior. Yearbooks of high school and college at the University of Chicago and of another neighborhood high school were used to examine smiling behavior in the formal (graduation) portraits of over 3,000 S. Smiling was operationally defined as an expression in which all or any part of the teeth were showing. Judgments of smiling or nonsmiling were made and recorded by sex for each individual photographed. In all, 15 samples were processed, including high-school and college seniors for the years 1931, 1939, 1956, 1962, and 1965. All but one of these samples were predominantly or exclusively Caucasian; the single largest sample was entirely black. Chi-square computations were made for each sample and for the total sample.

In each sample, as well as the total sample, a larger proportion of females was classified as smiling. For most of these samples, the difference in frequency was significant, and where significance was not reached, the trend persisted. The results of this study are summarized in the following table. (Samples of Australian Aboriginals and Navajo have been added to McLean's data.)

Samples	Percentage Smiling		X^2	$p <$
	Males	Females		
College Seniors				
(U. of Chicago)				
1965	22	36	8.72	.005
1962	38	83	23.30	.0005
1956	29	46	2.80	.05
1939	15	49	43.02	.0005
1931	3	16	20.56	.0005
H. S. Seniors				
(Hyde Park H. S.)				
1966 (black)	57	69	8.70	.005
(U. of Chicago Lab School)				
1965	50	75	11.04	.0005
1962	48	61	2.35	.10
1956	43	64	1.80	.10
1939	0	47	26.49	.0005
1931	8	18	2.99	.05
H. S. Juniors (Lab)				
1965	38	69	12.57	.0005
H. S. Sophomores (Lab)				
1965	39	68	11.65	.0005
H. S. Freshmen (Lab)				
1965	42	71	13.96	.0005 ·
Junior H. S. Seniors (Lab)				
1965	39	70	12.85	.0005
Total	31	56		
Australian Aboriginal				
(Kormilda College, 1972)	69	78	1.49	.10
Navajo (Methodist Mission H. S.,				
1962–1970)	13	24	2.76	.05

STUDY 14: The Relation of Gazing and Smiling Behaviors to Status and Sex in Interacting Pairs of Children

Susan Beekman (1970)

Beekman studied children's smiling and gazing behaviors in relation to their sex and status in the classroom dominance hierarchy. The 32 Ss were drawn from two first- and third-grade classes in the University of Chicago Lab School. These children had participated in a larger study for which each child ranked his classmates on a dominance hierarchy defined as "toughness." The Ss chosen for this study were the eight members of each class whose peers had ranked them nearest the top or bottom of the classroom hierarchy. These high- and low-status boys and girls were paired in all possible combinations of status and sex, making a total of six cross-sex and six same-sex pairs for each class. The order in which the pairs interacted was randomized as much as possible.

The interaction of the pairs consisted of a drawing phase in which the children were asked to draw a picture together and an interview phase during which an adult asked them a series of questions regarding their picture and the relationship between them. Both phases of interaction were videotaped. The videotaped records were then analyzed for percentage of total interaction time spent in seven types of smiling and gazing behaviors. Since more time was spent gazing and smiling in the interview phase, and essentially the same trends appeared in both phases, data were reported for all 48 pairs in the interview phase and for 24 pairs in the drawing phase. Results are given below for each of the gazing and smiling variables.

PERCENTAGE OF TIME SPENT GAZING AT PEER In all same-sex pairs of different status, the low-status child spent a greater percentage of time ($p < .04$) gazing at the high-status partner than the latter spent gazing back (see Part 1 of Beekman's table). In same-sex pairs of similar status, the relative percentage of time spent gazing was not consistently related to their perception of which child was tougher.

In cross-sex pairings (see Part 2 of the table), the girls spent more time gazing at the boys than vice versa ($p < .05$). An examination of 16 children's behavior across the four possible conditions revealed the following general pattern: (1) High-status boys tended to spend less time gazing than any of their partners; (2) both low-status boys and high-status girls tended to spend more time gazing than the boys with whom they were paired but less time than the girls with whom they were paired; and (3) low-status girls tended to gaze more than any of their partners except other low-status girls.

Pairs of high- and low-status boys did very little gazing during the drawing phase. All other findings for the interview phase held for the drawing phase.

PERCENTAGE OF TIME SPENT IN MUTUAL GAZING In same-sex pairs, the mean percentage of time spent in mutual gazing was greater for children of similar status than for pairs with unequal status (except in the case of first grade girls). In the first-grade group, mutual gazing was greater for same-sex pairs than for cross-sex pairs, but the reverse was true for third-grade boys. The results for the drawing phase were the same as for the interview.

PERCENTAGE MUTUAL GAZING GREATER THAN CHANCE This measure was calculated by multiplying the percentage of time S^1 gazes at S^2 times the percentage of time S^2 gazes at S^1 and subtracting this number from the actual percentage of mutual gazing of the pair. The value of this variable was about half that of variable 2 for most interactions and followed a similar pattern. In same-sex pairs, the percentage mutual gazing greater than chance was increased in similar status pairs for both age groups. The

Mean Percentage Gazing At Peer
Part 1 Same-sex, unequal status pairs

		High-status child	Low-status child
First grade	Boys	7.22	19.52
	Girls	11.90	16.80
Third grade	Boys	3.65	8.50
	Girls	13.19	27.06

Part 2 Cross-sex Pairs

	Boys	Girls
First grade	8.82	17.35
Third grade	12.27	18.31

Mean Percentage Smiling
Part 3 Same-sex, unequal status pairs

		High-status child	Low-status child
First grade	Boys	51.25	42.54
	Girls	21.78	47.60
Third grade	Boys	20.50	25.83
	Girls	34.69	70.34

Part 4 Cross-sex pairs

		Pairs with high-status girls	Pairs with low-status girls
First grade	Boys	21.21	28.11
	Girls	13.88	39.41
Third grade	Boys	27.91	26.95
	Girls	25.93	51.55

comparison of same- and cross-sex pairs on this variable followed the pattern described for mutual gazing.

PERCENTAGE OF TIME SPENT SMILING   As shown in Part 3 of the table, a low-status girl smiled more than her high-status counterpart, but this was not the case for pairs of low- and high-status boys.

In cross-sex interactions (Part 4), low-status girls almost always smiled more than their partners, except when they were paired with other low-status girls. High-status girls nearly always smiled less than their partners, except when interacting with other high-status girls. Nearly all boys smiled more than high-status girls and less than low-status girls.

PERCENTAGE OF TIME SPENT SMILING BROADLY   The patterns here resemble those reported for variable 4.

NUMBER OF GIGGLES PER MINUTE   Similar relationships held as for variables 4 and 5 in same- and cross-sex interactions. Low-status girls giggled more frequently than their high-status counterparts, although no such pattern appeared for the boys.

PERCENTAGE OF TIME SPENT TALKING   The mean percentage of time spent talking was greater for high-status than for low-status first graders, but this was not the case in the third grade. At both grade levels the mean percentage of time spent talking was greater for boys than for girls. This relationship was reversed in the drawing phase.

STUDY 15:   Competitive Behavior in Sex-Segregated and Sex-Integrated Children's Groups

Carol Lynn Cronin (1977)

Two experiments were conducted to examine the competitive behavior of young adolescents in sex segregated and sex integrated situations. The first experiment was an athletic competition. It was hypothesized that girls would compete actively against one another but would be inhibited when competing against boys; that is, those girls who performed well competing against other girls would show a drop in performance when competing against boys. A dodgeball game was organized on a school playground. Fifty-four 9-, 10-, and 11-year-old middle-class black children volunteered to play (24 girls and 30 boys). Same-sex baseline games determined high- and low-skill boys and girls. During the ensuing tournament two observers noted points scored (successful dodges) by individuals and competitions by individuals for the loose ball after every throw. In the first 15-minute game, high-skill girls scored significantly more points than low-skill girls (X^2 test, $p < .02$). In each pairing of a girls' group with a boys' group, boys scored significantly more points than girls (X^2 test, $p < .02$). High- and low-skill girls were indistinguishable when competing against boys.

Total Points, Chances, and Percentages in Oral Contests

Round	Participants	Total Points Scored	Possible Points (Chances)	Percentage of Possible Points
1	High boys	14	27	52
	Low boys	9	27	53
2	High girls	22	30	73
	Low girls	23	30	77
3	High boys	13	27	48
	Low girls	17	27	63
4	High boys	16	27	59
	High girls	20	27	74
5	Low boys	11	27	41
	Low girls	15	27	56
6	Low boys	10	27	37
	High girls	16	27	59

Dodges, Hits, and Retrievals in Same-Sex and Mixed-Sex Games

Game	Participants (N)	Dodges Total	Dodges Mean	Dodges Standard Deviation	Hits Total	Hits Mean	Hits Standard Deviation	Retrievals Total	Retrievals Mean	Retrievals Standard Deviation
1	High girls (9)	37	9.6	15.6	8	.9	.9	59	6.6	3.8
	Low girls (8)	26	1.0	2.8	4	.5	.8	41	5.1	2.9
2	High boys (11)		3.4	3.5	15	1.4	1.5		5.7	3.2
	Low boys (10)		2.6	5.9	9	.9	1.3		3.0	1.6
3	High girls (10)		.4	1.0		.3	.5	36	3.6	2.6
	Low boys (10)		6.7	11.9		1.2	.9	51	5.1	3.5
4	High girls (10)		.6	1.4	4	.4	.5		2.3	1.8
	High boys (10)		5.8	7.4	17	1.7	1.7		6.6	2.7
5	Low girls (7)		0	0		.6	.5		3.7	4.4
	Low boys (6)		11.8	25.1		1.0	.6		9.0	6.1
6	Low girls (8)		0	0		0	0		.5	.8
	High boys (11)		3.5	2.8		1.7	1.5		4.6	3.5

X^2 Test Significant (p < .02) for each game

182

The second experiment was an academic competition. Even though girls had a skill advantage over boys, it was hypothesized that boys would not show any inhibition when competing against girls. Girls were again expected to show inhibition when competing against boys. A spelling contest was organized in the same school, and 19 girls and 18 boys, aged 9 to 11, volunteered. A written test determined boys' and girls' skill levels. An oral contest, organized the same way as in experiment revealed that both boys and girls showed consistent performance levels against all opponents, and there was no evidence of inhibition in the academic situation for either sex. Boys consistently outvolunteered girls $(p < .05)$ no matter their skill level. Several other measures, as well, indicated that no matter how poorly they spelled, the boys were more eager to compete than were the girls.

STUDY 16: Parental Manipulation of the Sex Ratio of Offspring in Humans

Thomas Figurski (1977)

Author's summary

By virtue of their greater gametic potential, healthy males have greater reproductive success (RS) than healthy females. Conversely, unhealthy males, victims of fierce male competition, have less RS than unhealthy females. Thus, natural selection would favor those parents who could adjust the sex ratio of their offspring according to the conditions of health so that more males would be produced in superior conditions and more females in poor conditions (Trivers and Willard, 1973). This is a prime example of parental manipulation of progeny to the advantage of parental RS and at the expense of some individual potential offspring (Alexander, 1974).

To test this hypothesis empirically for humans on a global scale, national life expectancy, representative of health conditions, was correlated with the national sex ratio at birth for 29 countries across the world. Results indicated a significant relationship between the two variables, with a Pearson's r of approximately $+.6$.

STUDY 17: The Importance of Good Looks in Dominance

Ellen Rozenfeld (1976)

The study investigated what cues derived from those available in photographs would enable individuals most accurately to determine the dominance hierarchy existing among six adolescent boys.

Photographs of six thirteen-year-old boys were obtained. The dominance rank order between the boys had previously been established through observation and inquiry (Savin-Williams, 1977). Two photos of each boy, one showing only the face, one the full body, were mounted on cards. Thirteen female and 6 male Ss aged 15 to 52 were presented with the six

Continent	Political Division	Life Expectancy			Sex Ratio at Birth	
		Male	Female	Date	Date	
Africa	Cape Verde	48.3	51.7	1970–75	1970–74	1.031
	Seychelles	61.9	68.0	1970–72	1970–72	1.060
	South Africa	49.8	53.3	1970–75	1969–71	1.028
	Southern Rhodesia	49.8	53.3	1970–75	1970–72	1.033
	Tunisia	52.5	55.7	1970–75	1970–72	1.048
America, North	Canada	69.34	76.36	1970–72	1970–72	1.061
	Greenland	58.9	65.7	1966–70	1967–70	1.058
	Panama	64.26	67.50	1970	1969–71	1.042
	Puerto Rico	68.92	76.05	1971–73	1971–73	1.046
	Trinidad and Tobago	64.08	68.11	1970	1969–71	1.025
	United States	68.2	75.9	1974	1973–74	1.053
	Bahamas	64.0	67.3	1969–71	1969–71	0.987[a]
America, South	Argentina	65.16	71.38	1970–75	1969–70	1.023
	Chile	60.48	66.01	1969–70	1969–71	1.038
Asia	Hong Kong	67.36	75.01	1971	1970–72	1.067
	Israel	70.13	73.27	1974	1973–74	1.058
	Japan	71.16	76.31	1974	1973–74	1.063
	Malaysia, West	63.36	68.01	1972	1971–73	1.053
	Soviet Union	64	74	1971–72	1970–73	1.050
	Singapore	65.1	70.0	1970	1969–70	1.065
	Yemen, Democratic	43.7	45.9	1970–75	1969–70	1.298[a]
Europe	England and Wales	67.8	73.8	1968–70	1968–70	1.058
	France	68.6	76.4	1972	1971–73	1.053
	Germany, Federal Republic of	67.61	74.09	1971–73	1971–73	1.057
	Portugal	65.29	72.03	1974	1973–74	1.055
	Romania	66.83	71.29	1972–74	1972–74	1.060

	Sweden	72.11	1970–74	77.51	1970–74	1.061
	Switzerland	70.29	1968–73	76.22	1968–73	1.059
Oceania	American Samoa	65.0	1969–71	69.1	1969–71	1.057
	Fiji	68.5	1970–75	71.7	1970–74	1.073
	New Zealand	68.55	1970–72	74.60	1970–72	1.049

[a]Extreme ratio omitted from calculation of Pearson's r to avoid unwarranted influence.

cards and asked to rank the boys in hierarchies based on dominance, looks, and body build.

Eight out of the 19 Ss' rankings of hierarchies based on dominance as well as on looks were significantly correlated with the established dominance hierarchy. In 13 cases, in fact, the correlations between the looks and established dominance hierarchies were greater than or equal to the correlations between the perceived and the established dominance hierarchy. None of the 19 rankings of body build was significantly correlated with the established dominance hierarchy.

Results were interpreted to suggest that looks, unlike body build, play an important role in both the perception and the formation of dominance orders.

STUDY 18:   Sex and Racial Influences in a Seventh-Grade Class

Jerry Westermeyer (1975)

Westermeyer investigated sex and racial influences on social organization and friendship selection within a class of seventh graders aged 12 to 14. The class (16 males and 15 females) consisted of 10 black, 9 white, and 11 Spanish-speaking students. Individuals were asked to list their 5 best friends and to rank order 10 of their classmates on 4 dimensions: best looking, most athletic, dominant, and most intelligent. In addition, 15 of the boys and 11 of the girls responded to a TAT-like stimulus card (a picture of the head of an Arab man).

Sex significantly influenced all hierarchies. Both sexes more frequently voted for boys on the dominance and athletics hierarchies ($p < .01$); for the opposite sex on the looks hierarchy ($.01 < p < .02$); and for their own sex on the intelligence ($p < .01$) and friendship ($p < .001$) hierarchies. Dominant boys ranked high on the looks and athletics hierarchies but not on the intelligence hierarchy. The dominance hierarchy appeared a strong influence on friendship organization among boys. In contrast, dominance had little influence on female friendship patterns.

Racial grouping strongly influenced the looks, friendship, athletics, and intelligence hierarchies. The dominance hierarchy was least affected by race.

Analysis of TAT data revealed sex differences congruent with trends observed in the hierarchy data. Males more frequently wrote stories involving physical harm to the man's face. Females more often chose names for the central figure and wrote about family relationships. TAT data were not analyzed for racial differences.

STUDY 19:   The Female Approach to Dominance

Nancy Solow (1976)

Solow analyzed the nature of dominance relations among five adolescent girls (mean age 13.3) during their participation in a five-week summer

SEX DIFFERENCES

Dominance	Boy Votes	Girl Votes
To Boys	230	141
To Girls	10	84
	p < .01	

Athletics	Boy Votes	Girl Votes
To Boys	237	152
To Girls	2	73
	p < .01	

Intelligence	Boy Votes	Girl Votes
To Boys	140	42
To Girls	97	183
	p < .01	

Looks	Boy Votes	Girl Votes
To Boys	99	122
To Girls	135	103
	.01 < p < .02	

Friendship	Boy Votes	Girl Votes
To Boys	235	9
To Girls	5	216
	p < .001	

RACIAL DIFFERENCES

Dominance

To	Others	Blacks		Others	Whites		Others	Spanish
Others	292	122		254	97		116	54
Blacks	23	28		76	38		184	111
	$p < .01$			NS			NS	

Athletics

	Others	Blacks		Others	Whites		Others	Spanish
Others	278	101		288	105		112	44
Blacks	37	48		41	30		187	121
	$p < .001$			$p < .001$			$.05\ p < .02$	

Looks

	Others	Blacks		Others	Whites		Others	Spanish
Others	282	66		261	77		229	83
Blacks	16	84		63	63		71	76
	$p < .001$			$p < .01$			$p < .001$	

Intelligence

	Others	Blacks		Others	Whites		Others	Spanish
Others	296	143		192	51		170	75
Blacks	16	7		135	84		130	87
	NS			$p < .001$			$p < .05$	

Boys Friendship

	Others	Blacks		Others	Whites		Others	Spanish
Others	125	37		163	44		83	31
Blacks	25	53		17	16		67	59
	$p < .001$			$p < .01$			$p < .01$	

Girls Friendship

	Others	Blacks		Others	Whites		Others	Spanish
Others	49	22	Others	122	30	Others	103	57
Blacks	31	38	Whites	28	45	Spanish	47	23
	$p < .001$			$p < .001$			NS	

camp. Analysis was based centrally on behavioral observations made by the cabin counselor of verbal and physical dominance displayed by the girls. Sociometric ratings by the girls of the dominance order and the cabin counselors' ratings of the girls on various characteristics were also obtained.

Analysis revealed the existence of a linear and transitive dominance hierarchy. The hierarchy was found to be stable over time with regard to ranking of individuals, average number of interactions per hour, and individual involvement in and success at dominance encounters. Great individual variance was observed in the nature of dominance across settings. No overall difference across settings on the distribution of dominance interactions was observed, however, when all dyadic interactions were considered.

Girls used basically verbal rather than physical types of social power. They showed individual preferences for types of verbal assertion and frequently varied the types of interaction by the individual with whom they were involved. Ratings of the girls on pubertal status, intelligence, and athletic ability correlated positively with the dominance order ($r = .89; .92; .41$), whereas the counselor's ratings of beauty and how much she liked the girls correlated negatively with the order ($-.21; -.37$).

Discussion of the observed results suggested the hierarchy retained a feminine flavor, reflecting the feminine facility for verbal expression as well as feminine sensitivity and reactivity to situational cues and environmental changes. Analysis of individual styles of dominance, such as those of "maternal martyr" or "manipulative attention seeker," suggested that dominance styles incorporated feminine personality constellations.

STUDY 20: An Exploratory Study of Perceptions of Peer Hierarchies in Early and Middle Adolescence

Joan Miller (1977)

Miller examined age and sex differences in the perceived structure of peer hierarchies over early and middle adolescence. It was hypothesized that such perceptions would evidence certain parallels with the structure of dominance hierarchies found among nonhuman primates as well as reflect the impact of cognitive, affective, and social processes specific to human adolescence. Such effects were demonstrated in relation to (1) the dimensions around which hierarchies were most delineated; (2) sex differences in dominance; and (3) age and sex differences in accuracy of perception of the rankings of self and others.

The sample included 19 female and 22 male seventh graders (mean age 13.1) and 19 female and 26 male tenth and eleventh graders (mean age 16.5). Assigned to class subgroups of approximately 10, students ranked members of their group on (1) having attention paid to one's opinions; (2) having many friends; (3) looks; (4) smartness; and (5) toughness. Self-report scales provided measures of adolescents' affective involvements around the dimensions.

Hierarchies were found consistently most delineated on toughness among early but not among middle adolescents. The strength of the association between male sex and toughness was weaker among middle than among early adolescents.

In all cases, males overrated more than females, though this trend reached statistical significance only on friends ($p < .05$) and looks ($p < .01$) among middle adolescents. Sex differences in accuracy of perceiving others occurred on four out of five dimensions among early adolescents, with no such sex differences observed among middle adolescents. Both male and female early adolescents were found to overrate significantly more than male and female middle adolescents on looks ($p < .01$) as well as to show significantly lower accuracy than the older adolescents in perceiving the rankings of others on this dimension ($p < .01$ for males; $p < .05$ for females). Such an effect was posited to occur because of early adolescents' egocentrism around looks, an area of particular affective vulnerability given the onset of puberty. A model of overrating as reflecting both competitive and defensive affective orientations was proposed.

STUDY 21: The Onset of Children's Preference for Same-Sex Play Neighbors

Brandon Taylor (1974)

Observations were conducted in a nursery school where children were grouped according to age; three groups were observed: 16 two-year olds, 18 three-year olds, and 20 four-year olds. Children were observed twice indoors and twice during outside recess. The sex of each child and his first, second, and third spatially nearest neighbors were recorded. The change between the two-year-old group and the three-year-old group indicates that the onset of same-sex play preference is between two and three years.

		Percentage observations		
		Age Two	Age Three	Age Four
Child observed	Nearest neighbor			
Boys	Boy	57	64	59
	Girl	33	33	37
	Teacher	10	3	4
Chi-square[a]		NS	$p < .001$	$p < .05$
Girls	Boy	38	7	41
	Girl	76	77	56
	Teacher	15	16	3
Chi-square		NS	$p < .001$	$p < .05$

[a]The numbers of each sex in each group were unequal; the Chi-square values were computed with this in mind.

STUDY 22: Sex Differences in the Classroom

Mary Martini (1974)

Martini analyzed social interaction through "behavior records" of twenty-two second- and third-grade children from two open classrooms in a

Catholic elementary school on the North Side of Chicago. The data averaged 43 observations (two minutes each) per child. Extensive detail on the coding method and on the data themselves is included. Girls were observed to interact with other children more frequently than boys, and all tended to interact (73% of the time) with others of the same sex. Boys tended to interact predominantly with only one other person, while girls initiated more interactions with teachers. There were also sex differences in the topics of verbal interactions, as well as in the "structure" of the interactions.

STUDY 23: Sex Differences in the People versus Object Continuum

Ed Fahrmeir (1968)

The study examined the content of drawings made by the Ss early in the course of Omark and Edelman's study (1977). The content of the drawings was classified into the following categories: (1) human figures; (2) animals; (3) flora and natural scenes; and (4) inanimate objects.

	Classification of drawings by subject matter[a]							
	Boys				Girls			
	1	2	3	4	1	2	3	4
Nursery school	1.5	2.0	0	3.0	4.0	0.5	0	3.0
First grade	4.0	7.0	5.5	21.0	8.5	1.5	7.0	3.5

[a] Each drawing was made by two people; divided drawings were given .5 credit per half.

The pattern in nursery school is unclear. First graders had definite preferences: boys heavily favored inanimate objects; girls preferred human figures and natural scenes.

STUDY 24: Sex Differences in Style and Content in Children's Drawings

Mark Lawrence (1968)

Children's drawings (collected in the course of the Omark-Edelman research) were analyzed for sex differences in content by counting the occurrences of action, vehicles, smiles, perspective, females, males, guns, flowers, gentle animals, fierce animals, houses, decorative furnishings, suns, and people. Sex differences were noted for the action, perspective, male, and female categories, as well as for some of the other categories for some of the groups. Probabilities are based on the Mann-Whitney U-Test.

	(80♀, 35♂) Kindergarten		(61♀, 49♂) First grade		(42♀, 43♂) Third grade		Significantly more
	u score	probability	u score	probability	u score	probability	
Action	2.54	0.006	4.87	0.001	3.52	0.001	Boys
Vehicles	1.67	0.05	4.48	0.001	3.78	0.001	Boys
Smiles	—	NS	4.18	0.001	1.90	0.04	Girls
Perspective	—	NS	1.28	0.10	2.89	0.002	Boys
Females	4.65	0.001	3.82	0.001	1.90	0.04	Girls
Males	1.97	0.02	1.28	0.10	1.45	0.08	Boys
Guns	—	NS	2.51	0.007	2.21	0.02	Boys
Flowers	1.48	0.07	1.37	0.09	2.33	0.01	Girls
Gentle animals	—	NS	1.42	0.08	2.65	0.004	Girls
Fierce animals	—	NS	1.74	0.04	—	NS	Boys
Houses	—	NS	2.06	0.02	1.01	0.10	Girls
Decorative furnishings	—	NS	—	NS	1.29	0.10	
Suns	—	NS	1.36	0.09	1.24	0.11	
People	—	NS	—	NS	—	NS	

STUDY 25:   Sex Differences in Attention Structure among Sixth Graders

Richard Costanzo (1973)

Sixth-grade children (16 male, 11 female) were asked to write letters in class to anyone they wished; it was stated that the letter would not be seen or graded by the teacher. The letters were scored for themes (interpersonal or not), people mentioned, competitiveness, length, and sex of addressee. The last was of interest: letters tended to be addressed to same-sex individuals. Boys also wrote less about themselves and peers than did girls and more about "famous people."

STUDY 26:   Sex Differences in Parenting in the Middle Years

Robert B. Snow (1976)

The study investigated father-child versus mother-child dyadic relationships in the middle years. Ten young adult males and 10 young adult females (mean age 20) completed a questionnaire assessing a range of aspects of the parent-child relationship. Their parents (fathers mean age 47; mothers mean age 45) later were individually interviewed on the same questions as well as on more general adult developmental issues. Measures of the "content" as well as of the degree of "consensus" in parent and child responses were then obtained.

The quality of interaction with children rather than the amount was found to distinguish fathers from mothers. Fathers as compared to mothers appeared less obligated, less varied in active participation in showing care, and less empathetic; they gave and received fewer total indications of affection and showed less mutuality with their young adult children.

Mothers consistently evaluated their interpersonal skills lower than they were rated by their daughters, whereas fathers evaluated their interpersonal skills higher than they were rated by their sons. Such findings of greater discrepancy in same-sex rather than cross-sex parent-child dyads were interpreted, particularly in the case of males, as a manifestation of competition.

The overall results, the author proposed, indicate mothers are more multidimensional and complex in their parenting than are fathers. Mother-child relations are characterized by greater mutuality and reciprocal influencing than are father-child relations. Results, the author showed, are congruent with ego psychological as well as biosocial models of sex differences.

STUDY 27:   A Longitudinal Study of Dominance in Boys

Glenn E. Weisfeld (1977)

A cohort of boys ranked each other on "toughness" three times: in first, second, and fifth grade. In ninth grade, the same boys were ranked by male classmates on dominance, defined as ability to get one's way; leadership;

and popularity. Toughness ranks in grade school were correlated with dominance, leadership, and popularity at the .04 level or better for all three intervals: fifth grade to ninth, second to ninth, and first to ninth. Spearman rank order correlation coefficients ranged from .52 to .79. Another cohort was followed from third to ninth grade, with similar results. The same two cohorts of boys were also ranked by their female classmates on toughness in grade school and on desirability as dates and as party guests in high school. Toughness in first, second, and fifth grade was correlated with desirability in ninth grade for one cohort, and toughness in third grade was correlated with desirability in tenth grade for the other cohort. Thus, dominance interactions early in grade school may affect access to resources—including females—in high school. The grade-school data in this study were collected by Omark and Edelman and used with permission.

STUDY 28: Sense of Humor: A Study of Male-Female Differences in Children

Henry Post (1973)

Post hypothesized that significant differences in sense of humor between the sexes would point toward significant differences in male-female temperament, personality, ego investment, values, and concerns.

Ten boys and ten girls, aged nine to twelve, were given ten cartoons and instructed to rank order them from most to least humorous. Each child was then asked to draw a picture either from a movie or from a television show that was "really funny."

The girls' favorite cartoons involved puns, spoken lines, static scenes, and a neat, clean, and functional drawing style; boys, on the other hand, selected cartoons that depicted considerable physical activity, for example, one character hitting another over the head. The second part of the experiment, drawing a movie or television scene, revealed basically the same trends: girls drew situations involving an interpersonal encounter that indicated *how* people did things and involving spoken lines, whereas boys drew scenes of violence and action indicating *what* people were doing. Another striking sexual difference was evident in pictures showing human figures. Ninety percent of the boys drew simple stick figures; 90% of the girls drew complete figures with faces.

STUDY 29: Social Hierarchies in Same-Sex Peer Groups

Richard Parker (1976)

The study investigated the nature of dominance hierarchies in same-sex classrooms. It was hypothesized that there would be no significant differences between all-girls' and all-boys' classes in the amount of agreement about a toughness hierarchy or in the amount of overrating by individuals of their own hierarchical positions.

Dominance relations were investigated in an all-female and in an all-male class at first, second, and third grade levels in a Roman Catholic elementary school (mean 20 students per class). Sociometric data on toughness, smartness, and friendship hierarchies were obtained and observations made of playground and classroom behavior.

No significant differences were observed between all-girls' and all-boys' classes in the amount of agreement about a toughness hierarchy or in the amount of overrating made by individuals of their own position in the hierarchy. Results contrasted, however, with those observed in cross-sex classrooms (Omark and Edelman, 1977). Same-sex classes overrated at about twice the level of mixed-sex classes and, relatedly, showed only random agreement about a hierarchy.

Three implications were drawn. On a theoretical level, the results were interpreted as documenting the variability of behavior in different ecological contexts. On a substantive level, the equality of overrating in same-sex classes was related to studies suggesting that all-female educational institutions produce more confident and assertive women than do coed educational institutions. Finally, the lack of agreement on a hierarchy within all-male classes, in contrast to the pattern among males in mixed classes, suggested that the presence of females helps congeal the hierarchical structure.

STUDY 30:   Mate Choice in the Human Female: A Study of Height Preferences

Francis Lang (1972)

Lang looked at male height as a variable in the human female's choice of a mate. She attempted to validate and account for the hypothesis that universally females tend to choose males who are taller than themselves. Forty female university students served as S. Four cards were used to solicit TAT-like stories; on each card the same young couple was depicted. In the four versions, the male was either short or tall and either mustached or clean-shaven. Each S was shown one version of the card and asked to write a brief story about the picture.

The short, clean-shaven version elicited the same type of response from all 10 Ss. The male was pictured as "anxious" or "weak" and the female became the "dominant" and "more confident" member of the pair. Although the couple was seen as being temporarily together, their relationship would not be a successful one.

In contrast, the tall, clean-shaven man was the more self-confident of the pair and the woman became the more self-conscious. The male was described as "protective," "reassuring," "understanding," "sympathetic," and "knowing"; the female was "concerned," "ambivalent," "naive," and "unsettled." Despite the woman's insecurity, this association did not seem to be marred by the conflict and discomfort of the relationship with the short man. The couple was most often viewed as a date or as lovers.

The short mustached man had all the inadequacies attributed to his clean-shaven counterpart and was "sneaky" and "sleazy" as well.

The tall man with a mustache provided an interesting combination of attributes. He was still the tall, dominant male involved in a dating or romantic relationship but was also somewhat sleazy.

Thus, the preferences were clear. In all 20 stories, the Ss responded negatively to the male's relative shortness. Although the mustached men were not favored, the tall mustached man had an advantage over the clean-shaven but short male.

A brief questionnaire administered to the Ss verified females' preference for taller males. When asked whether they believed that females usually prefer taller men, 78% answered yes. Of those women who disagreed, all showed a clear preference on the TAT task for the taller male, both mustached and clean-shaven.

When asked whether they had ever dated a man of their height or shorter, 90% replied that they had, but of these 36 women only two were *currently* involved with a shorter man. Many of the rest indicated that they had only one date with a shorter man.

Finally, the 36 women who had dated a shorter man were asked to describe how they felt with him. Two-thirds of these Ss gave a negatively oriented response, expressing a general feeling of awkwardness and self-consciousness that was most acute in public places. Of the twelve women who reported no self-consciousness with shorter men, eight had been shown a short man in the TAT card and all eight had reacted with negative stories—suggesting that at some level they shared the other women's height preference.

STUDY 31:   Height Differentials in Male and Female Dyads

Maureen Travis (1975)

The study investigated sex differences in the relationship between friendship choice and height. Past research showing the greater involvement of males over females in dominance hierarchies and the positive association between height and dominance and that between dominance status and male friendship led to two hypotheses. Males would tend to choose friends close to their own height. Females, in contrast, would choose friends randomly on the basis of height.

As they entered a campus bar ten female dyads and 25 male dyads (median age 23) were asked their height, weight, age, and the height of their two closest friends. The investigator ranked all Ss into four categories of body build.

Scoring differences under three inches as "similar," no sex differences were observed in the relationship between friendship choice and height. Both males and females tended to choose and to be with friends of the same approximate height ($z = -2.54$; $p < .05$). The effects of body build and age upon height differentials in friend dyads could not be calculated because of the limited number of Ss who fell into extreme categories.

The author proposed that dominance may be important in both female and male same-sex relations and height important therein as an indicator of dominance. Various other explanations of the link between height and friendship choice were suggested.

STUDY 32:   Infant Reactions to Adult and Child Strangers

Joan Laser (1969)

Laser investigated the hypothesis that infants would be more fearful toward an adult than toward a child stranger. Subjects were 8 male and 12 female infants between the ages of 6 and 12 months. The author served as an adult stranger; an eight-year-old girl served as a child stranger during the procedures (conducted in the Ss' homes). The mother put the infant in a familiar place and left the room. The child or the adult stranger—the order was reversed each time—entered the infant's room, walked around for five seconds and finally approached the infant. The stranger stared down at the infant with a small, closed-lip smile for 35 seconds, without changing her expression or moving. She then left the room. After a few seconds, the second stranger entered and repeated the identical procedure. During this process, the author rated the infant on smiling, facial expression, movement, and crying. The infants' mothers also were interviewed.

Using each infant as his or her own control, Laser observed that infants smiled more to the child than to the adult stranger (Sign test, $p = .006$). In 14 out of 20 cases in which differences occurred in facial expressions to the two strangers, more fear was shown toward the adult than toward the child (Sign test, $p < .001$). More avoidance movement occurred to the strange adult and more approach to the strange child (Sign test, $p < .001$). All instances of crying (seven occasions) occurred in the presence of the adult and none in the presence of the child stranger. Neither age nor family background predicted the infants' reactions to the two strangers.

The results were discussed as showing not only less fear but also a positive approach reaction toward the child stranger, a reaction rarely displayed toward the adult. The differential reactions to strangers, it was suggested, may reflect height differentials or other characteristics facilitating recognition of the young in a species. The author additionally proposed that the reactions may be seen as adaptive in facilitating the infants' ability eventually to leave the parents and to enter more fully into the peer group.

STUDY 33:   Infants' Fear of Strangers: Reactions to a Red or White Mask

Sandra Horowitz (1975)

Horowitz examined differences in fear reactions displayed by infants to a stranger wearing either a red or a white mask. On the basis of research showing the marked responsiveness of infants to red as a visual stimulus and the association of red with dominance and danger among animals and man, it was hypothesized that a red mask would elicit a greater fear response from infants than would a white mask.

Ten male and ten female infants ranging in age from 6 to 15 months were visited in their homes by a female E. Subjects were divided into two groups containing equal numbers of male and female infants of fairly comparable age. Infants were placed in their beds by their mothers, who left the room. The masked E then entered the bedroom, approached and stared down at the infant for not more than one minute. The latency to crying was timed. The shorter the latency, it was assumed, the greater the fear response. All individuals in one group were approached by the E as she wore a bright red mask; infants in the other group were approached by the E wearing a white mask.

A Mann-Whitney U-Test indicated that the latency to crying was significantly shorter in the red-mask condition ($p < .01$; one-tailed). This effect occurred among both male and female infants.

STUDY 34:   Aspects of Visual Interaction in Human Social Life

Alice J. Dan (1969)

Visual encounters are important, this study asserts, in interpersonal events for most primates because visual contact carries a social message, cuing the intention of actors in social situations, particularly in dominance relations. Dan assessed the effects of staring on human behavior in a "natural" situation. Two hypotheses were stated: (1) staring should catch the attention of the subject; and (2) sex differences in response should exist, with males reacting more quickly than females because of an increased sensitivity to dominance competition (staring).

An observer stared directly into the face of a S (20 males and 20 females, ages not given, but presumably college age) for two minutes in a school cafeteria, recording the time taken for the S to notice, as well as any facial or bodily reactions during the two minutes.

The first hypothesis was supported: 37 of the 40 Ss appeared to notice the staring observer, usually by brief glances with little facial expression. Only eight Ss returned the stare, seven of whom were of the same sex as the observer. The second hypothesis was not supported; rather, there was a strong tendency, regardless of sex, to respond more quickly when the observer was of the same sex. Reaction time was also shorter if the S was sitting alone and if the observer was to the left of the S. An interesting, peripheral finding was that the bearded male observer elicited the longest delay in return glancing, perhaps because beardedness is a sign of dominance and thus provokes less uncertainty and competition. All observers reported they felt tense whenever their direct gaze was returned, especially if the S was of their sex. This tension was quickly dissipated if the S smiled.

Replications of this study should employ an independent measure of dominance status of the Ss to note any differences related to dominance in stares returned; ask the Ss post hoc for their subjective interpretation of the visual interaction and vary characteristics of the observer such as attractiveness, size, age, and, especially, beardedness.

STUDY 35: An Evolutionary Approach to Staring Encounters and to the Development of Dominance Hierarchies

Murray S. Edelman (1968)

Edelman focused on one aspect of nonverbal behavior—the staring encounter—from an evolutionary-developmental perspective. In a review of the ethological literature, it was seen that the stare threat has the adaptive function of resolving and reinforcing the dominance hierarchy among group members while suppressing physically harmful interactions. Within this framework, starting encounters were investigated during the period of initial peer-group formation.

A group of nursery-school boys and a group of first-grade boys were arranged in pairs within their own class and instructed to outstare each other. The winner of the staring interaction was found to have a statistically significant relationship with the pair's decision of "Who is the toughest?" and the teacher's ratings of who would win an argument. This relationship held only among the first graders; the nursery-school sample did not show a hierarchical structure on any of the three measures.

The results were discussed in terms of the child's developing ability to relate to a hierarchical structure. Edelman suggested that the developing ability to exhibit a submissive gesture and to know who is the "toughest" serves an adaptive function for the ages in which serious injury becomes increasingly possible.

STUDY 36: Form Perception, Innate Form Preferences, and Visually Mediated Head Turning in the Human Neonate

Carolyn G. Goren (1970)

Four experiments on the perceptual preferences of 36 human newborns were performed, Goren employing a new method for measuring stimulus preferences based on visual following. Various stimuli were presented in an arc in front of the infant's face; the E started at the midline and moved the stimulus slowly to the right or to the left once the infant had fixated on the stimulus. Degrees of head turning elicited by each stimulus were estimated with the help of a large protractor placed around the infant's body.

Experiment 1 demonstrated an unlearned preference for a facelike configuration: a schematic face was followed significantly more than a moderately scrambled face and the latter was followed significantly more than a scrambled face.

Experiment 2 showed that newborns follow the two most complex of a series of three checkerboards significantly more than the least complex checkerboard.

Experiment 3 demonstrated that a real human face is followed significantly more than a three-dimensional mannequin head and a photograph of the mannequin. Contrary to expectations, however, the photograph was followed significantly more than the mannequin.

Experiment 4 indicated that infants showed more following of a schematic face than of six eyes, two large eyes, normal eyes, or a mouth stimulus. No differences in following of the six large eyes and the two large eyes were observed, though both elicited more following than the two normal eyes.

The results indicated that the ability to organize visual input into a "whole" appears to be present within the first 24 hours after birth. The results of the four experiments were interpreted within an ethological framework in which neonatal interest in the face pattern was seen as adaptive in the formation of early social attachments.

STUDY 37: An Ethological Perspective on Eye Contact in Newborns

Jay Magaziner (1974)

This project grew out of a filmed event that occurred during a study of the newborn's visual preference for the human face. Magaziner sought to document infants' preference from the first hours of life for the eyes in particular and to study the interaction in a face-to-face encounter between a newborn and his or her caretaker. Ten male and ten female black newborns were tested while they were crying. None of the infants' mothers had been given more than 50 mg. of Demerol within six hours of delivery.

The hypothesis was that a crying newborn will cease crying when picked up, turn toward the caretaker, open his or her eyes and look at the caretaker's face, and fixate on the caretaker's eyes. Moreover, these behaviors (some of which may occur simultaneously) are initiated by the infant.

Each infant was tested in a dimly illuminated room in a controlled, naturalistic situation. A 16 mm. movie camera was used to film the sequence. Crying was induced by removing the infant's clothing or by tapping the foot. Upon deciding that the crying was fairly well sustained, the E lifted the infant in such a way that the head was supported in the crook made by the elbow but was free to turn. The newborn was held slightly away from the E's body, giving the infant the greatest freedom of head and body movements. The E responded only to movements initiated by the infant—and then attempted to respond in a naturalistic way. The E nodded when eye contact was made, for the purpose of later coding from the film. The following system of coding was used: 0 = baby crying and is picked up (starting point); 1 = baby stops crying; 2 = baby turns toward E; 3 = baby opens eyes and looks at some part of E's face; 4 = baby fixed for at least 3 seconds on eyes of E (E nods).

The results confirmed the hypothesis that crying newborns follow the sequence of behavior outlined above. When picked up, all infants stopped crying; 95% turned to the E and 90% looked at E. Of these 90%, all fixed on the E's eyes after looking at the face. Of the two male infants who did not complete the sequence, one fell asleep as he was picked up and the other failed to open his eyes although he did orient his body toward the E.

The author suggested that the actions studied here represent an innate organization of behavior resulting in the orientation of the infant to the appropriate stimulus—a human caretaker. The result of this "natural" tendency to orient with the body and head and to fixate and follow with the head and eyes is that eye contact is established and maintained with the "other." That this contact is adaptive seems obvious in that it both elicits and rewards the caretaker's attention. An evolved capacity to elicit the caretaker's attention—and affect—is particularly crucial in a species whose members enter the world in such a helpless state.

STUDY 38: Infants' Reactions to Dilated and Constricted Pupils of an Adult Stranger in a Naturalistic Setting: A Preliminary Investigation

Janet Bare (1974)

The purpose of this study was to determine (1) whether human infants respond differently to two conditions of pupil size in the eyes of an adult stranger; and, if so, (2) whether infants respond more positively to the E in the dilated condition. It was hypothesized that the infants would smile more to large (dilated) pupils.

The Ss used were 16 normal Caucasian infants (half boys, half girls) who ranged in age from 9 to 23 weeks (mean = 14). Their mothers reported that they smiled socially and had not yet shown any fear of strangers. The same female E visited each infant twice, once with her pupils pharmacologically dilated and once with them constricted. The order of the visits was reversed for some of the Ss. A 10% solution of phenylephrine hydrochloride was used to achieve pupil dilation (pupil size of 7–8 mm.) and a 2% solution of pilocarpine hydrochloride induced constriction (pupil size of about 2 mm.). The E had blue eyes, in which the pupils were quite visible (normal pupil size about 5–6 mm.).

The babies were tested in their homes in a naturalistic social situation while their families were not within visual or auditory range. The E placed the infant on his back on a bed or couch already familiar to him and sat leaning over him so that her face was easily visible. When the baby seemed alert and comfortable, the E began the 7-minute test. During this interval, the E touched the infant while smiling, talking, and nodding to him—attempting to maximize and sustain his attention to her face. The test ended with the soft buzz of a timer; the E immediately recorded the number of smiles observed and scored the infant's performance on a scale of one to five for a selection of behaviors reflecting positive or negative social orientation. The positive items were nature of social response, attention span, general emotional tone, behavior constancy, and vocalization. Negative social orientation items were tension, fearfulness, and crying.

For the group of 16 infants, 73 smiles were recorded in the constricted condition and 104 in the dilated condition. Thus, the group performance was in general agreement with the hypothesis although the difference did not approach statistical significance. As a group, the infants had somewhat higher positive social orientation scores in the dilated condition and higher negative social orientation scores in the constricted condition—as expected—but these differences were not significant.

An examination of the data by sex revealed that the overall performance of males and females was quite different in the *dilated* condition. That is, although the number of smiles observed for males and females was nearly identical (39 and 36, respectively) in the constricted condition, the total smiles for females in the dilated condition was only 36, whereas that of the male sample increased to 68. This was not a highly significant difference, however, ($p < .08$, two-tailed, Mann-Whitney U). There was virtually no difference in negative social orientation for the two sexes in the dilated condition, but the boys' greater negative reaction to constricted pupils also approached significance ($p < .10$, two-tailed, Mann-Whitney U).

On the group of items with which positive social orientation was evaluated, the boys did score significantly higher ($p < .02$, two-tailed, Mann-Whitney U) in the dilated condition, in keeping with their greater tendency to respond in accordance with the hypothesis.

These results are not easily explained. It was the author's subjective impression, however, that some infants actually seemed to focus on her eyes, whereas others never did so. It is suggested that further research in this area should include a condition of normal pupil size and should provide a means for judging the infants' behavior "blind."

STUDY 39: An Empirical Investigation into the Effect of Beardedness on Perception of Social Situations

Richard Parker (1968)

The purpose of Parker's investigation was to explore the effect of male beardedness upon the perception of social situations and personal qualities. A set of four standard TAT cards was used as a control; an experimental set was made by adding a beard to a male figure in each of the control cards. The author predicted that the bearded versions (compared with the standardized responses evoked by the control set) would be perceived as more aggressive, forbidding, active, mature, virile, and dominant, in line with the ethological theory concerning the adaptive function of beardedness as a symbol of maturity, dominance, and aggression.

Half of the 12 male and 12 female undergraduate Ss were assigned to experimental TAT sequences; the other half were shown the controls. Each S was asked to "tell what is happening in the pictures." Stories were analyzed for consistent differences in content.

Although there were no appreciable differences between two of the experimental cards and their controls, the author reported that, upon questioning the Ss, it became apparent that the beards in these two cards were not perceptible. His tentative conclusion, based on the two remaining experimental cards, was that there was some evidence that beardedness did alter the Ss' perceptions of presumed situations and roles. In one case—the card with a young man and an older woman—the bearded man seemed more active, stronger, and superior; his beardless counterpart appeared of equal strength and activity and was not in a superior position relative to the woman. In the card portraying an older man and a bearded younger man, the stories were also different from the control version. In the experimental version, the younger man was much more frequently perceived as holding a position of equality or even dominance rather than the typical submissiveness attributed to his clean-shaven control version.

Upon extending the N in a follow-up study, the following distributions were obtained on the two promising cards (7BM, 6BM, and their bearded versions):

THEMES OF STORIES TOLD TO STANDARD AND EXPERIMENTAL CARDS

| | TAT Card 7 BM | | Experimental Card[a] | |
	Females	Males	Females	Males
Submission of younger person	6	9	5	2
Equality or dominance of younger person	4	1	5	8

| | TAT Card 6 BM | | Experimental Card[b] | |
	Females	Males	Females	Males
Both equally involved	8	8	2	3
Man acts, woman reacts	2	2	8	7

[a] Beard added to younger man's face.
[b] Beard added to man's face.

STUDY 40:   Dominance and Submission in Presidential Politics: A Sociobiological View

Robert W. Kubey (1976)

The study examined the relationship among presidential status, sex of offspring, and various physical characteristics of U.S. presidents. It was shown that more males (80) than females (55) were born to U.S. presidents and that the greatest proportion of male presidential offspring was born from 1853 to 1881. Out of the five bearded U.S. presidents, four served during those years and fathered the greatest number of sons. Considering all U.S. presidents, Kubey showed that bearded presidents fathered disproportionately more sons than nonbearded presidents ($p = .05$).

Such effects, it was speculated, derived from the greater importance of personal interaction between male politicians in determining access to power prior to the age of mass media. Attributes such as facial hair and male progeny, as aspects of threat display, then may have constituted important political prerequisites.

STUDY 41:   Threat Display

Sonya Hoard (1975)

Hoard studied the effect of the Afro hairstyle on the perceived image or status of black males. She reasoned that a mass of dark hair standing out from the scalp functions as an "intimidation display." Such threat displays presumably are attractive to the opposite sex since they are correlated with—and provide for—positions of dominance in the social order. In terms of contemporary racial tensions, "naturals"—especially exaggerated ones—may be threatening to the white establishment, whereas (at least to blacks) closely cropped hair may imply submission and subservience.

Hoard hypothesized, therefore, that black females would manifest some ambivalence about "supernaturals" on black males: a black female would consider a black male more threatening and attractive when he was pictured wearing a massive natural, but she also would have some misgivings about the social adaptiveness of the extreme hairdo.

Equal numbers of black and white male and female University of Chicago students were tested, making a total of 32 Ss. Each S was shown one card—of a TAT format in which the stimulus figures were two adult males and a dog; length of hair and skin color of the men were varied—and asked to make up a story based on the picture. Subjects were tested by a member of their own race; their stories were taped for later analysis. For purposes of analysis, dominance in each stimulus card was ascribed to the figure referred to most often by the S. Additionally, the theme of each S's story was noted, including the description of the two human figures.

Although inconclusive, this study suggested some interesting trends such as the fact that both blacks and whites appear to have the same stereotypes. In the stimulus pictures with black figures, the figure with the larger hairdo was associated with less success and less stability. In the racially mixed stimulus cards, the short hair evoked subservience; the long hair, hostility and confrontation. The author concluded with Guthrie's point that for purposes of social order a balance must be struck between appeasement and threat (Guthrie, 1970).

STUDY 42:   Baring One's Chest: Ethological and Evolutionary Perspectives

Ann Whitaker (1976)

Whitaker explored the adaptive significance of hair on mens' chests. It was predicted that males displaying hair on the chest would be perceived as more aggressive, dominant, and sexually attractive than males not displaying chest hair.

Ten male and ten female college students, aged 18 to 21, were asked to tell stories in response to four TAT cards. The cards depicted a male with (card 2) or without (card 1) chest hair, his shirt slightly unbuttoned, sitting on a bed with a female; and the same male with (card 4) or without (card 3) chest hair, sitting at a table with another male.

Both sexes perceived cards 1 and 2 as scenes in which the male was dominant and seductive in relation to the female. Female subjects felt that the relationship was fairly equal between the two males in cards 3 and 4 although they tended to view the male with chest hair as more sexy and masculine. For male subjects, card 3 was also viewed in terms of both males' being equal. Five of the male subjects, who appeared themselves not to have chest hair, however, seemed "threatened" by card 4 and tended to portray the second male in a submissive role in relation to the male with chest hair. The five male subjects with visible chest hair, in contrast, tended to portray the male with chest hair in card 4 as strong and aggressive.

STUDY 43:   An Inquiry into the Adaptive Significance of Pubertal Voice Change

Frank J. Winstan (1973)

The study investigated the adaptive value of the altered voice pitch of mature males as an indicator of status with respect to dominance relations, increasing thereby as well the attractiveness of males to females. It was predicted that adolescents would describe a high-pitch male as less dominant and as less sexually attractive and successful in his relationships with females than a low-pitch male.

An auditory episode test was designed, consisting of eight tape-recorded minidramas, including one to three voices. The principal character in each episode was an adolescent male with either a high- or a low-pitched voice; secondary characters were played by male and female adolescents. Each episode was designed to function as a relatively ambiguous projective device.

Subjects were 259 ninth-grade students (mean age 15.3) from two high schools in Montreal. Each subject was exposed to three episodes, administered in a classroom context. They then wrote stories and answered brief, multiple-choice questions about the episode. Responses to the eight episodes were coded according to the dimensions of specific relevance to each. Statistical analyses were performed separately by high school and by sex.

Despite methodological weaknesses in certain episodes, in general the major hypotheses were supported. Low voice pitch was found to function as a threat device, enchancing male status; a high voice pitch signaled subordinate status and immaturity. High voice pitch appeared to render males relatively unattractive to females in comparison with low voice pitch. Evolutionary implications of male voice pitch in dominance relations, male-female courtship, family relationships, and communication were discussed.

STUDY 44.   Courtship and Female Breasts

Debbie Miller (1969)

This study was prompted by the theory that states that female breasts serve as sexual releasers in human courtship situations. To test this statement, Miller compared the attitudes of men and women subjects toward large- and small-breasted young women. Two versions of a TAT-type picture were prepared. The sketch showed a young man and a young woman waiting beside a bus stop sign. The two versions were identical except for the addition of two small, rounded lines in the second card to depict larger breasts.

Subjects used were graduate students at the University of Chicago. Forty Ss (20 male and 20 female) were shown the small-breasted version; another 40 (20 male and 20 female) viewed the large-breasted picture. Each S was asked to (1) study the drawing for 2 minutes, (2) write a short paragraph about his or her feelings toward the woman in the picture, and finally, (3) mark an adjective checklist best to describe the woman.

Although the paragraphs did not furnish much data relevant to this study, the adjective checklist indicated that the males tended to see the large-breasted woman as a very provocative, sexual object who might possess "liberal" attitudes and who was "on the move" (Chi-square, $p < .05$).

STUDY 45:   The Effects of Blond Hair

John Bjork (1973)

In his study of the effect of hair color on the perceived age and status of males, Bjork reasoned that blond hair—more common among women and children (apparently, darkening is testosterone related)—would cause a man to be attributed with more feminine or innocent qualities. Bjork's specific hypothesis was that a man pictured with blond hair would more likely be described in terms that implied youthful and angelic qualities than the same figure with dark hair.

Three pairs of cards were used in a TAT format to test this hypothesis. The pairs were identical except that one of the male figures had dark hair in one version and blond hair in the other. Each of the pairs pictured two persons in interaction. In the first pair, two young men were talking; the stimulus figure appeared to be gesturing with his hand in order to make a point. The second and third pairs were adapted from standard TAT cards—an older woman and a younger man and an older man and a younger man. The young man's hair color was varied in the second pair and the older man's hair was altered in the third pair.

Subjects were 15 male and 15 female University of Chicago undergraduates. Each S was shown one of the versions of the three pairs of cards. The order was varied so that a S saw one experimental card presented between two control cards, or vice versa. The S was asked to make up a story for each card and to rate the stimulus figure on a series of paired adjectives. Finally, the S's hair color was rated as either light or dark.

The results were varied but indicated some trends that might support the original hypothesis. In the first pair of cards, the blond figure was seen in a slightly more positive light than his dark-haired version. In the older woman-younger man cards, the blond version was more often perceived as the woman's son; the figure with dark hair was more typically categorized as her husband or "another man." Finally, the older man with dark hair was sometimes described as a grandfather or as an authority of some sort giving advice. With blond hair, he was more typically a partner or someone of status equal to that of the younger man (who had dark hair in both versions). The author concluded that these trends, though not statistically significant, supported his original hypothesis.

STUDY 46: Moral Judgment/Behavior in Relation to the Kin/Non-Kin Distinction

Irene Sebastian (1973)

Sebastian examined Trivers's theory of kin and nonkin altruistic behavior, asking "Are there two moral codes, one for kin and one for nonkin?"

Thirty-three eighth-grade students were given Kohlberg's Situation III Moral Dilemma (woman dying from cancer; husband attempts to acquire lifesaving drug) with the relationship altered to father-daughter. All Ss were then given a questionnaire concerning their moral judgments. Three of the Ss were intensely interviewed to clarify the moral reasoning.

The results indicated that 79% of the Ss felt Heinz, the father, should steal the drug for his daughter. Only 55%, however, felt it would be right for Heinz to steal the drug if the person in need were his friend. No S responded that if given the choice between giving the drug to a sibling or to a friend, he or she would select the latter (five refused to make a decision). "Closeness" did not appear to explain the majority feeling that Heinz should steal for his daughter. Rather, he should steal because of family role obligation—irrespective of affection. There was some evidence from the interviews that Ss changed their moral reasoning, that is, moral stage, when considering kin versus nonkin. With kin, the primary issue was saving a life; with nonkin, more often the issue was stealing.

Thus, there appears to be, the study concludes, a different moral code for kin and nonkin.

STUDY 47: A Pilot Study of Altruistic Behavior and Genetic Relatedness in a College Age Sample

Paula Leven (1975)

The study investigated the adequacy of the kinship genetics model to account for individuals' reported willingness to engage in or accept altruistic help. Five situations involving altruistic cost in time or money were presented in questionnaire format to seven male and seven female college students. Subjects were asked to rate on a six-point scale the degree of altruistic help they would be willing to give (three situations) or accept from (two situations) individuals of varying degrees of genetic relatedness. In one of the situations, S were asked to rank order rather than rate the individuals.

Nonrelated individuals, such as spouse and best friend, ranked higher than predicted by the kinship genetics model. The cost of altruism appeared to be experienced as higher in situations involving sacrifice of money, when related individuals became more significant, rather than in situations involving sacrifice of time, when nongenetically related individuals were ranked higher. Findings on three scales, of higher rankings for child over mother, suggested that a vector of investment toward the young must be added to the kinship genetics model of altruism. No differences were found in general trends between individual ratings and forced choice rankings, though the latter caused greater distinctions to be made between closely related individuals. In general, the author concluded that the kinship genetics explanation of altruism "is either untenable or too vaguely articulated to predict altruistic behavior."

STUDY 48: Ethnic Stereotypes: Agreement between Jewish-Americans and Irish-Americans

John Harris (1976)

The study investigated (1) the degree to which distinct stereotypes are associated with Irish and Jewish ethnic groups; and (2) the degree to which stereotypes held by one group about the other converge with stereotypes applied by the second group to itself. It was hypothesized that the rank ordering of stereotypes would show substantial agreement when Irish or Jewish Ss were describing Jewish people as well as when Irish and Jewish Ss were describing Irish people. No agreement or a negative relationship was hypothesized to occur between the rank order of stereotypes utilized by each group when describing itself (control condition).

Sixteen Jewish-American and 16 Irish-American college graduates and graduate students (8 males, 8 females in each group) were administered a 126-item adjective checklist. Subjects were asked to indicate whether they felt each item described Irish people, Jewish people, both, or neither.

Correlations found between the rank ordering of stereotypes applied by the two ethnic groups confirmed the three hypotheses:

1. Responses of Irish and Jews when both are describing Jews: $r = .698$, $t = 6.013$, $p < .001$, one-tailed.

2. Responses of Irish and Jews when both are describing Irish: $r = .727$, $t = 6.541$, $p < .001$, one-tailed.

3. Responses of Irish and Jews when each group is describing itself: $r = -.44$, $t = -.02$, $p < .01$, one-tailed.

Some external evidence was cited suggesting there may be a basis in actual behavior for stereotypic attitudes applied to the two ethnic groups. A slight trend was also observed for each stereotyping group to attribute traits with a more negative loading to the other group and traits with a more positive value loading to itself.

STUDY 49: An Empirical Study of Selective Altruism in 40 Adolescent High-School Students

Gwen Haas-Hawkings (1976)

Forty adolescents (providing even representations of blacks and whites, males and females) from a Chicago public high school were studied for their selective preferences as to the beneficiary of a predefined altruistic act (saving a drowning individual). Three TAT-like stimulus pictures were designed to elicit choices between black and white when age was not a factor, young and old when race was not a factor, and young and old when race was a confounding factor. It was found that regardless of race or sex the S clearly chose intraracial altruism when age was not a factor. When race was not a factor, the preference was clearly for the young, and this tendency held up strongly even when race was a confounding factor.

STUDY 50: Anglo, Hopi, and Navajo Mothers' Face-to-Face Interactions with Their Infants

John W. Callaghan (1977)

Nineteen Anglo, 18 Hopi, and 15 Navajo mothers were asked to "get the attention of your baby" (all under six months old). The subsequent interaction was videotaped and the tapes analyzed for maternal and infant behaviors. For details see Callaghan (1977). Two summary tables are presented here.

INFANT BEHAVIORS
Differences between Group Total Scores:
Chi-square Test Probabilities

Mode	Groups[a]	Scores (adjusted for time)		X^2	p
Total behaviors	A × H	A = 1313.7	H = 900.7	77.03	< .001
	A × N	A = 1313.7	N = 995.1	43.96	< .001
	H × N	H = 900.7	N = 995.1	4.70	< .04
Total behaviors	A × H	A = 1040.6	H = 709.2	62.76	< .001
excluding	A × N	A = 1040.6	N = 653.2	88.60	< .001
vocalizations	H × N	H = 709.2	N = 653.2	2.30	< .14
Total arm	A × H	A = 620.3	H = 449.6	27.23	< .001
movement	A × N	A = 620.3	N = 438.9	31.07	< .001
	H × N	H = 449.6	N = 438.9	.13	NS
Arm movement:	A × H	A = 529.1	H = 337.4	42.41	< .001
nondirected-	A × N	A = 529.1	N = 378.7	24.92	< .001
random activity	H × N	H = 337.4	N = 378.7	2.38	< .14
Reaches/grasps	A × H	A = 64.8	H = 90.8	4.34	< .05
	A × N	A = 64.8	N = 29.4	13.30	< .001
	H × N	H = 90.8	N = 29.4	31.36	< .001
Leg movement	A × H	A = 156.6	H = 99.5	12.73	< .001
	A × N	A = 156.6	N = 61.7	41.26	< .001
	H × N	H = 99.5	N = 61.7	8.86	< .006
Arches back/	A × H	A = 105.8	H = 45.0	24.51	< .001
tenses	A × N	A = 105.8	N = 31.3	40.48	< .001
	H × N	H = 45.0	N = 31.3	2.46	< .13
Head movement	A × H	A = 79.8	H = 67.4	1.04	NS
	A × N	A = 79.8	N = 54.5	4.77	< .04
	H × N	H = 67.4	N = 54.5	1.37	NS
Cries/grimaces	A × H	A = 160.4	H = 70.1	21.48	< .001
	A × N	A = 160.4	N = 219.3	9.14	< .005
	H × N	H = 70.1	N = 219.3	76.92	< .001
Smiles	A × H	A = 45.1	H = 20.4	9.31	< .005
	A × N	A = 45.1	N = 10.8	21.05	< .001
	H × N	H = 20.4	N = 10.8	2.95	< .09

[a]A = Anglo; H = Hopi; N = Navajo in this and the next table.

MATERNAL BEHAVIORS
Differences between Group Total Scores:
Chi-square Test Probabilities

Mode	Groups	Scores[a] (adjusted for time)		X^2	p
Total behaviors	A × H	A = 2708.5	H = 2226.8	47.02	< .001
	A × N	A = 2708.5	N = 1539.1	321.95	< .001
	H × N	H = 2226.8	N = 1539.1	125.58	< .001
Total behaviors within groups: M.G. × $\overline{\text{M.G.}}$	A	M.G. = 888.	$\overline{\text{M.G.}}$ = 2236.	.82	NS
	H	M.G. = 710.	$\overline{\text{M.G.}}$ = 1767.	12.12	< .001
	N	M.G. = 325.	$\overline{\text{M.G.}}$ = 805.	2.97	< .09
Vocalizations	A × H	A = 1377.7	H = 720.1	206.14	< .001
	A × N	A = 1377.7	N = 302.4	688.22	< .001
	H × N	H = 720.	N = 302.4	170.63	< .001
Vocalizations within groups: M.G. × $\overline{\text{M.G.}}$	A	M.G. = 535.	$\overline{\text{M.G.}}$ = 1054.	28.29	< .001
	H	M.G. = 332.	$\overline{\text{M.G.}}$ = 469.	105.52	< .001
	N	M.G. = 58.	$\overline{\text{M.G.}}$ = 164.	.02	NS
Repositions baby	A × H	A = 213.3	H = 129.5	36.93	< .001
	A × N	A = 213.3	N = 104.9	20.49	< .001
	H × N	H = 129.5	N = 104.9	2.58	< .12
Repositions baby within groups: M.G. × $\overline{\text{M.G.}}$	A	M.G. = 57.	$\overline{\text{M.G.}}$ = 189.	2.52	< .12
	H	M.G. = 17.	$\overline{\text{M.G.}}$ = 127.	14.38	< .001
	N	M.G. = 25.	$\overline{\text{M.G.}}$ = 52.	1.07	NS
Tactual behavior	A × H	A = 617.3	H = 723.7	8.44	< .007
	A × N	A = 617.3	N = 582.9	.99	NS
	H × N	H = 723.7	N = 582.9	15.17	< .001
Tactual behavior within groups: M.G. × $\overline{\text{M.G.}}$	A	M.G. = 133.	$\overline{\text{M.G.}}$ = 579.	28.92	< .001
	H	M.G. = 222.	$\overline{\text{M.G.}}$ = 583.	1.65	NS
	N	M.G. = 99.	$\overline{\text{M.G.}}$ = 329.	2.49	< .13
Movement	A × H	A = 500.3	H = 653.6	20.37	< .001
	A × N	A = 500.3	N = 548.9	2.25	< .15
	H × N	H = 653.6	N = 548.9	9.12	< .005
Movements within groups: M.G. × $\overline{\text{M.G.}}$	A	M.G. = 163.	$\overline{\text{M.G.}}$ = 414.	.09	NS
	H	M.G. = 139.	$\overline{\text{M.G.}}$ = 588.	16.03	< .001
	N	M.G. = 138.	$\overline{\text{M.G.}}$ = 265.	12.41	< .001

[a] MG = behavior occurring when mother and infant are in mutual gaze; $\overline{\text{M.G.}}$ = not in mutual gaze.

Bibliography

Aberle, D. F. Matrilineal descent in cross-cultural perspective. In D. M. Schneider and K. Gough (eds.), *Matrilineal Kinship*. Berkeley, Ca.: University of California Press, 1961.

Ainsworth, M. D. *Infancy in Uganda*. Baltimore, Md.: Johns Hopkins University Press, 1967.

Alexander, R. D. The evolution of social behavior. *Annual Review of Ecological Systems 5* (1974): 326–383.

Altmann, S. Personal communication, 1977.

Barkow, J. Personal communication, 1969.

Bardwick, J. M. Psychological conflict and the reproductive system. In E. L. Walker (ed.), *Feminine Personality and Conflict*. Belmont, Ca.: Brooks/Cole, 1970.

Basehart, H. W. Ashanti. In D. M. Schneider and K. Gough (eds.), *Matrilineal Kinship*. Berkeley, Ca: University of California Press, 1961.

Bateman, A. J. Intra-sexual selection in *Drosophila*. *Heredity 2* (1948): 349–368.

Beach, F. A. The descent of instinct. *Psychological Review 62* (1955): 401–410.

Befu, H. *Japan: An Anthropological Introduction*. San Francisco: Chandler, 1971.

Benedeck, T. *Psychosexual Functions in Women*. New York: Ronald, 1952.

Benedict, R. Synergy: Some notes of Ruth Benedict. Selected by A. H. Maslow and J. J. Honigman. *American Anthropologist 72* (1970): 321–333.

Birren, J. E. (ed.). *Handbook of Aging and the Individual*. Chicago: University Chicago Press, 1959.

Blanck, S. Dimorphism in seated postures. Committee on Human Development, University of Chicago, 1971.

Bleed, P. Early flakes from Sozudai, Japan: Are they man made? *Science 197* (1977): 1357–1359.

Block, J. H. Issues, problems, and pitfalls in assessing sex differences: A critical review of "The Psychology of Sex Differences." *Merrill-Palmer Quarterly 22*, no. 4 (1976): 283–309.

Blurton-Jones, N. Personal communication, 1976.

Bock, R. D. Word and image: Sources of the verbal and spatial factors in mental test scores. *Psychometrika 38* (1973): 437–457.

Bock, R. D., and Kolakowski, D. P. Further evidence of sex-linked major-gene influence in human spatial visualizing ability. *American Journal of Human Genetics 25*, no. 1 (1973): 1–14.

Borden, T. Altruism in two perspectives. M. A. thesis, University of Chicago, 1975.

Bowlby, J. *Maternal Care and Mental Health.* Geneva: WHO Monograph no. 2 (1952).

Brazelton, T. B. *Neonatal Behavioral Scale.* Philadelphia: Lippincott, 1973.

Brazelton, T. B., and Freedman, D. G. The Cambridge neonatal scales. In J. J. van der Werf ten Bosch (ed.), *Normal and Abnormal Development of Brain and Behavior.* Leiden: Leiden University Press, 1971.

Broverman, D. M.; Klaiber, E. L.; Kobayashi, Y.; and Vogel, W. Roles of activation and inhibition in sex differences in cognitive abilities. *Psychological Review 75* (1968): 23–50.

Brown, J. L. Alternate routes to sociability in jays with a theory for the evolution of altruism and communal breeding. *American Zoologist 14,* no. 1 (1974): 63–80.

———. *The Evolution of Behavior.* New York: Norton, 1975.

Bry, Adelaide. *The Sexually Aggressive Woman.* New York: Wyden, 1975.

Burlinghame, D., and Robertson, J. Nursery school for the blind. Film (16mm.; sound), Hampstead Child Therapy Clinic, London, 1967.

Callaghan, J. W. Anglo, Hopi, and Navajo mothers face-to-face interactions with their infants. M. A. thesis, University of Chicago, 1977.

Callan, H. *Ethnology and Society.* Oxford: Clarendon, 1970.

Campbell, B. *Human Evolution.* Chicago: Aldine, 1966.

Carnegie Commission on Higher Education. *Opportunities for Women in Higher Education: The Current Prospects for the Future and Recommendations for Action.* New York: McGraw-Hill, 1973.

Carpenter, C. R. A field study of the behavior and social relations of howling monkeys. *Comparative Psychology Monograph 10* (1934): 1–168.

———. A field study in Siam of the behavior and social relations of the gibbon. *Comparative Psychology Monograph 16* (1940): 1–212.

Caudill, W., and Frost, N. A comparison of maternal care and infant behavior in Japanese-American, American, and Japanese families. In U. Bronfenbrenner and M. A. Mahoney (eds.), *Influences on Human Development.* Hinsdale, Il.: Dryden, 1975.

Caudill, W., and Scarr, H. A. Japanese value orientations and cultural change. *Ethnology 1* (1962): 53–91.

Caudill, W., and Weinstein, H. Maternal care and infant behavior in Japan and America. *Psychiatry 32* (1969): 12–43.

Chance, M. R. A., and Jolly, C. *Social Groups of Monkeys, Apes, and Men.* New York: Dutton, 1970.

Chance, M. R. A., and Larson, R. (eds.). *The Structure of Social Attention.* New York: Wiley, 1976.

Chagnon, N. A. *Yanomamo: The Fierce People.* New York: Holt, Rhinehart & Winston, 1972.

———. *Studying the Yanomamo.* New York: Holt, Rhinehart & Winston, 1972.

———. Personal communication, 1978.

Chagnon, N. A., and Irons, W. (eds.). *Evolutionary Biology and Human Social Behavior.* North Scituate, Ma.: Duxbury, 1978.

Chiang, I. *The Chinese Eye: An Interpretation of Chinese Painting.* London: Methuen, 1960.

Chisholm, J. S. Cradleboarding practices among the Navajo. Ph.D. dissertation, Rutgers University, 1977.

———. Personal communication, 1978.

Chisholm, J. S., and Richards, M. Swaddling, cradleboards, and the development of children. *Early Human Development,* in press.

Clignet, R. *Many Wives, Many Powers.* Evanston, Il.: Northwestern University Press, 1970.

Cloninger, C. R.; Reich, T.; and Guze, S. B. The multifactorial model in disease transmission: pt. III: Familial relationship between sociopathy and hysteria (Briquet's syndrome). *British Journal of Psychiatry 127* (1975): 23–32.

Coon, C. S. *The Origin of Races.* New York: Knopf, 1962.

Court Brown, W. M. The development of knowledge about males with an XYY chromosome complement. *Journal of Medical Genetics 5* (1969): 341–359.

Crandall, V. Sex differences in expectancy of intellectual and academic reinforcement. In R. K. Unger and E. L. Denmark (eds.), *Woman: Dependent or Independent Variable.* New York: Psychological Dimensions, 1975.

Crick, F. H. C.; Garnett, L; Brenner, S; and Watts-Tobin, R. J. General nature of the genetic code for proteins. *Nature 192* (1961): 1227–1232.

Crow, J. F. Ionizing radiation and evolution. *Scientific American,* September 1959, pp. 2–11.

———. Inbreeding and heterosis. In I. H. Herskowitz (ed.), *Study Guide and Workbook for Genetics.* New York: Mcgraw-Hill, 1960.

Dale, R. R. A comparison of the academic performance of male and female students in schools and universities. *Journal of Biosocial Science,* supp. 2 (1970): 95–99.

Darlington, C. D. *The Evolution of Genetic Systems.* New York: Basic Books, 1958.

———. *The Evolution of Man and Society.* New York: Simon & Schuster (Clarion), 1969.

Dart, R. The cultural status of the South African man-apes. *Smithsonian Report for 1955.* Washington, D.C.: Smithsonian Institute, 1956.

Darwin, C. *The Descent of Man.* New York: Modern Library (Random House), original edition, 1871.

Davenport, W. Sexual patterns and their regulation in a society of the Southwest Pacific. In F. A. Beach (ed.), *Sex and Behavior.* New York: Wiley, 1965.

Dawkins, R. *The Selfish Gene.* New York: Oxford University Press, 1976.

De Bary, W. T. (ed.). *Introduction to Oriental Civilizations,* Vol. 1: *Sources of Japanese Tradition.* New York: Columbia University Press, 1958.

Deck, L. P. Buying brains by the inch. *Journal of College and University Personnel Association 19,* no. 3 (1968).

DeVore, I. (ed.). *Primate Behavior: Field Studies of Monkeys and Apes.* New York: Holt, Rhinehart & Winston, 1965.

Dion, K. K.; Berscheid, E.; and Walston, E. What is beautiful is good. *Journal of Personality and Social Psychology 22* (1972): 156–162.

Donaldson, R. A study of sex differences in play in various cultures. Paper, International School of America, 1972.

Draper, P. Cultural pressure on sex differences. *American Ethnologist,* November 1975, pp. 1–14.

Dube, L. *Matriliny and Islam; Religion and Society in the Laccadives.* Dehli: National Publishing House, 1969.

Eccles, Sir J. C. *Brain and Conscious Experience.* New York: Springer-Verlag, 1966.

Eibl-Eibesfeldt, I. *Ethology: The Biology of Behavior.* New York: Holt, Rhinehart & Winston, 1970.

Einstein, A., and Infeld, L. *The Evolution of Physics.* New York: Simon & Schuster, 1938.

Elkin, A. P. *The Australian Aborigines.* New York: American Museum of Natural History, 1964.

Endo, S. *Silence*. Trans. William Johnston. Tokyo: Sophia University Press, 1969.

Erikson, E. H. Sex differences in the play configurations of pre-adolescents. *American Journal of Orthopsychiatry 21* (1951): 667–692.

Farina, A.; Fischer, E. H.; Sherman, S; Smith, W. T.; Groh, T; and Mermin, P. Physical attractiveness and mental illness. *Journal of Abnormal Psychology 86* (1977): 510–517.

Fisher, R. A. *The Genetical Theory of Natural Selection*. Oxford: Clarendon, 1930.

Fiske, A. A biological framework for the study of social organization. Committee on Human Development, University of Chicago, 1973.

Fogel, A. Gaze, face, and voice in the development of mother-infant face-to-face interaction. Ph.D. dissertation, University of Chicago, 1976.

Ford, C. S., and Beach, F. A. *Patterns of Sexual Behavior*. New York: Harper, 1951.

Fowler, H. T. An investigation into human breeding system strategy. Paper read to Animal Behavior Society meeting, Pennsylvania State University, June 1977.

Fox, Robin. *Kinship and Marriage*. Baltimore, Md.: Penguin, 1967.

Freedman, D. G. Development of the smile and fear of strangers: With an inquiry into the inheritance of behavior. Film (16mm.; sound), Psychological Cinema Register, PCR–2140, University of Pennsylvania, 1963.

————. Smiling in blind infants and the issue of innate versus acquired. *Journal of Psychology and Psychiatry 5* (1964): 171–184.

————. A biological view of man's social behavior. In W. Etkin (ed.), *Social Behavior from Fish to Man*. Chicago: University of Chicago Press, 1967.

————. *Human Infancy: An Evolutionary Perspective*. New York: Wiley (Halsted), 1974.

————. The development of social hierarchies. In L. Levi (ed.), *Society, Stress, and Disease*, Vol. 2: *Childhood and Adolescence*. New York: Oxford University Press, 1975.

————. Infancy, biology, and culture. In L. P. Lipsitt (ed.), *Developmental Psychobiology*. New York: Wiley (Halsted), 1976.

Freedman, D. G.; King, J. A.; and Elliot, O. Critical period in the social development of dogs. *Science 133* (1961): 1016–1017.

Freedman, D. G., and Omark, D. R. Ethology, genetics, and education. In F. A. J. Ianni and E. Storey (eds.), *Cultural Relevance and Educational Issues*. Boston: Little, Brown, 1973.

Freedman, M. B. Studies of college alumni. In N. Sanford (ed.), *The American College*. New York: Wiley, 1962.

Friday, N. *My Secret Garden: Women's Sexual Fantasies*. New York: Simon & Schuster (Pocket Books), 1974.

Frisch, J. E. Individual behavior and inter-troop variability in Japanese macaques. In P. C. Jay (ed.), *Primates; Studies in Adaptation and Variability*. New York: Holt, Rhinehart & Winston, 1968.

————. Lecture series, Department of Anthropology, University of Chicago, Spring 1970.

————. Personal communication, 1975.

Fujiki, N., et al. A study of inbreeding in some isolated populations. *Japanese Journal of Human Genetics 4* (1968): 205–225.

Fuller, J. L. *The Nayars Today*. New York: Cambridge University Press, 1976.

Fuller, J. L., and Thompson, W. R. *Behavior Genetics*. New York: Arley, 1960.

Gardner, R. Rivers of sand. Film (16mm; sound), Psychological Cinema Register, 90075, University of Pennsylvania, 1974.

Geber, M., and Dean, R. F. A. Psychomotor development in African children: The effect of social class and the need for improved tests. *Bulletin of the World Health Organization* 18 (1958): 471–476.

Ginsburg, H. Paper read to Psychonomic Society, Washington, D.C., November 1977.

Goldstein, K. *The Organism*. New York: American Book, 1939.

———. The smiling of the infant and the problem of understanding the "other." *Journal of Psychology* 44 (1957): 175–191.

———. *Human Nature in the Light of Psychopathology*. New York: Schocken, 1963.

Goodall, J., and Van Lawick, H. Miss Goodall and the wild chimpanzees. Film (16mm; sound), Psychological Cinema Register, 31269, University of Pennsylvania, 1967.

Goren, C. G.; Sarty, M.; and Wu, P. Visual following and pattern discrimination of face-like stimuli by newborn infants. *Pediatrics* 56, no. 4 (1975): 544–549.

Gottesman, I. I. Developmental genetics and ontogenetic psychology. In A. D. Pick (ed.), *Minnesota Symposium on Child Psychology*, Vol 8. Minneapolis: University of Minnesota Press, 1974.

Gottlieb, G., and Kuo, Z. Development of behavior in the duck embryo. *Journal of Comparative and Physiological Psychology* 59, no. 2 (1965): 183–188.

Gowin, E. B. *The Executive and His Control of Men: A Study in Personal Efficiency*. New York: Macmillan, 1915.

Green, N. An exploratory study of aggression and spacing behavior in two preschool nurseries: Chinese-American and European-American. M.A. thesis, University of Chicago, 1969.

Grzimek, B. (ed.). *Animal Life Encyclopedia*. New York: Van Nostrand Reinhold, 1972, 13 volumes.

Guthrie, R. D. Evolution of human threat display organs. In T. Dobzhansky (ed.), *Evolutionary Biology*, Vol. 4. New York: Appleton Century, 1970.

Gutmann, D. Men, women, and the parental imperative. *Commentary* 56 (1973): 59–64.

Hallet, J.-P. The Pygmies of the Ituri Forest. Film (16mm; sound), Encyclopedia Britannica, 1975.

Hamilton, W. D. The evolution of altruistic behavior. *American Naturalist* 97 (1963): 354–356.

———. The genetical evolution of social behavior. *Journal of Theoretical Biology* 7 (1964): 1–52.

———. Book review of *The Selfish Gene*. *Science* 196 (1977): 575.

———. Personal communication, 1978.

Hardin, G. *Nature and Man's Fate*. New York: Holt, Rhinehart, 1959.

Harpending, H., and Purefoy, F. Personal communication, 1978.

Hausfater, G. Dominance and reproduction in baboons (*Papio cyncephalis*): A quantitative analysis. Ph.D. dissertation, University of Chicago, 1973.

Hebb, D. O. Heredity and environment. *British Journal of Animal Behavior* 1 (1959): 43–47.

Hediger, H. *Observations sur la psychologie animale dans les parques nationaux du Congo Belge*. Brussels: Institut des parques nationaux du Congo Belge, 1951.

Heider, K. G. *The Dugum Dani*. Chicago: Aldine, 1970.

Helfer, R., and Kempe, C. (eds.). *The Battered Child.* Chicago: University of Chicago Press, 1968.

Hershkovitz, P. *Living New-World Monkeys (Platyrrhini).* Chicago: University of Chicago Press, 1977.

Hess, E. H. Imprinting. *Science 130* (1959): 133–141.

———. *The Tell-Tale Eye.* New York: Van Nostrand Reinhold, 1976.

Hess, R. D. Social class and ethnic influences on socialization. In P. H. Mussen (ed.), *Carmichael's Manual of Child Psychology.* New York: Wiley, 1970.

Heston, L. L. Psychiatric disorders in foster-home reared children of schizophrenic mothers. *British Journal of Psychiatry 112* (1966): 819–825.

Heston, L. L., and Shields, J. Homosexuality in twins. *Achives of General Psychiatry 18* (1968): 149–160.

Hilsdale, P. Marriage as a personal existential commitment. *Journal of Marriage and Family Living 24* (May 1962): 137–143.

Hinde, R. A. Interaction of internal and external factors in canary reproduction. In F. A. Beach (ed.), *Sex and Behavior.* New York: Wiley, 1965.

Hoffman, L. R., and Maier, N. R. F. Social factors influencing problem solving in women. *Journal of Personality and Social Psychology 4* (1966): 382–390.

Hook, E. B., and Porter, I. H. (eds.). *Population Cytogenetics.* New York: Academic Press, 1977.

Horton, R. African traditional thought and Western science, pt. II. *Africa 37* (1967): 155–177.

Hrdy, S. B. Infanticide as a primate reproductive strategy. *American Scientist 65*, no. 1 (1977): 40–49

Humphry, M. *The Hostage Seekers: A Study of Childless and Adopting Couples.* New York: Humanities, 1965.

Hutt, C. *Males and Females.* Baltimore, Md.: Penguin, 1972

Imanishi, K., and Altman, A. (eds.). *Japanese Monkeys: A Collection of Translations.* Atlanta, Ga: Emory University Press, 1965.

Itani, J. Paternal care in the wild Japanese monkey. *Primates 2* (1959): 61–93.

———. On the acquisition and propagation of a new food habit in the troop of Japanese monkeys at Takasakiyama. In K. Imanishi and A. Altman (eds.), *Japanese Monkeys: A Collection of Translations.* Atlanta, Ga: Emory University Press, 1965.

Izawa, K. Unit groups of chimpanzees and their nomadism in the savanna woodland. *Primates 11* (1970): 1–46.

Jay, P. C. (ed.). *Primates.* New York: Holt, Rhinehart & Winston, 1968.

Jenni, D. A. Evolution of polyandry in birds. *American Zoologist 14* (1974): 129–144.

Jensen, G. Sex differences in developmental trends of mother-infant monkey behavior (*M. nemestrina*). *Primates 1*, no. 3 (1966): 403.

Junker, K. S. *The Child in the Glass Ball.* New York: Abingdon, 1964

Kagan, J. *Change and Continuity in Infancy.* New York: Wiley, 1971.

Kaufmann, J. H. Social relations of adult males in a free-ranging band of rhesus monkeys. In S. A. Altmann (ed.), *Social Communication among Primates.* Chicago: University of Chicago Press, 1967.

Kawai, M. On the system of social ranks in a natural troop of Japanese monkeys. In K. Imanishi and A. Altmann (eds.), *Japanese Monkeys: A Collection of Translations.* Atlanta, Ga.: Emory University Press, 1965.

Kenyatta, J. *Facing Mount Kenya.* London: Secker & Warburg, 1938.

Kerouac, J. *On the Road.* New York: New American Library (Signet), 1958.

Kessen, W. (ed.). *Childhood in China*. New Haven, Ct.: Yale University Press, 1975.

Kimura, D. Functional asymmetry of the brain in dichotic listening. *Cortex 3* (1967): 163–178.

———. Spatial localization in left and right visual fields. *Canadian Journal of Psychology 23* (1969): 445–458.

Kinsey, A. C.; Pomeroy, W. B.; and Martin, C. E. *Sexual Behavior in the Human Male*. Philadelphia: Saunders, 1948.

Kinsey, A. C., et al. *Sexual behavior in the Human Female*. Philadelphia: Saunders, 1953.

Kirkpatrick, C., and Cotton, J. Physical attractiveness, age, and marital adjustment. *American Sociological Review 16* (1961): 81–86.

Koford, C. B. Group relations in an island colony of rhesus monkeys. In C. H. Southwick (ed.), *Primate Social Behavior*. Princeton, N.J.: Van Nostrand, 1963.

Kohlberg, L. Development of moral character and moral ideology. In M. L. Hoffman and L. W. Hoffman (eds.), *Review of Child Development Research*. New York: Russell Sage, 1964.

Koyama, N. Changes in dominance rank and division of a wild Japanese monkey troop at Arashiyama. *Primates 11* (1970): 335–390.

Kronhausen, P., and Kronhausen, E. *The Sexually Responsive Woman*. New York: Grove, 1964.

Krut, L. H., and Singer, R. Steatopygia: The fatty acid composition of subcutaneous adipose tissue in the Hottentot. *American Journal of Physical Anthropology 21* (1963): 181–188.

Kubey, R. W. Dominance and submission in presidential politics: A sociobiological view. Committee on Human Development, University of Chicago, 1977.

Kuchner, J. Chinese and European-Americans: A cross-cultural study of infants and mothers. Ph.D. dissertation, University of Chicago, 1979.

Kummer, H. Personal communication, 1965.

———. Personal communication, 1968.

———. *Primate Societies: Group Techniques of Ecological Adaptation*. Chicago: Aldine/Atherton, 1971.

Kuo, Z. Y. Ontogeny of embryonic behavior in Aves, pt. IV: The influence of prenatal behavior upon postnatal life. *Journal of Comparative Psychology 14* (1932): 109–121.

Kurland, J. A. Sisterhood in primates: What to do with human males. Paper read to American Anthropological Association meeting, November 1976, Washington, D.C.

Lao-tze. *Tao Teh King*. (Trans. A. J. Bahm). New York: Ungar, 1958.

Lehrman, D. S. A critique of Konrad Lorenz's theory of instinctive behavior. *Quarterly Review of Biology 28* (1954): 337–363.

Leiderman, P. H.; Babu, B.; Kagia, J.; Kraemer, C.; and Leiderman, G. F. African infant precocity and some social influences in the first year. *Nature 242* (1973): 247–249.

Leonard, J. E., and Ehrman, L. Recognition and sexual selection in *Drosophila*: Classification, quantification, and identification. *Science 193* (1976): 693–695.

Leonard, M. R. Problems in identification and ego development in twins. *Psychoanalytic Study of the Child 16* (1961): 300–318.

Levi, C. *Christ Stopped at Eboli*. New York: Farrar, Strauss, 1963.

LeVine, R. A. Socialization, social structure, and intersocial images. In H.

Kelman (ed.), *International Behavior: A Social Psychological Analysis.* New York: Holt, Rhinehart & Winston: 1965.

———. Outsiders' judgments: An ethnographic approach to group differences in personality. *Southwestern Journal of Anthropology 22* (1966): 101–116.

———. Personal communication, 1969.

———. Patterns of personality in Africa. In A. DeVos (ed.), *Responses to Change: Society, Culture, and Personality.* New York: Van Nostrand Reinhold, 1976.

Levy, R. *Tahitians: Mind and Experience in the Society Islands.* Chicago: University of Chicago Press, 1973.

Lewis, M.; Kagan, J.; and Kalafat, J. Patterns of fixation in the young infant. *Child Development 37* (1966): 331–341.

Lewontin, R. C. The apportionment of human diversity. *Evolutionary Biology 6* (1972): 381–398.

———. *The Genetic Basis of Evolutionary Change.* New York: Columbia University Press, 1974.

Linblad, J. Personal communication, 1962.

Lipsitt, L. P., (ed.). *Developmental Psychobiology.* New York: Wiley (Halsted), 1976.

Lorenz, K. Companionship in bird life. In C. H. Schiller (ed.), *Instinctive Behavior.* New York: International Universities Press, 1957.

———. *On Aggression.* New York: Harcourt, 1966.

Lugard, Lady F. L. *A Tropical Dependency.* London: Nisbet, 1905.

Maccoby, E., and Jacklin, C. *The Psychology of Sex Differences.* Stanford, Ca.: Stanford University Press, 1974.

MacDougall, D. To live with herds (the Jie). Film (16mm; sound), Oak Park, Il., Film Images, 1973.

Malinowski, B. The natives of Mailu. *Transactions of the Royal Society of South Australia 39* (1915): 494–706.

———. *The Sexual Life of Savages.* New York: Halcyon House, 1929.

Martini, M. Personal communication, 1977.

Masters, R. E. L. *Patterns of Incest.* New York: Julian Press, 1963.

Matsumoto, Y. S. Notes on primogeniture in postwar Japan. In R. J. Smith and R. K. Beardsley (eds.), *Japanese Culture: Its Development and Characteristics.* Chicago: Aldine, 1962.

Mayr, E. Where are we? *Cold Spring Harbor Symposium on Quantitative Biology 24* (1959): 1–14.

Mech, D. L. *The Wolves of Isle Royale.* Washington, D.C.: U.S. Government Printing Office, 1966.

Meggitt, M. A. *Desert People: A study of the Walbiri Aborigines of Central Australia.* Sydney: Angus & Robertson, 1962.

Money, J., and Ehrhardt, A. A. *Man and woman, Boy and Girl.* Baltimore Md.: Johns Hopkins University Press, 1972.

Morris, D. *The Human Zoo.* New York: McGraw-Hill, 1967.

Mourant, A. E.; Kopec, A. C.; and Damaniewska-Sobczak, K. *The Distribution of the Human Blood Groups and Other Polymorphisms, 2d. ed. New York: Oxford University Press, 1976.*

Munroe, R. L., and Munroe, R. H. Effect of environmental experience on spatial ability in an East African society. *Journal of Society Psychology 83* (1971): 15–22.

Murdock, G. P. World ethnographic sample. *American Anthropologist 59* (1957): 664–687.

Murray, H. A. *Explorations in Personality.* Cambridge,: Ma. Harvard University Press, 1938.

Myrdal, G. *An American Dilemma.* New York: Harper, 1944.

Nakane, C. *Garo and Khasi: A Comparative Study of Matrilineal Systems.* The Hague: Mouton, 1967.

Nei, M., and Roychoudbury, A. K. Genic variations within and between the thre major races of man: Caucassoids, Negroids, and Monogoloids. *American Journal of Human Genetics 26* (1974): 421–443.

Nisselius, J. K. Behavioral assessment of the Navajo newborn. M.A. thesis, University of Utah, 1976.

Novikoff, A. B. The concept of integrative levels and biology. *Science 101* (1945): 209–213.

Nozawa, K. Poulation genetics of Japanese monkeys, pt.I: Estimation of effective troop size. *Primates 13* (1972): 381–393.

Omark, D. R.; Omark, M.; and Edelman, M.S. Formation of dominance hierarchies in young children: Action and perception. In T. Williams (ed.), *Psychological Anthropology.* The Hague: Mouton, 1975.

Omark, D. R., and Edelman, M. S. The development of attention structures in young children. In M. R. A. Chance and R. Larson (eds.), *Attention Structures in Primates and Man.* New York: Wiley, 1977.

O'Nell, C. Personal communication, 1969.

Pannor, B., and Sorosky, R. Open adoption. *Social Work 21* no. 2 (1976): 97–100.

Parker, R., and Freedman, D. G. Sex differences in children at play. Film (16mm; sound), Psychological Cinema Register, PCR–2245, University of Pennsylvania, 1971.

Patterson, O. Context and choice in ethnic allegiance: A theoretical framework and Caribbean case study. In N. Glazer and D. P. Moynihan (eds.), *Ethnicity: Theory and Practice.* Cambridge, Ma.: Harvard University Press.

Pepper, S. C. *World Hypotheses.* Berkely, Ca.: University of California Press, 1961.

Peter, Prince of Greece and Denmark. *Studies in Polyandry.* The Hague: Mouton, 1963.

Pirsig, R. M. *Zen and the Art of Motorcycle Maintenance.* New York: Morrow, 1974.

Poincaré, H. *Science and Method.* New York: Dover, 1914.

Provine, W. B. *The Origins of Theoretical Population Genetics.* Chicago: University of Chicago Press, 1972.

Pusey, A. Personal communications, 1971.

Rainwater, L. Crucible of identity: The Negro Lower-class family *Daedalus 2* (1966): 172–216.

Randall, R., and Murray, A.-M. *New Dimensions in Adoption.* New York: Crown, 1974.

Reischauer, E. O. *The Japanese.* Cambridge, Ma.: Harvard University Press (Belknap), 1977.

Richards, A. I. Some types of family structure amongst the Central Bantu. In A. R. Radcliffe-Brown and C. D. Furde (eds.), *African Systems of Kinship and Marriage.* New York: Oxford University Press, 1950.

Rimland, B. *Infantile Autism: The Syndrome and Its Implications for a Neural Theory of Behavior.* New York: Appleton-Century-Crofts, 1964.

———. Personal communication, 1974.

Roberts, D. F. The development of inbreeding in an island population. In L.

N. Morris (ed.), *Human Populations, Genetic Variation, and Evolution.* San Francisco: Chandler, 1971.

Robertson, D. R. Social control of sex reversal in a coral fish. *Science 177* (1972): 1007–1009.

Roe, A. *The Making of a Scientist.* New York: Dodd, 1953.

Roheim, G. The psychoanalytical interpretation of culture. In W. Muensterberger (ed.), *Man and His Culture: Psychoanalytic Anthropology after Totem and Taboo.* London: Rapp and Whiting, 1969.

Roiphe, A. Article on lesbian faction at Sarah Lawrence. *New York Times Magazine,* 20 March 1977.

Rose, R. M.; Holaday, J. W.; and Bernstein, I. S. Plasma testosterone, dominance rank, and aggressive behavior in male rhesus monkeys. *Nature 23* (1971): 366–368.

Rosenthal, D., and Kety, S. S. (eds.). The transmission of schizophrenia. *Journal of Psychiatric Research 6* (1968): Supplement no. 1.

Roth, P. *Portnoy's Complaint.* New York: Random House, 1969.

Sade, D. S. Determinants of dominance in a group of free-ranging rhesus monkeys. In S. A. Altmann (ed.), *Social Communication among Primates.* Chicago: University of Chicago Press, 1967.

————. Inhibition of son-mother mating among free-ranging rhesus monkeys. *Scientific Psychoanalysis 12* (1968): 18–38.

————. Life cycle and social organization of rhesus monkeys. Paper prepared for the International Society for the Study of Behavioral Development, Pavia, Italy, September 1977.

Sahlins, M. D. On the sociology of primitive exchange. In M. Banton (ed.), *The Relevance of Models for Social Anthropology.* London: Tavistock, 1965.

————. *The Use and Abuse of Biology.* Ann Arbor, Mi.: University of Michigan Press, 1976.

Sarich, V. M. The origin of hominids: An immunological approach. In S. L. Washburn and P. C. Jay (eds.), *Perspectives on Human Evolution.* New York: Holt, Rhinehart & Winston, 1968.

Savin-Williams, R. C. Dominance-submission behaviors and hierarchies in young adolescents at a summer camp. Ph.D. dissertation, University of Chicago, 1977.

Schaffner, B. (ed.). *Group Processes.* New York: J. Macy Foundation, 1954.

Schaller, G. B. *The Mountain Gorilla.* Chicago: University of Chicago Press, 1963.

Scheffler, H. W. *Choiseul Island Social Structure.* Berkeley, Ca.: University of California Press, 1965.

Scheinfield, D. Dominance, exchange, and achievement in a lower-income black neighborhood. Ph.D. dissertation, University of Chicago, 1973.

Schneider, D. M., and Gough, K. (eds.). *Matrilineal Kinship.* Berkeley, Ca.: University of California Press, 1961.

Schneirla, T. C. Instinctive behavior maturation-experience, and development. In B. Kaplan and S. Wagner (eds.), *Perspectives in Psychological Theory.* New York: International Universities Press, 1960.

Schull, W. J., and Neel, J. V. *The Effects of Inbreeding on Japanese Children.* New York: Harper, 1965.

Schumpeter, J. A. *Imperialism and Social Classes.* New York: Kelley, 1951.

Schusky, E. L. *Variations in Kinship.* New York: Holt, Rhinehart & Winston, 1974.

Scott, J. R. Personal communication, 1977.

Selander, R. K. Sexual selection and dimorphism in birds. In B. G. Campbell (ed.), *Sexual Selection and Descent of Man, 1871–1971*. Chicago: Aldine, 1972.

Selye, H. *The Stress of Life*. New York: McGraw-Hill, 1956.

Shafer, R. Athabaskan and Sino-Tibetan. *International Journal of American Linguistics 18* (1952): 12–19.

Shaffer, L. F., and Shoben, E. J., Jr. *The Psychology of Adjustment*. Boston: Houghton Mifflin, 1956.

Sigall, H., and Candy, D. Radiating beauty: Effects of having a physically attractive partner on person perception. *Journal of Personality and Social Psychology 28* (1973): 218–224.

Simmons, L. W. (ed.). *Sun Chief*. New Haven, Ct.: Yale University Press, 1942.

Simon, R. J., and Alstein, R. J. *Trans-racial Adoption*. New York: Wiley, 1977.

Simon, W., and Gagnon, J. Psychosexual development. *Trans-Action/Society 6* (5 March 1969): 13.

Singer, R. Lecture and slide presentation, Department of Anatomy, University of Chicago, May 1968.

Sorokin, P. A. *Social and Cultural Mobility*. New York: The Free Press, 1959.

Spieth, H. T. Mating behavior within the genus *Drosophila* (*Diptera*). *Bulletin of the American Museum of Natural History 99* (1952): 395–479.

Spitz, R. A., and Wolf, K. M. The smiling response: A contribution to the ontogenesis of social relations. *Genetic Psychology Monographs 34* (1946): 57–125.

Spuhler, J. N. (ed.). *Genetic Diversity and Human Behavior*. Chicago: Aldine, 1967.

Stebbins, G. L., Jr. *Variation and Evolution in Plants*. New York: Columbia University Press, 1950.

Stern, C. *Principles of Human Genetics*, 3d. ed. San Francisco: Freeman, 1973.

Sugiyama, Y. Social organization of hanuman langurs. In S. Altmann (ed.), *Social Communication among Primates*. Chicago: University of Chicago Press, 1967.

Sumner, W. G. *Folkways*. Boston: Ginn, 1906.

Tanner, N., and Zihlman, A. Women in evolution, pt. I: Innovation and selection in human origins. *Signs 6* (1976): 585–608.

Teitelbaum, M. S., and Mantel, N. Socioeconomic factors and the sex ratio at birth. *Journal of Biosocial Science 3* (1971): 23–41.

Terman, L. M., et al. *Genetic Studies of Genius*, Vol. 1: *Mental and Physical Traits of a Thousand Gifted Children*. Stanford Ca.: Stanford University Press, 1925.

Terman, L. M., and Tyler, L. E. Psychological sex differences. In L. Carmichael (ed.), *Manual of Child Psychology*. New York: Wiley, 1970.

Thomas, E. M. *The Harmless People*. Baltimore, Md.: Penquin, 1959.

Thorpe, W.H. *Learning and Instinct in Animals*, 2d ed. London: Methuen, 1963.

Thrasher, R. M. *The Gang: A Study of 1,313 Gangs in Chicago*. Chicago: University of Chicago Press, 1963.

Tidball, M. E., and Kostiakowski, V. Baccalaureate origins of American scientists and Scholars. *Science 193* (1976): 646–652.

Tiger, L. *Men in Groups*. New York: Random House, 1969.

Tiger, L., and Shepher, J. *Women in the Kibbutz*. New York: Harcourt, 1975.

Torda, F. Heterosexual, marital, and maternal orientations of late adolescent Negro and white girls. Ph.D. dissertation, University of Chicago, 1969.

Triseliotis, J. P. *In Search of Origins.* London: Kegan Paul, 1973.

Trivers, R. L. The evolution of reciprocal altruism. *Quarterly Review of Biology 46* (1971): 33–57.

———. Parental investment and sexual selection. In B. G. Campbell (ed.), *Sexual Selection and the Descent of Man.* Chicago: Aldine, 1972.

Trivers, R. L., and Willard, D. E. Natural selection of parental ability to vary the sex ratio of offspring. *Science 179* (1973): 90–92.

Trotsky, L. *My Life.* New York: Grosset & Dunlap, 1930.

Turnbull, C. *The Mountain People.* New York: Simon & Schuster, 1972.

———. *Wayward Servants.* New York: Natural History Press, 1965.

Van Lawick, Baron H. *Solo: The Story of an African Wild Dog.* Boston: Houghton Mifflin, 1974.

Van den Berghe, P. L., and Barash, D. P. Inclusive fitness and human family structure. *American Anthropologist 79* (1977): 809–823.

Waddington, C. H. *Organizers and Genes.* New York: Cambridge University Press, 1947.

Wade, M. Book review of *The Selfish Gene.* Evolution 32 (1978a): 220–221.

———. The evolution of social interactions by family selection. Department of Biology, University of Chicago, 1978b.

———. A critical review of the models of group selection. *Quarterly Review of Biology 53* (1978c): 101–114.

Ward, P. C. Infanticide. *Encyclopedia Americana 15* (1977). New York: Encyclopedia Americana.

Warren, N. African infant precocity. *Psychological Bulletin 78* (1972): 353–367.

Webster, S. Cognatic dissent groups and the contemporary Maori: A preliminary reassessment. *Journal of the Polynesian Society 84* (1975): 121–152.

Weinrich, D. J. Human reproductive strategy, pt. II: Homosexuality and non-reproduction: Some evolutionary models. Ph.D. dissertation, Harvard University, 1976.

Westermarck, E. *The History of Human Marriage.* London: Macmillan, 1891.

White, S. H. Evidence for a hierarchical arrangement of learning processes. In L. P. Lipsitt and C. C. Spiker (ed.), *Advances in Child Development and Behavior, Vol 2.* New York: Academic Press, 1967.

Whitney, G. Genetic substrates for the initial evolution of sociability, *American Naturalist 110* (1976): 867–875.

Wickler, W. *The Sexual Code.* New York: Doubleday, 1972.

Wightman, W. P. D. *Science and Monism.* London: George Allen and Unwin, 1934.

Williams, G. C. *Adaptation and Natural Selection.* Princeton, N. J.: Princeton University Press, 1966.

———, (ed.). *Group Selection.* Chicago: Aldine/Atherton, 1971.

Wilson, E. O. *Sociobiology: The New Synthesis.* Cambridge, Ma.: Harvard University Press, 1975.

Winstan, F. J. An inquiry into the adaptive significance of pubertal voice change. M.A. thesis, University of Chicago, 1973.

Witkin, H. A., et al. Criminality in XYY and XXY men. *Science 193* (1976): 547–555.

Wolf, A. Childhood association and sexual attraction: A further test of the Westermarck hypothesis. *American Anthropologist 72* (1970): 503–515.

Wolfe, T. *From Death to Mourning.* New York: Scribner's, 1935.

Woolpy, J. H. Socially controlled systems of mating. Ph.D. dissertation, University of Chicago, 1967.

Wright, S. The statistical consequences of Mendelian heredity in relation to speciation. In J. Huxley (ed.), *The New Systematics*. New York: Oxford University Press, 1940.

———. *Evolution and the Genetics of Populations*, Vol. 3: *Experimental Results and Evolutionary Deductions*. Chicago: University of Chicago Press, 1977.

Wynne-Edwards, V. C. *Animal Dispersion in Relation to Social Behavior*. Edinburgh: Oliver and Boyd, 1962.

———. Intergroup selection in the evolution of social systems. In G. C. Williams (ed.), *Group Selection*. Chicago: Aldine/Atherton, 1971.

Yolles, S. F. How different are they? *New York Times Magazine*, 5 February 1967.

Yoshiba, K. Local and intertroop variability in ecology and social behavior of common Indian langurs. In P. C. Jay (ed.), *Primates: Studies in Adaptation and Variability*. New York: Holt, Rhinehart & Winston, 1968.

Subject Index

Aboriginals, Australian
  cousin marriages of, 134
  harems and ecology, 41
  physical coordination of infants,
    158, 160
  and smiling, 57–58, 178
  walkabout, 134
Abouré
  and matriliny, 17
  polygyny of, 79
Adoption
  and child abuse, 22–23
  child's desire to find biological kin,
    117
  in homogeneous societies, 126
  inter-racial, by fertile parents,
    166–168
  among island peoples, 23, 119
  and parents' love, 21–22
  tribal nature of, 22
  See also Navajo; Polynesians
Afro-Americans
  behavior of infants compared to
    other races', 146
  coordination of, compared to
    Caucasians', Africans', 158
  and divorce, 17, 18
  and hair styles, 205
Age
  and nonbiological altruism, 210
  veneration for, 111–112
Aggression
  and altruism, 128 fn
  avoidance, 42, 45, 58–59, 61, 64,
    94–95, 122–123
  among birds, 23–26, 122–123
  chromosomes and, 25–26
  and dimorphism, 31–33
  female-female, 29–41
  female, in predators, 31

female vs. male tendency for, 16,
    25–26, 32, 58–59
  and food supply, 31, 42
  and hierarchies, 30
  infants and, 41–42
  and kinship, 33–34
  and mating, 34–35, 39–41
  male-male, 30–33, 41–43
  male mortality and, 59–60
  population control and, 30, 122–123
  among primates, 30–33
  See also Competition; Beards;
    Display; Dominance; Dominance-
    submission hierarchies; Eyes; Sex
    differences; Status hierarchies
Ainu, isolation of, 124
Alpha, female
  appearance, 47
  difficulty identifying, 70
  in different-sex groups, 71–72
  nature of, 47, 70, 168
  See also Dominance-submission
    hierarchies; Status hierarchies
Alphas, males
  and appearance, 38–39, 46, 71, 169
  charisma of, 38–39, 46
  effect on patterns of others, 36–37
  nature of, 46, 47, 70–71
  nonaggressive, 42
  self-confidence of, 39, 41, 46
  and testosterone levels, 39
  See also Dominance-submission
    hierarchies; Status hierarchies
Altruism, biological
  and adopted children, 21–22
  and age, 210
  and aggression, 128, fn
  and chromosomes, 25–26
  and ethnicity, 114
  and evolution, 120

227

Author Index